Reconstructions in Early Modern History

Series Editors: John Morrill and Pauline Croft

Power and Protest in England 1525–1640

ALISON WALL

A member of the Hodder Headline Group
LONDON
Co-published in the United States of America by
Oxford University Press Inc., New York

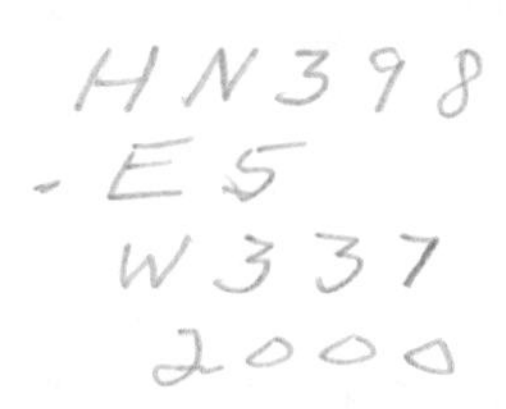

First published in Great Britain in 2000 by
Arnold, a member of the Hodder Headline Group,
338 Euston Road, London NW1 3BH

http://www.arnoldpublishers.com

Co-published in the United States of America by
Oxford University Press Inc.,
198 Madison Avenue, New York 10016

British Library Cataloguing in Publication Data
A catalogue entry for this book is available from the British Library

Library of Congress Cataloging-in-Publication Data
A catalog record for this book is available from the Library of Congress

ISBN 0 340 76122 9 (hb)
ISBN 0 340 61022 0 (pb)

1 2 3 4 5 6 7 8 9 10

Production Editor: James Rabson
Production Controller: Bryan Eccleshall
Cover Design: Terry Griffiths

Typeset in 10/12pt Sabon by Phoenix Photosetting, Chatham, Kent
Printed and bound in Great Britain by MPG Books Ltd, Bodmin, Cornwall

To Christopher

Contents

Preface

Early modern England experienced religious, political and social turbulence, and yet until 1640 avoided the terrible strife and civil wars which beset neighbouring states. How was this achieved; how did power really work on the ground in England? The family provided a model for state patriarchy, but how was power contested in family life? And, crucially, how did ordinary men and women respond to those who ruled them? These questions have long interested me, and when I started to explore them, it seemed that keeping order in a nation without regular police or army must have required harsh suppression, provoking dissent. So the study was originally called 'resistance to authority'. But further exploration suggested that persuasion might have been more important than coercion. Royal and civic imagery, hard work by JPs and villagers, even pulpit homilies could help deflect discontent. Protest appeared to be episodic, directed against specific grievances strong enough to overcome a common desire for peace.

Since I had been working on this subject intermittently between teaching and other writing, it was a pleasure when the editors of this series offered the opportunity to prepare a book on power in action and popular reactions. I would like to thank Christopher Wheeler at Arnold for inviting me to write, and for his interest and warm encouragement, and John Morrill and Pauline Croft for their enthusiasm and for reading the text.

Archivists and librarians have been essential to this study. My thanks go especially to those of the Wiltshire County Record Office, Essex Record Office, Chester Record Office, the Public Record Office, Henry E. Huntington Library, California, and the Bodleian Library, and to former and present librarians at Christ Church, Oxford, John Wing and Janet McMullin, for unfailing cheerful assistance. Nicholas Mayhew, Keeper of the Heberden Coin Collection, Ashmolean Museum, Oxford, kindly showed me the Tudor and Stuart coins.

My debt to other historians is clear in the notes and bibliography; many of them have helped as well with discussion and references. Among them all,

I especially thank Felicity Heal, Clive Holmes, Kevin Sharpe, Robyn Priestley and Alex Shephard. I thank Iain Cameron, my colleague at Sydney, and the lively finalists and postgraduates in the late 1980s who took our seminar on 'Authority and rebellion'; and I am grateful to Christ Church Oxford for providing a welcoming academic community since I moved to England. Earlier variations on the theme of Chapter 8 were given at the Universities of Perth, Auckland and Sussex, and I would like to thank the audiences for their questions, particularly Judith Richards and William Lamont.

My greatest debt is to my husband, Christopher Haigh. I thank him for his support, for discussion of the book at every stage, even on Sunday country walks as well as companionable trips to county archives, and for his critical reading and helpful comments on the manuscript.

Alison Wall
Oxford
May 2000

Abbreviations

BIHR	*Bulletin of the Institute of Historical Research*
BL	British Library
DNB	*Dictionary of National Biography*
EcHR	*Economic History Review*
EHR	*English Historical Review*
ERO	Essex Record Office
HEH	Henry E. Huntington Library, San Marino, California
HJ	*The Historical Journal*
HMC	Historical Manuscripts Commission
HR	*Historical Research*
JBS	*Journal of British Studies*
L&P	*Letters and Papers, Foreign and Domestic, of the Reign of Henry VIII*, ed. J. Brewer, J. Gairdner and R. Brodie (1862–1932)
P&P	*Past and Present*
PRO	Public Record Office
TRHS	*Transactions of the Royal Historical Society*
WCRO	Wiltshire County Record Office
WAM	*Wiltshire Archeological and Natural History Society Magazine*

Introduction

The history of early modern England was, for many years, history from the centre: narratives of kings and queens, the activities of parliament and its members, the Church and religious change – which of course are still important. Then interest spread to include wider areas, geographically and socially: the provincial aristocracy and gentry, county politics, family relationships, crime and social conditions. Enquiry into the regions produced a series of books suggesting that early modern society was disorderly and violent. There were articles and books on revolt and protest, which made the English seem an undisciplined people. Book titles pressed the theme – *In Contempt of all Authority*, *Rebellion and Riot*, *Tudor Rebellions*, *Village Revolts*, *Rebellion, Popular Protest and the Social Order in Early Modern England*, *Revel, Riot and Rebellion*, and *An Ungovernable People*. We were told in 1981 that between the Great Revolt of 1381 and the Monmouth Rebellion of 1685 England saw three centuries of recurrent regional uprisings – not to mention the Civil Wars. In articles, Lawrence Stone discussed interpersonal violence, and Joel Samaha sedition.[1] 'An ungovernable people' indeed.

Some sixteenth-century observers too noted the wilful indiscipline and dangerous volatility of people both high and low. In 1583, William Lambarde, a concerned justice of the peace who wrote handbooks for local governors, warned the Kent magistrates and jurors of the chaos which would follow 'if every man breaketh loose without fear of God, restraint of conscience, estimation of law, or regard of charity'. After the outbreak of war with Spain, he told them 'now will your sons and servants strive to draw their necks out of the yoke of due obedience'. In 1587 things were no better, he lamented: 'in so working a sea of sin and wretchedness as this age is, the ship of commonwealth shall be in peril'. In 1605 and 1608 Lord Chancellor Ellesmere castigated JPs throughout the country for forgetting their oath to God and their duty to king and country, for lurking around London and leaving vagrants uncorrected and the poor unaided in their parishes. Was there no authority sufficiently effective to control incipient chaos? Were the people really so rebellious?[2]

Those who ruled certainly faced a difficult task in keeping order. They had no professional police or standing army, and the feudal bonds of allegiance were eroded. Who really did wield power at each level of society? How did they acquire and seek to promote their authority? We need to look beyond the formal administrative structures, to explore conceptions of political power and public duty. In a hierarchical system with the monarch at the head, kings and queens were expected to rule, but they were not simply dictators. Quentin Skinner, Johan Sommerville, Glenn Burgess and others have explored theoretical notions of sovereignty and modes of political discourse in early modern England.[3] But serious discussion of ideas of the commonwealth and the sovereign's place were limited to the small educated minority of men who had the leisure to contemplate and who perhaps could influence the political sphere. The monarchs needed to gain the loyalty of all their subjects: not only nobles and gentry in their castles and manor-houses, but ordinary men and women – behind the plough, at the loom, around the well, and especially in the alehouse. Moreover, from 1547 to 1603 the Tudors experienced what was seen as novel and dangerous rule: the throne occupied by a child, and then by two women in succession. After 1603, the throne of England was occupied by a Scot. Major religious changes occurred in each reign, except perhaps that of James I. Perhaps it would not be surprising if crises were endemic.

King James might proclaim that monarchs were chosen by God to rule, and write books expounding high views of royal authority and the subject's duty of obedience. But Tudor and Stuart monarchs could only rule if they could secure the co-operation of subjects, and they needed the willing assistance of many. With only a few paid officials at the centre and even fewer in the regions, practically all transmission of governing power depended on delegation through people interested enough to take part. Why would they bother? Patronage was one of the most important incentives, and the crown held the key to rewards of many kinds: titles of nobility or knighthood, appointments to posts which brought income or status, or gifts of land or privileges encouraged public service. So some nobles and commoners jostled for positions which would bring these prizes. The most hard-working ministers in government grew rich as well as enjoying the less tangible rewards of power. Thomas Wolsey built a palace and lived like a king, and Thomas Cromwell also did well. Protector Somerset built Somerset House, his palace in the Strand. Elizabeth's most assiduous chief minister Lord Burghley acquired and built country mansions, and so did his son Robert Cecil. James I's boyfriends Somerset and Buckingham were given money and estates – but they laboured too at governing, Buckingham almost to the point of assuming sovereign power. These men worked energetically at the centre, and also at regulating lesser powers across the realm. Aristocrats, sometimes willingly, sometimes not, held high office in the north, on the border with Scotland, in the Marches of Wales, or in their counties.

Studies of the exercise of power in the counties emphasise the dependence of the crown and the Privy Council on the unpaid labour of rural squires. They have often assumed that all leading gentry held the vital administrative and legal post of justice of the peace. Every law made by parliament, every proclamation by a monarch, had to rely on such men, including whoever was sheriff, for implementation across the country. As Tudor and Stuart monarchs and Privy Councils sought to control ever more aspects of life, from religious observance and military preparedness to labour relations, drinking ale or assisting the poor, so the demands on the JPs increased. William Lambarde in 1587 moaned about 'not loads, but stacks of statutes' which gentlemen had to administer in their counties. Why would they bother? In fact, not all did, but, conversely, not all those who wished to do so succeeded in getting or maintaining a position of authority. The gentry indulged in a great deal of intrigue and pressure to acquire the prime post: to be appointed by the Lord Chancellor as a justice of the peace. They also used their contacts locally and among the monarch's chief advisers in order to secure dismissal of rivals. But, as we shall see, their use of power was not only selfish: many sought to serve the public good – as they saw it.

The town-dwellers and villagers of early modern England also bore responsibility for managing social cohesion. As mayor or member of a borough corporation, some citizens had to organise the communal activities of daily life, and the turning of laws and judicial decisions into public compliance. In towns too there were struggles for power, and those who achieved membership of urban government needed to exploit costume, ceremonial and buildings to advertise their authority. In the villages, those who took their turns as constable or officer of the watch had onerous tasks. According to a study of village constables, those selected rarely refused.[4] But if they had faced continuous resistance and riot, would they have agreed to serve? Only when Charles I increased their burdens in the 1630s, so that they had to coerce villagers to serve in and pay for the militia, fulfil the demands of the Book of Orders of 1631, collect ship money, and support the unpopular war against the Scots in 1637, were fewer willing to undertake the tasks of enforcement. Apparently, willingness to co-operate affected individual choices about whether to serve in office – but even unwillingness suggests that duty was taken seriously.

Part I of this book discusses such questions about power: who actually held it, how they sought or lost it, and the methods by which it was promoted among the people.

Part II considers the nature of authority in the early modern family. The hierarchy of the state drew on the theory of patriarchy in the family as a metaphor for submission to monarch, and to the crown's officers at all levels. James made it explicit when he called himself the father of his people; Elizabeth depicted herself in speeches as the careful housewife, and in 1563 promised to be a natural mother of her subjects. Female monarchy itself generated a cleavage between the theories of patriarchy and the present reality. Sermons and books written by men proclaimed male authority and the duties of wives, children and servants to obey. But how far did people actually follow such texts in daily lives which rarely conformed to the model of the polemicists – that of the husband going out in the world bringing in the money, and the wife confined to domesticity? Studies of agricultural life, and of women at work in rural and urban contexts have suggested that women, men, and the young led more interrelated lives than that. Laura Gowing, Tim Stretton, Ralph Houlbrooke and others have shown that women were not always confined under male guardianship and could use the law themselves.[5] A woman's position in family authority was always highly ambiguous, since if she owed subjection and deference to father or husband, she also had control over children, servants and apprentices. The issue of power relationships within the family was then as now a delicate one, and a changing one too, perhaps not susceptible to clear-cut formal instruction. Perhaps men were not always imperious, and wives and children were often undeferential; perhaps the family was not such a good pattern for the state after all?

Part III takes up themes concerning power in action across the country, and responses to it. Keith Wrightson pointed out that parliaments and proclamations legislated for, and political moralists wrote and preached, a notion of order and a pattern of authority which was harmonious – but such notions needed to be translated into action among the people. Wrightson suggested, however, that many did not share their superiors' conceptions, and there were also variations between the approach of gentry JPs and that of constables, jurors, and those who were expected to submit to rule.[6] The sixteenth and early seventeenth centuries faced unusual strains: dynastic uncertainties, revolutionary changes in religion, harvest failures, unprecedented population growth, continuous inflation, and episodes of expensive and generally unsuccessful foreign war. Each of these stresses created exceptional difficulties in maintaining authority, and Lord Chancellors moaned that the local office-holders were failing to do so.

But the local governors cannot have failed so dismally. The ship of commonwealth may have been in peril, or rocked in rough seas in the mid-1530s, in 1549, 1553, the late-1560s, late-1580s and mid-1590s, and the 1620s – but it did not sink, or at least not until 1642 when civil war began to overturn the established government. It has sometimes been assumed that the plaints of Privy Councillors were true, and that little was done by those appointed to run the localities, or that well-organised and effective systems of social discipline were constructed only in the later seventeenth century. The surviving archives of local government from the mid-sixteenth century onward, studied in conjunction with private working papers, diaries and correspondence, suggest that, on the contrary, men in authority across the realm were working hard to achieve a well-ordered society and to find effective remedies for the social and other problems confronting them. In Wiltshire and Essex, in Middlesex and Staffordshire, the work of these men can be glimpsed, and a closer look at the record can reveal systematic attention to the most pressing problems from at least the mid-sixteenth century. In Essex, petty sessions reported regularly and quarter sessions dealt with huge work loads. In Wiltshire, treasurers handled systems for relieving poverty well before the Poor Law acts of 1598 and 1601, and the justices discussed the best way to handle difficult cases: several would confer even over such matters as what help to allow to a poor old man who had his hovel destroyed by fire in the thatch, or to a soldier wounded in warfare. The devotion of gentlemen to tedious administration, to organising the repair of potholes in the highways, as well as maintaining order, suggests an answer to some of the questions raised above.

Not everyone wished to obey the demands of the state, whether they were expressed in parliamentary statute or justice's warrant. Yet it is notable that in 1534, amid unprecedented change, nearly every person who was required to take the Oath of Succession did so. Despite much grumbling and reluctance, virtually the whole adult male population did as it was told. The forced loan of 1626 was widely condemned in public by the politically aware, and 70 gentlemen refused to pay and went to prison – but almost everyone eventually paid up, reluctantly. Even the unpopular Ship Money was collected, though with increasing difficulty, until 1639. Somehow, the state persuaded its subjects to accept much of what it demanded.

Nevertheless, people grumbled and complained about those who directed them.[7] Geoffrey Elton has demonstrated popular hostility to Henry VIII's rejection of Queen Katherine and of the pope, to his marriage with Anne Boleyn and to the dissolution of monasteries. The number of martyrs to Henry's religious changes and new marriage was roughly similar to the number of Protestant martyrs under Mary Tudor – around 300, which means that most people gave in to new policies, if unwillingly. There was anger too at the king's minister Thomas Cromwell, who had dealt with punishment of the severest critics. In 1536, the York articles of the Pilgrimage of Grace complained to the king that 'we your true subjects think that your grace takes of your counsel . . . such persons as be of low birth and small reputation'.[8] In all reigns the literate and politically aware could produce sarcastic rhymes and scurrilous libels, which show how those in power were perceived to fail. The *Poems and Songs Relating to the Duke of Buckingham* show serious discontent in their ironic railing at the chief minister's power-seeking and the failures of his policies.[9] Ordinary people in the villages and towns vividly, and often rudely, expressed their dismay when the state's demands conflicted with their own needs: they could blame monarch, Councillors, gentry, or constables with excretory insults. Yet this abuse also shows what people expected of those with power over them, even if it were only the temporary power of a constable in his year of office.

The disorders of young people probably lay behind a sizable proportion of arguments between constables and unruly village elements: youth is often implied in the descriptions of participants. Shakespeare's shepherd complained 'I would there were no age between ten and three-and-twenty, or that youth would sleep out the rest; for there is nothing in the between but getting wenches with child, wronging the ancientry, stealing, fighting'.[10] The apprentices and journeymen of London frequently misbehaved on the streets at holidays like Twelfth Night and Shrove Tuesday. Does that mean that they rejected authority overall? More seriously, when the pressure of new policies or economic grievances became too great, or ambition and opportunism beckoned, some people actually rose in rebellion, and more in riots. The rioters against agricultural capitalism in 1607 under their leader 'Captain Pouch' were castigated by the Lord Chancellor and others as 'levellers', implying that they wished to level English society.[11] But perhaps they simply sought to level the newly-created enclosures that had altered their farming methods and threatened their livelihood.

How dangerous were these protests? Were the English really 'in contempt of all authority'? Was there an endemically disordered and rebellious state of affairs in England from the reign of Henry VIII to the 1630s? Despite the divisions of a hierarchical society, with extremes of wealth and poverty, religious revolution, agricultural change and foreign pressures, all the risings were quickly contained – until in 1641 the combined grievances against Charles I led towards real rebellion.

Until then, squalls and storms beset Lambarde's 'ship of commonwealth'; it strained but it did not sink. Women and children defied men, even utilised the central and local law courts supposedly closed to them. Kings and Councillors, justices and constables were sometimes reviled, rebellions were raised and riots erupted. The writings and the voices of governors and governed – concerned Councillors, ambitious nobles, hard-working JPs, affronted constables, troubled townsmen, worried villagers and farmers – show how early modern men and women dealt, in practice, with authority.

PART I

1

Monarchy

When we look back on the sixteenth century, the long reigns of Henry VIII and Elizabeth seem at first sight settled and almost pre-ordained. Henry's father Henry Tudor had overcome the uncertainty of a crown won on the battlefield, without direct hereditary title; Henry VII had conciliated the powerful, combined innovation in government with traditional kingship, and safely passed on the throne to a son. Henry VIII's long reign was followed by his three children in turn. But there were very real problems in each case, since Henry's only male heir Edward was a child king when he acceded in 1547 and died in 1553, aged 15; Mary, the first woman to reign since the ill-fated brief rule of Matilda in 1141, had to fight her way to the throne. However, the period between 1547 and 1558 has often been dismissed, as merely an anomalous interlude of 'crisis', with Mary's death after only five years as queen opening the way for Elizabeth's triumphant 45–year rule. Elizabeth saw off the invasion threat from a Spanish king who believed her to be a bastard, and in her later years England experienced an exceptionally creative phase of poetry, music, and drama. She made England safe for the Stuarts. During Elizabeth's last years, James VI of Scotland faced doubts about whether or not he was the rightful successor to her throne, but after she died in 1603, he acceded peacefully, ruled confidently, and was followed naturally by an adult son. This all seemed like a steady and safe inheritance.

But these rulers were never as secure as they now seem. True, by 1509 England had a very long history of centralised monarchical rule: the Wars of the Roses had disputed only who should be king, not the system of monarchy or the powers of the crown. Yet through the sixteenth and early seventeenth century both inherent weakness and explicit challenges created a continuing problem of authority, as each monarch was nervously aware. The real fragility of Tudor and Stuart rule informed every royal policy. Foreign alliances or war, relations with Parliament and the court, management of the provinces, provision for labour regulation or poverty among the people, all were influenced by the need to maintain royal power. Ironically, Charles I was probably the only ruler in our period who felt secure, and he ended facing rebellion and execution.

The difficulty of securing both the life of the monarch and obedience to him or her lay partly in the lack of formal coercive force. In early modern England there was a small central bureaucracy, no regular army, and no organised police force. Kings and queens could be very vulnerable, and they knew it. So how could they they establish their authority, how could they persuade the nation to accept and abide by it? More important, since most of the people lived outside London, how could they even tell them what to think or do? They needed to control the great magnates who had tenants enough to challenge the crown if they chose; but also to command allegiance from the 'middling sort' in town and country, and the rural majority. More than that, they needed co-operation in governing, from highest to lowest. They did not always succeed in achieving these objectives, but they rarely forgot to try.

Theory and tradition sanctioned royal power, with the help of God. God's ordained plan was continually invoked in support: Henry VII's Act of Succession in 1485 named 'Henry, by the grace of God, King'. That was the form in which the current sovereign was invoked in statutes and official documents; people were to be reminded that God had a part in politics. The notion that James I met opposition because of his provocative theory of the divine right of kings ignores the widespread acceptance, throughout the sixteenth century, of the divine origin of kingly authority. This did not mean that every action of a monarch was God-given; it meant rather that God had ordained the rule of the realm by king or queen. In the earlier part of Henry VIII's reign, at least, most people both low and high, simply accepted the divine origin of monarchy without thinking about it, even while they might wish to criticise royal actions, or royal ministers.

That the king's power came from God perhaps needed specific emphasis in the 1530s, when Henry claimed power over the Church and used parliament to confirm his claims and to lay heavy penalties on those who denied them. The 1533 Act in Restraint of Appeals refers to the realm governed by a king unto whom all 'bear next to God, a natural and humble obedience'. The statute declaring Henry supreme head of the Church of England outlined the king's power to order the Church 'to the pleasure of Almighty God', and a 1539 statute reminded his people that the king is 'by God's law supreme head immediately under Him of this whole Church and Congregation of England'. That God gave the king power in the state was uncontroversial: the claim that He gave the king power over the Church was more problematical, and met opposition from clergy, nobles, royal officeholders and the common people, to the extent of inspiring a major rebellion in 1536. During the 1530s and 1540s, Henry VIII changed direction on many religious and political matters, but he never withdrew his divine justification.

The nine-year-old Edward inherited his father's place of authority under God, although in practice his power was exercised by others. Surprisingly, neither Protector Somerset nor the duke of Northumberland used it cautiously. Each in turn moved quickly to alter the nation's official religious practice towards Protestantism. It was partly to safeguard the new religious laws, as well as his own power, that Northumberland tried to install his daughter-in-law, Jane Grey, as monarch when Edward died in 1553. But Henry's elder daughter Mary overcame Northumberland's forces and took the throne, as her father intended. Henry VIII had regulated the succession by statute and by his will, giving Mary and then Elizabeth clear right after Edward and his heirs (if any). So there were cogent reasons for asserting Mary's right to rule, and the 1554 Act concerning the regal power appeals to the rhetoric of divine right – that the imperial crown has 'by the divine providence of Almighty God' descended to her. Those who joined Mary to enforce her succession against Jane Grey claimed God's intention, and not just military success. Such reminders of God's part in the governance of England continued to appear in official statements during Mary's brief reign.

Elizabeth was scarcely more secure when she became queen in 1559. She inherited a nation with divided religious beliefs – a dissension which had international implications, and a war with much larger and richer neighbours. She came to the throne amid some doubts about female monarchy, and about her legitimacy as the child of Henry's second marriage to Anne Boleyn. To committed Catholics, she was a bastard, and Mary Queen of Scots claimed her title. Elizabeth thus needed all the justification she could summon. Of course, she too was queen 'by the grace of God' (as well as Henry's will, and parliamentary statute). But she had to convince the nation to accept her, and especially all who took office in government, central and local, secular and ecclesiastical. For them, she prescribed the Oath of Supremacy, a formal oath of allegiance accepting her authority over the nation and over the Church. She meant to exercise the control over the Church which Henry VIII had taken from the pope, and to emphasise that even as a woman she could do so. The oath aimed to ensure the loyalty of those in power by a net of formal obligation. Not everyone took the oath, nor could it ensure universal loyalty. However, it succeeded in gaining at least outward adherence from most officials in Church and state, giving Elizabeth time to establish her government and the Protestant religion. Perhaps she was lucky to have 45 years of rule in which to try.

James I articulated an explicit divine right in his writings, and in addressing parliament. But in practice he took it no further than his predecessors, and he certainly never acted as a tyrant or absolute monarch: he was far too much of a realist. James saw his duty, as next under God, to care for the nation as a father, and he assumed the duty of his subjects was to obey without question. There lay some of the problems of his reign: not so much in an increased emphasis by the sovereign on God-given authority, but in the increased willingness of some politicians to question his edicts. Yet despite squabbles with the House of Commons in 1606, 1610, 1614, and 1621, and criticism elsewhere, James did manage to rule fairly peacefully. It was his son who failed, by neglecting the practical realities of dealing with people, to make divine right kingship work.

From his accession in 1625, Charles I expected parliament to do as he wished, and not to require negotiation and subtlety. He defended the duke of Buckingham in the face of widespread bitter criticism of the favourite, and quickly punished many of those who questioned government policies by making them sheriffs so that they could not sit in parliament nor on the bench of JPs for a year. The court became more formal and restricted, with a new emphasis on high art. Charles imposed the policies he favoured – the Book of Orders of 1631, revenue-raising, Laudian innovations – without securing the co-operation of the political elite, and during the 1630s many of them became disillusioned with Stuart rule. Charles treated dissent harshly: Hugh Pyne in Somerset was lucky to survive his expression of contempt for the king in 1629, the government at first wanted him hung for it; puritan pamphleteers were publically mutilated in 1637.[1] Charles made occasional progresses, notably in 1633 when he travelled north for his coronation in Scotland, but he made less effort than had his predecessors to provide at least the appearance of contact with the people.

God gave sovereigns to the realm and expected them to be obeyed, but the practical insecurity of early modern monarchy meant that monarchs had to work at persuading their subjects to follow orders. They tried a range of methods. There remain questions about how large a proportion of the population could be reached by them. Preaching could be one of the most potent weapons. It could be used to preach royal policy in all the 9,500 parishes of England: it provided the widest and fastest dissemination possible, but it was not uniformly effective. Religious division reduced the effectiveness of the pulpits. The ecclesiastical alterations of the 1530s, and piecemeal changes in the organisation and doctrine of the English Church, created opposition from many of the clergy as well as laymen and women. But Henry's government issued precise instructions on what the priests were to teach their people, and ordered justices of the peace to report any who failed to do so. Further religious change in the reigns of each of his three successors meant that ministers in many parishes opposed the royal wishes, and would not willingly preach to support them. One attempt to overcome the problem was the setting of formal Homilies on doctrine by Edward VI's government. These were printed sermons to be read in all churches, to spread the same ideas everywhere. The Homily on Obedience emphasised that all authority in the realm derived from royal power. Elizabeth reimposed the 1547 Homilies in 1559, and added a further set in 1563.

Preaching obedience to authority aimed to reach everyone, since all should attend church. But it could only work universally if everyone did go to church each week, and they did not. Some men and women found more pressing things to do, especially at the busiest seasons of the agricultural year; harvest, or sowing time. Or they preferred sleep, the alehouse, or games on their day of rest. The pendulum of the English reformations meant that some people stayed away from church because of doctrinal objections, and governments could not coerce them all. Those who attended church did not always listen attentively to what they were told, and congregations squabbled, dozed or gossiped through sermons and homilies. But, over time, something stuck and lessons were learned. For the churches taught national loyalty almost as much as Christian faith: the Homilies taught obedience, the royal arms set up on a board taught respect, and royal festivals taught gratitude: there were special prayers each 17 November to celebrate Elizabeth's accession, and then on 5 August and 5 November to celebrate James's escapes from plotters.

Royal proclamations were another way for the sovereign's authority to reach the people rapidly. A proclamation announced the accession of each new ruler: few people knew immediately when a monarch had died and a new ruler was installed, and the news took time to spread within and beyond the capital. Change of reign was always dangerous, for the bonds of obedience were loosened and new loyalties had to be learned. Northumberland knew it well, and tried to prevent the transfer of loyalty to Mary Tudor after the death of Edward VI in 1553. When Elizabeth was dying in 1603, 'great peturbation' was reported, fears that the 'masterless men and malcontents may rise', and the armed guard at the palace was increased.[2] There had long been anxiety, since Elizabeth would not name her successor; in the event James King of Scotland succeeded smoothly. A change of monarch was important news, and when it seemed likely, every traveller carried rumour or information from inn to inn along the highways, and London letter-writers posted speculation to their country correspondents. But it was the proclamation of the successor which confirmed the rumours, declared the sovereign's title and rights, and demanded allegiance.

As well as confirmation of accessions to the throne, proclamations were vital working tools of royal rule: they announced the sovereign's orders on issues which needed immediate action, and reminded people of their duty in times of crisis or uncertainty, though they could not create new offences or penalties.[3] Some told people things they needed to know, such as those declaring the value of coins in the currency changes of 1550, 1554, and 1560. Others told people what they were to think, such as the proclamation in 1535 against Bishop Fisher, who had refused to assent to the king's new Supremacy Act. Mary used proclamations as propaganda for the return to Catholicism, and for her marriage to Philip of Spain. Proclamations provided the way to order rapid action in times of harvest crisis or fears of invasion, and dealt with offences, such as one against the people who helped the Jesuit Edmund Campion in 1580. Most covered mundane, local or even individual questions – food prices, fishing rights in the Thames, or an outlawry, and copies of these went only to the relevant places. Many proclamations responded to urgent needs or petitions from affected groups, such as food or wine merchants, or clothiers. The proclamations temporarily closing the London theatres were a response to plague epidemics in the capital.

How widely did proclamations reach? Hundreds of different proclamations were issued – at least 437 from Henry VII to Edward's death in 1553, 64 in Mary's short reign, 382 in Elizabeth's long one. Under James I, proclamations managed much government regulation during the long intervals between parliaments. The form of a proclamation was meant to impress with regal importance: it was carefully drafted, and the writ to proclaim was sealed with the Great Seal. Nearly all were in English, rather than Latin. Messengers on foot or on horseback carried proclamations out to towns and villages, there to be published in the churches and read out with a loud voice by local officials in market places or places 'of great resort of the people'. In London they were proclaimed by the common cryer. Often copies were posted up, usually on church doors. The more elaborate ones, such as the announcement in London of the peace treaty with France in 1546 were accompanied by trumpets and bonfires to ensure attention. In some cases we know how many copies were made: for one proclamation of 1534, 20 were handwritten on parchment, and sealed, for sheriffs and the most important local officials, and 300 were printed to be sent to others. For more local matters, only a few were printed. But for the proclamation of January 1542 on the royal style, when Henry VIII proudly declared himself King of Ireland, 600 printed copies were made; for a proclamation against hawking in the same year, three printings of 400 copies each seemed necessary. The largest printing in Elizabeth's reign was one of 700 copies, while under James there were issues comprising 1,000, or even 1,300 copies. With 9,500 parishes and around 800 large and small market towns, not every place received one, but the officials in all the major towns would see a copy, and presumably inform others. Most of the population could not read, but they might hear one read out at church, or at the market cross in one of the 300 or so chief market towns. And these people could inform others: news about food prices, value of money, or politics spread rapidly in alehouses and in village and town streets, especially on market days. A proclamation could become public in London a day or two after the date of the writ, while distant places had to wait several days for a messenger to ride out. Eventually then, the king or queen could make their will known to a good proportion of their subjects even in distant rural areas. But it is impossible to know exactly how many subjects heard directly, or how much the orders became distorted in transmission.

Not all proclamations were strictly followed. Henry VIII's Statute of Proclamations of 1539 (repealed in 1547) was passed to insist that the king 'shall be obeyed', and to coerce offenders, claiming that obstinate persons were refusing to acknowledge what the kingly power given by God allowed Henry to command. Announcement of a revised value for coins demanded adherence for practical reasons, however unpopular it might be, as in the revaluation of 1551; whereas a religious edict troubled consciences and provoked resistance. Some proclamations were afterwards transformed into statutes by parliament, enforceable (or not) through the normal judicial or administrative means. The Privy Council could enforce proclamations, and tried to do so against banned preachers who continued to preach in Elizabeth's reign. But it was hard to control ideas by proclamation, or indeed by any other means. The successful distribution of the Martin Marprelate tracts against the bishops in the 1580s – despite official bans – demonstrated that the government could not secure compliance if some were determined to press their own opinions.

Two of the Tudor monarchs understood well the uses of self-advertising in a dangerous and uncertain world. Henry VIII and Elizabeth exploited the visual imagery of majesty very deliberately to convey the impression of high power and authority through pictures, by royal ritual, and, for Henry, by building palaces. Many of the paintings and engravings of the monarchs still survive, making it possible to trace the purposeful creation of a quite new image of regal monarchy from the middle of Henry's reign.[4] It is probably no coincidence that this happened around 1532, when Henry knew he would be facing enormous uncertainties over the reception of his divorce and break from the pope. He feared opposition from foreign powers, and from his subjects high and low, and sought to bolster his power in whatever way he could. Until then there were few portraits of Henry VIII, and those that survive have no propagandist value. For most people accustomed to the famous later image, those early portraits would come as a shock. The 1520 portrait depicts a nervous, unimpressive, young man, with a slightly receding chin, and suspicious expression, looking sideways and apparently avoiding the eye of the beholder. He looks shy. The two 1525 Hornebolte watercolours similarly show a Henry without majesty: he is side-on, rather chinless and a little pudgy, wearing a simple black velvet cap with no plume. In one he is beardless, intensifying the timid impression, the other shows him with a beard but still very weak. We should assume that this was much as Henry VIII appeared, since presumably court painters did not attempt to depict him worse than he was.[5]

But Henry was lucky, or clever, to find an artist of the Holbein's talent to create a new image just when he most needed one. This is an entirely different Henry, barely resembling the earlier: now he stands full-length, looking confidently forward. The face is transformed – broader and bearded – and the artist gives his body extra bulk, showing him with legs apart and arms encased in huge brocade sleeves to give him extra mass. In the lost Holbein privy chamber mural, which we know from copies, the king wears a plumed hat, in others he wears a crown and ermine. But in all versions he dominates, standing tall, or surrounded by figures who are smaller, or kneeling before him, as in the picture of him granting a charter to the City of Gloucester in 1541.[6] His clothing and surroundings are rich and magnificent. Holbein was paid to depict glory in a kingly figure who radiated power, and he succeeded. The new powerful image dominated royal iconography for the rest of the reign, and became accepted as the image of Henry for ever after.

The Holbein mural of kingly power in Henry's privy chamber, and the portraits, aimed to impress those who had audience with the king, or visited his court. Relatively few people actually saw these pictures, but they included many who mattered: foreign ambassadors, English nobles, gentry, and royal servants. Other versions spread the new image of majesty more widely. The title-page illlustration to the English Great Bible of 1539 contained a semi-divine royal iconography, showing Henry VIII at the top, handing the *verbum dei* to Archbishop Cranmer and to Thomas Cromwell, with the social hierarchy down to the common people shown at the bottom.[7] This reinforced the king's position at the head of both religious and secular power. The Great Bible was supposed to be set up in all parish churches for the people to read, and it took the image to a much wider potential audience – 'potential' because most of the population could not read nor were they likely to look at the Bible themselves. It would be overstatement to call this mass propaganda, yet some of the people in all social groups had the opportunity to see it.

The newly developed iconography came to permeate the material elements of Henry's rule, too. The portraits on the Great Seal, which was used for the wax seal on all important documents in the king's name, changed from traditional stereotype to the new style. The new Seal showed the bulky square-faced monarch majestic on a broad throne on one side, with 'supreme head of the church of England', in Latin, round the rim; the other side showed him on horseback in armour ready for war. The Holbein king also appeared in the initial-letter illustrations of official documents: the Plea Rolls image changed to the new broader, bearded Henry, and this new version was used in charters, such as the Gloucester city one mentioned above. Although they would not reach the mass of the population, these images spread the idea: the city government would see the charters, sheriffs and other local governors the Great Seal, lawyers and some clients the legal documents. Such persuasion of men with local power in the distant towns mattered, since they were far less likely than the nobles to attend court and there be impressed with royal authority.

As well as personal portraiture, the Tudors used symbols and heraldic devices – the portcullis, the Tudor rose, greyhound, red dragon, and the ship of state. These armorial devices and symbols proclaimed regality and the Tudor heritage, and the royal arms and badges adorned all sorts of surfaces – the livery of royal servants, manuscripts, armour, cannon, buildings, hangings, furniture, banners for ships and processions. These official images became fashionable, and private gentlemen proclaimed their loyalty by using them in their own houses.

The pictorial representation of royal grandeur to encourage obedience continued after Henry's death in 1547, although it was far more difficult to represent Henry's successors as authority figures. Edward was a nine-year-old boy when he came to the throne, not at all majestic. Yet even the delightful 1539 portrait of the baby Edward had already depicted him wearing a plumed velvet hat like Henry VIII, gesturing as if to his people with one hand, and holding an orb-like object – the trappings of a Holbein king would be his. The 1550 picture of Edward, now at Petworth, shows him slim and young-faced, but standing solidly like his father, with the wide sleeves to suggest impressive size, and richly embroidered fabrics for his clothes and furnishings. He was displayed as his father's son, who would grow into his father's grandeur.[8]

Mary Tudor was perhaps unlucky to be painted by Hans Eworth, and Antonio Moro, who lacked Holbein's gift for propagandist royal portraits.[9] This was particularly unfortunate for her, because a woman regnant desperately needed to invoke a majestic image. There had been no sovereign queen since the short ill-fated reign of Matilda 400 years earlier, and the patriarchal theory of woman's place as silent and submissive created problems for one who ruled a nation. Perhaps Mary herself did not even grasp the necessity fully, for in one of Eworth's portraits she wore a plain dark velvet dress which conveyed little of riches or power. In another, although she wore a big brocade dress and prominent jewel, the image is spoilt by her rather dour facial expression, small chin and pinched mouth. Probably it was a more realistic picture than the Holbein versions of Henry VIII, but cannot have greatly impressed contemporaries. In contrast to their court portraits, the Great Seals of Edward, and of Mary and Philip made greater effort at majesty. Edward is shown in an ermine collar, crowned and enthroned, sitting straight and tall with legs wide, holding orb and sceptre. He appears smaller on the obverse horseback war-leader side, but there were Tudor emblems everywhere, including Tudor roses on the horse's armour. On their seal, Philip and Mary are robed with ermine, crowned, each with a hand on the orb, appearing more or less equal. This did not reflect their relative positions in the English state, however, since Philip was excluded from full regal power. Even more surprisingly, the mounted figures on the obverse show Philip in the foreground, partly obscuring Mary. Considering the hostility to Philip among the English governing classes, this was unwise, apart from detracting from the idea of Mary as a confident ruler.

Queen Elizabeth did not immediately revert to anything like the exaggerated regal style of her father's image.[10] She faced a similar problem to Mary, in that woman's expected role was one of subservience not authority. Early portraits and miniatures did little for her – they simply show her standing, dressed in dark clothes, no more impressive than other aristocratic ladies. It took time to develop ideas of majesty that fitted a female ruler, and to portray those ideas in paintings, engravings and seals. But later in her reign there was a deliberate policy to control pictures and copies, with approved images of the queen, and a plan for a model version for artists to follow.

There was no one court painter, yet images of Elizabeth from 1569 onward all show a truly majestic figure, with the richest embroidered gowns and jewellery, in a regal standing pose and either crowned or with elaborate hair arrangements. Moreover, a complex set of symbols and allegories promoted the queen's attributes as ruler. They show her as true successor to the Tudor throne; as purity; as the goddess of peace; and as the embodiment of imperial ambition. In the renowned 'Ditchley' portrait by Gheeraerts in 1592, she is identified with England itself, standing on the map. In portraits from the end of her reign, her ageing is concealed: the face is usually the formalised schema of Hilliard's miniatures, but the dress, jewellery, and allegorical imagery become even more luxuriant.

Many of the paintings of Elizabeth were for the houses of important people in her court and government, such as Hatton and Robert Cecil, who might hope to impress the queen with their enthusiastic loyalty when she visited. Sir Francis Drake, Sir Christopher Hatton, Sir Francis Walsingham, and Sir Thomas Heneage, ambitious courtiers all, were themselves all painted between 1587 and 1594 wearing cameos of the queen. Majestic imagery adorned official documents such as charters and the Great Seal of 1584, but now the frontispieces of books, engravings, and even costume medallions of the queen's supposed likeness were copied from Hilliard's or Isaac Oliver's designs. The majestic imagery of Queen Elizabeth was promulgated more widely than her father's had been, as a part of official policy. Still, such items were too expensive for most of her subjects, and the elaborate and allusive iconography was comprehensible only to the educated few. Yet the queen and her government decided that the image was important, giving attention to the portraits and patterns and encouraging their proliferation. Perhaps it did indeed help to secure the obedience of sycophantic courtiers and loyal commoners; or perhaps Elizabeth just hoped that it might, and painters and miniaturists enjoyed the profits.

King James I held a view of his regal rights which was similar to that of his predecessors. But he thought its articulation in speeches to parliament sufficed, and did not feel the need to use portraiture to support his authority. Rather, he relied on the court and the pageantry within it. James held lavish and expensive masques designed by Ben Jonson and Inigo Jones for his inner group of favourites and fawners, but each masque was usually performed only once, and seen by the fortunate few within the court. The best-known portrait of James is probably the 1621 Mytens one of the seated king gazing sideways, with a tired and sorrowful expression. The fabrics of his clothes are satin and velvet, but without decoration, and his garments and pose lack the defiant magnificence and emphasis on bulk of the Henry or Elizabeth pictures.[11] James appears a little more decisive pictured on horseback, or in the de Critz standing portrait, but still he is represented without grandeur: the effect on contemporaries is unknown. His son Charles I likewise did not favour the huge embroidered garments for portraits: he dressed quite simply and his thin face and small stature did not convey an image of grandeur. Nevertheless, van Dyck tried: he showed King Charles on horseback in a dignified, commanding pose, with a serious stately expression. These pictures may have helped his reputation of majesty within a narrow court circle, but they reflected his own dignified self-image rather than seeking to project greatness to his subjects.

Royal portraits hung in palaces and private great houses, and were seen by few. Even copies, medallions, or engravings were not seen by the mass of the population. But one form of royal image reached every level of society but the destitute. Coins carried a design picturing the monarch.[12] Oddly, for the first sixteen years of Henry VIII's reign the stylised crowned portrait of Henry VII remained in use. But from the middle of Henry VIII's reign, the approach altered: designers now tried harder to portray majesty on coins, and recoinages acknowledged the monarch's ageing with new portraits. The larger coins – gold sovereigns, half sovereigns and crowns, silver shillings – were big enough for wonderfully detailed portraits, and the mints at London, York, Bristol and Canterbury produced excellent currency. After 1526, Henry VIII appears more like his Holbein image, while commercial need and new designs led to a big increase in coins minted. The value of silver coins minted in 1522–3 was some 17,000 pounds; the yearly average 1527–30 reached 70,000 pounds. Gold coins also increased in number. In 1545–7, the coinage debasements led to massively increased output, with coins worth over 440,000 pounds minted in 1545–6, more than at any other time up to the end of Elizabeth's reign.[13] The larger coins carried a different, chunkier, older face of the king, along with the some of the traditional Tudor emblems: the Tudor rose at his feet. But the debased coins created anger and distress among the people, and so the image cannot have been good for the king's reputation then.

The numerous coin issues of Edward VI's brief reign show a fascinating progression in imagery designed for maximum political effect. They start with a boyish profile head, as on the 1547–9 half sovereign coin; the 1549–50 coin shows a somewhat more grown-up youth, crowned, with longer hair. On the gold crown of 1550–3, Edward is shown crowned, with the orb and sceptre, while the silver crown and half-crown coins of 1551, and the pattern prepared for a new crown coin in 1553, all carried a more imposing young monarch on horseback, as if ready to assume kingly roles in ceremonial or war. The coin images were evidently important: the public was being prepared for real rule by Edward, and the maturing image shows how important his advisors considered the coins to be. In contrast, Mary was fully adult, yet did not resolve the difficulty of promoting female rule visually, and this is evident in her coins as in her portraits. She was shown crowned, and enthroned, but facially weak and even pudgy, while the coins for Philip and Mary, facing each other in profile, have her wearing a modest coif, not especially regal, with the crown floating over them both. This had less impact than the single portraits of monarchs, since two faces had to fit on the same small surface!

(a)

(b)

(c)

Fig. 1 (a): Pattern for a new Edward VI coin (1553), with a young king on horseback, no longer shown as a child. (**b**) Elizabeth milled shilling, same design as the three half-pence coin. (**c**) James I spur-ryal (*c.* 1605), king in ship of state, with shield.
(Photographs: courtesy of the Ashmolean Museum, Oxford, Heberden Coin Collection)

Right from the beginning, Elizabeth's coins were more impressive, showing her with an elaborate crown and, in some, brandishing a sceptre. Most representations were in profile. The early Elizabethan sixpenny coin carried a crowned profile of the queen, in a strong although not particularly flattering image, but one which lasted well in use, with the crown remaining visible. Most of these coins even show the somewhat hooked nose, with a very firm expression. The small three half-pence coin with her face in profile and quite long hair, with the crown above, also retained the image clearly, even on well-worn examples, while the 1601 full-face design flattered her a little more. One design depicted the elaborately dressed queen in a Tudor ship, symbolising her active command of the ship of state, and her supreme authority as captain. The higher value coins such as the gold half-sovereign were milled coins of better quality, able to depict a more elaborate crown, and a very clear and commanding profile of the queen. In a reign as long as Elizabeth's a great many coins were minted; the designs were mostly similar, and all provided a strong image of the queen's face and crown.

The main surprise of James I's coin designs is that he appears so much more dignified and regal than in, for instance, the now well-known Mytens painting. The 1604–19 crown coin shows James in profile on horseback, a sword drawn up by his shoulder, while on the rose ryal coin he has a tidy beard and sits enthroned with the monarchy's emblems, especially the portcullis, prominent; the 1619–25 issue is similar but with an older king wearing a higher ruff (a concession to fashion perhaps). James I's own court might have been undignified, but his image to the people was serious and kingly.

On his coins, Charles I also appears in striking kingly postures, looking quite aggressive, with sword drawn, perhaps reflecting the war at the start of his reign. On several of the crown and half-crown coins he is on horseback. Shillings are less formal: Charles has longer hair, and a laced collar, although he wears a large crown.

More important in the persuasive role of the coin images are the smaller low-denomination coins, since by far the greatest number of the monarch's subjects handled them. These coins too had clear, strong images which remained visible despite daily use. The Ashmolean Museum coin collection contains multiple examples, in various states of wear, providing evidence for a remarkable standard of coin production and endurance. Henry VIII's 1526–44 little half-groats (only slightly more in circumference than the present 5p) carry the king's profile and big crown in prominent relief, even on well-worn copies; the shield on the obverse stands out rather less. On the groat (about the size of our 10p), Henry's powerful face and crown are retained even more clearly; and even on very worn examples of the Bristol-minted groats of 1544–7 the full-face image stands out in relief quite strongly. The pennies and half pennies fared worse, and on really worn pennies the crown is almost all that remains; or on Edward's pennies a rose on one side and shield on the other. The rest of Edward's lesser coins, especially those of the fine coinage of 1550–3 retain the boyish face and his crown extremely well, even when obviously much used. Philip and Mary's profiles on the groat, facing each other, are likewise fairly clear, with the crown above, and Philip's rather pointed face showing up strongly.

Queen Elizabeth's reform of the coinage meant that these better-made coins showed her image remarkably clearly on almost all examples. Not surprisingly, the larger, higher-value gold and silver coins lasted well: her silver ryal ship image stayed wonderfully vivid, as did the coat of arms and the ship motif on the smaller gold angel. The silver crown coin showed a more elaborate profile and the regal sceptre. The more common three-half pence mentioned above retained the strong if unflattering profile and prominent nose, as well as the long hair of a female monarch beneath her crown. Even the well-used pennies of the 1580s retained a surprisingly sharp portrait, despite very worn edges. The better Edwardian and Elizabethan coins still circulated right up to 1694, yet the picture usually remained. The same is true of early Stuart shillings, sixpences, even half-groats. James I's dignified gravitas on a shilling, or even a sixpence or half-groat, comes over still. The coins may be considered the strongest promotion of the monarch; the image and emblems of monarchy were available to almost all the people, assuming they chose to look at them.

By word and by image – sermons and proclamations, portraits and coins – subjects were encouraged to admire, fear and obey. Monarchs used other means to the same end, including ritual and buildings. Palaces could expound powerful sovereignty: they were large and solid, and visible to all who passed by.[14] In London, the citizens could view the might of the Norman Tower with awe, as a mighty fortress, a prison and a place of execution. It had royal lodgings, with privy chamber and council chamber, but monarchs stayed there mainly for ceremonial reasons, notably before commencing the traditional coronation procession from the Tower to Westminster Abbey. Henry VIII's great Palace of Whitehall sprawled over 23 acres, but except for the two grand gatehouses, it lacked exterior display to excite the humbler passers-by. Inside, however, the grander rooms of state offered space and formality, and it housed the monarch and many officials, with the administrative offices. The palaces outside London, especially Greenwich, Richmond, and Hampton Court, with their towers and decoration, were obviously majestic and stood out from the fields around them, especially when seen from the river.

Henry VIII owned many other great houses and had sixty altogether when he died. Some came by inheritance, some by forfeit from the dissolved monasteries, others by exchange or purchase. He loved building as much as he enjoyed using the palaces. Some, including Oatlands and Nonsuch, were intended for hunting parties. Royal houses also served as stages for the rituals of monarchy: the peripatetic court's role in distributing office and favour and welcoming the crown's leading subjects needed great spaces. Foreign ambassadors and visitors had to be impressed by conspicuous demonstrations of dignity and wealth. Henry embellished the buildings he acquired, both inside and out, indulging his love for display.

He provided enough palaces to last for two centuries: his successors enjoyed them and struggled to maintain the more important ones. James and Charles built only a few smaller more classical buildings, designed by Inigo Jones, in and around London. The 1619 banqueting house in Whitehall, with its new Palladian lines, looked gently imposing from the outside, but few Londoners saw the opulent Rubens ceiling within. The Queen's House at Greenwich, built in 1616 for James's queen, Anne of Denmark, and lavishly completed and furnished by Charles for Henrietta-Maria in 1635, was semi-private and remote from most Londoners, while the new chapel in St James's Palace was more private still. It was the nobility and gentry who saw the king or queen in these wonderful surroundings, and who, having the power to threaten the crown, needed to be convinced of its strength. The aim of these buildings was not to excite awe among the London masses.

But sometimes Londoners did see significant demonstrations designed to impress them with royal might. Royal entries to the city and coronations flamboyantly displayed the ruler in lavish processions through the streets from the Tower to Westminster.[15] They were magnificent occasions, street drama on the grandest scale, as the long procession of richly dressed nobles and gentlemen of the court walked or rode before and after the monarch, even the horses draped with heraldic royal emblems. At Elizabeth's coronation in January 1559, the new queen was dressed in cloth of gold and carried in a litter trimmed with gold brocade reaching to the ground. Her gentlemen pensioners walked on either side wearing crimson damask, while the accompanying footmen wore crimson velvet, ornamented with silver, and with the red and white Tudor rose and the letters ER. The nobility, all richly robed and jewelled, rode their best horses. Colourful banners of heraldic devices hung everywhere, and along the way elaborately staged pageants showed allegorical scenes of praise and promise. The visual impact must have been tremendous. As well as sight, there was much sound to excite the watchers: loud instruments at the pageants, musical greetings along the route and, at Westminster, organs, fifes, trumpets, drums and bells. Salutes by gunfire added to the noise, and there were bonfires and celebratory feasting.

The funerals of monarchs were more sombre occasions, but they too displayed to Londoners the pageantry and heraldry of ceremonial. A procession four miles long accompanied Henry VIII's huge funeral chariot through the streets in 1547. All the important dignitaries of state and church took part, together with representatives of foreign powers. The hooded mourners wore long black gowns and carried immense banners with colourful heraldic illustrations. In 1603 Elizabeth's coffin, draped in purple velvet and supporting a royally robed effigy, was drawn by horses with flags at their heads, and black heraldic carapaces. Twelve nobles carried great banners with the armorial bearings of her royal ancestors back to Henry II, while others carried banners with the symbolic greyhound, dragon, and lion; there were regional banners too. Illustrations of Elizabeth's funeral procession now in the British Library give us some idea of its portentous visual impact, and of its drama.[16] What they cannot convey is the additional effect of movement – of the slow march – and of the sounds: slow beating drums, and tolling church bells. Funerals of other members of the royal families followed heraldic and symbolic ceremonial, if a little less lavishly performed, and in 1612 that of James I's popular eighteen-year-old son Henry, heir to the throne, evoked much sorrow.

Celebration of royal births and marriages, and royal entries into London especially, provided further occasions for lavish pageantry on the streets. Mary I enjoyed such ceremonies in quick succession. In August 1553, she made her inital entry into London upon her accession, and made the most of the opportunity for a spectacular display of her authority. She wore regal purple velvet, many rich jewels, and rode a horse that was also dressed, in gold. The royal trumpeters, heralds, and over 700 nobles and gentlemen rode with her, and all the ambassadors with their servants, and many ladies too. The procession, including the aldermen and guards, was said to number 3,000 in all. Having finally secured the throne, she demonstrated her sovereignty with maximum use of traditional royal display. Her coronation nine days later was magnificent, but perhaps made less propaganda for new, female monarchy than it might have done, since in the ceremony of the day preceding the coronation itself she dressed as queens consort had done, in white, rather than as kings, in purple.[17] For the arrival of her husband Philip of Spain in 1554, there were 'demonstrations of joy' carefully planned by City office-holders; not by the queen herself or her government. In November 1558, Elizabeth set out for her pre-coronation entry into London on becoming queen, along with a thousand lords, gentry, and ladies, and was welcomed by speeches, singing, trumpets playing, and 'such shooting of guns as never was heard afore'.[18] Pageants provided by the craft companies as she and her entourage rode into the City of London centred on Tudor dynastic themes, using the union of the red and the white rose. A description of the event was printed almost immediately, to underline its importance. Lesser pageantry welcomed Elizabeth to Norwich two decades later – or would have done except that she had to rush through it because of rain! Royal progresses, when the court moved about on a summer tour to different royal palaces or to the houses of selected nobles or gentlemen, maintained some of the same elements. One of the best-known late Tudor paintings shows a rather formulaic Queen Elizabeth dressed in one of her amazing gowns, jewels and coronet, in a litter, surrounded by the great men of the realm, and some court ladies. Often the monarch rode on horseback, with a great entourage. Such extraordinary royal appearances in public must have strongly impressed those who watched. But these occasions were just that – extra-ordinary. For more than a generation, from 1559 to 1603, there was no coronation or royal funeral, not even a royal birth or marriage. There were diplomatic visits, and the great Armada celebration, but they lacked the dynastic and emotional content of the royal events.

In contrast to Elizabeth, James I aimed less for display and ceremonial; he was a more private monarch. Although he travelled frequently, his journeys to country houses were occasions for his own diversion, for hunting and visiting. He moved between palaces, with frequent excursions to hunt at Royston, Oatlands, and Newmarket; courtiers accompanied the king, or visited wherever he happened to be, and Councillors complained at the difficulties of administering when the king was so often away. James stayed with prominent gentry or aristocrats, to denote his favour – and also to help spread the cost of his court. James did make formal civic entries too, for instance to Lincoln in 1617. Too late to help his authority, his funeral in 1625 was very costly and magnificent; although the letter-writer John Chamberlain thought it confused and disorderly.[19]

Charles I preferred more formal ceremonial than had his father, but it reached only a restricted audience. For instance, he dined in public so that courtiers could watch; but he disliked and avoided mingling with crowds.

Display was mainly for London and nearby counties; none of the monarchs under discussion travelled very far from the capital in their progresses and ceremonial entries. Just occasionally other areas received a royal visit. James I made propaganda stops during his journey south from Scotland in 1603 to claim the English throne, and he travelled north-east in 1617. Charles I journeyed to Scotland and back in 1633 for his belated coronation as King of Scotland, with ceremonial stops along the way. But generally the Tudors and early Stuarts travelled in a limited trajectory about the south-eastern royal palaces and houses of aristocrats and gentry, with some visits a little towards the west. Elizabeth included Wiltshire in the 1570s, James made a progress through Hampshire in 1607. The rest of the country outside a radius of 100 or so miles from London saw a monarch only once in a generation, or never, and did not have the opportunity to enjoy the spectacle, or learn the lesson it sought to instil.

There was one unrepresentative section of the people that received very direct attention from the monarchs, in a ceremony symbolising royal mystery and power. The Tudor and Stuart kings and queens fulfilled the traditional magic of monarchy by touching for the King's Evil. The monarch's touch promised a cure for the disease (as well as the gift of a special gold angel coin). For medieval French and English kings the touch had provided a potent demonstration of sacred monarchy. It was an especially important legitimating symbol, for the Tudors who held the crown by conquest, not by legitimate descent, and for the Stuarts, who were Scots. Such displays of public concern for subjects might also help to create loyalty in the sufferers, and among the watching crowds. Elizabeth apparently decided to touch in the 1570s to emphasise her God-given sovereignty, after excommunication by the pope attempted to deny her right to rule. On summer progress and at

Easter she touched: nine at Kenilworth in 1575, thirty-eight on Good Friday 1597.[20] James I and Charles I both thought the rite essential and performed it regularly; Charles planned to touch at Easter and Michaelmas despite his fastidious dislike of the common people, although in 1632 he forbade people to approach him for it. In 1636 he perhaps belatedly recognised the need to conciliate his subjects and bestowed the rite.[21] The King's Evil, or scrofula, was a form of tuberculosis affecting mainly poor people, who took the hope of cure by royal touch very seriously. The patients were very carefully selected in advance; and in fact the likelihood of at least temporary improvement was quite high, since the journey in the open, and the hopeful expectation of cure assisted remission of symptoms. The royal magic appeared to work, and showed God's approval of monarch and people.

Each of these monarchs used some of the strategies of their predecessors to convince subjects of the mystique of royal power, while varying the emphasis. Henry projected power. Mary tried to cope with the novelty of depicting female monarchy; Elizabeth had much more time to develop it and sought to promulgate a regal imagery and a reputation for care of her people. James favoured a relaxed style with the people around him, while using proclamations and coin images to reach out more widely. Charles tended to believe that his royal will sufficed: the stiff images of him by van Dyck in the 1630s presumably reflect his attitude. But none of them could rule by royal will alone – they always depended on nobles, gentry and lesser officials to disseminate their power through the realm.

2
Nobility

The monarchy worked hard to establish acceptance of its authority, but the king or queen needed assistance to keep the country in obedience. The nobility and gentry could provide it. The great families, with extensive lands and tenantry, expected to take part in governing both at the centre and across the land; schematic views of England's polity in this period show 'the nobility' as a bloc, sharing in the counsels of the crown and providing the pivotal power in the counties, with 'the gentry' working at the next level. But the reality was much more complicated. Some nobles did exercise great authority both in national and local life, others had little, for success or failure in court favour or faction led to sudden reversals. Even among the greatest noble families, continuity in political authority was surprisingly rare during this period, due to shifting political rivalries, individual preference, and factors of age and succession. Around a third of noble families failed to produce a male heir at all, and some peers died when the heir was a child too young to exercise power. The creation of new aristocrats was therefore essential; the important question was who rose, and why, and how much authority they acquired. Lawrence Stone, in *The Crisis of the Aristocracy 1558–1641*,[1] exaggerated the overall decline of the nobility, since many families suffered debt briefly but recovered, as others have argued. Stone's comparisons are problematic because James I and Charles I suddenly increased the total size of the peerage, making more available peers from whom to choose office-holders. Stone also emphasised the changing role of the nobility, which became more court-based and lost its private military forces and territorial influence, thereby becoming less of a threat to the crown. The great feudal retinues were reduced, as the Tudors encouraged a courtier nobility, but that need not mean wholesale decline of the whole order. Even if no one noble family sustained its power from Henry VIII's reign to Charles I's, that does not mean that aristocratic authority declined. Peers both recent and by old inheritance continued to influence the crown, the administration, the parliaments and the counties. Every monarch on accession found an existing nobility in place. The strict definition of a noble was that the male family head was called by the monarch to sit in the House of Lords; in practice the major hereditary aristocratic families could not be omitted from Parliament. So it was a small and well-defined group, unlike the much more extensive gentry class. But the new king or queen did not have to treat all equally and give power to all – there was a choice.

The Tudor and early Stuart monarchs promoted 'old' aristocrats to positions of authority. And they chose new ones, out of friendship, or the need for military leadership, or to try to control localities, or to restrain rivals. Each monarch searched for loyalty in servants about the throne, although sometimes failed to find it. So a monarch's choice did not always mean continuity in the royal counsels, especially under the suspicious and changeable Henry VIII. Henry used attainder and execution far more than his successors. It was a fate which might await failure, as well as any hint of treason, and it contributed to the frenetic atmosphere of tension at court, as well as to rapid turnover of titles. But he raised many. Friendship could spur the choice, as when Henry VIII made Charles Brandon duke of Suffolk in 1514. Such men had to work for their position – to be useful in government or military command, and Suffolk served in France before and after his elevation. Henry endowed Suffolk with lands to help him exert control in East Anglia, and when Lincolnshire seemed dangerous he moved him there. Suffolk risked his place in Henry's confidence by secretly marrying the king's sister (suggesting a desire to usurp the throne), but regained it to continue as an important Privy Councillor. When the execution of the marquess of Exeter created a power vacuum, the king endowed John Russell with abbey and other lands in the south-west, raising his prestige there and at court.[2]

Some administrators did their duty in peace and received titles without obvious involvement in roller-coaster intrigue. William Paulet, a financial administrator with good City links, remained in office through all the upsets of other men's careers. He survived as Lord Treasurer from 1550 through the political tensions and alterations of office-holders in the reigns of Edward VI, Mary, and Elizabeth right until his death in 1572, becoming earl of Wiltshire in 1550, and first marquess of Winchester in 1551.

The old nobility played a rather different role from the new under Henry VIII. The monarch could call on them to deal with specific problems, but few sought the highest administrative office. The Talbots, earls of Shrewsbury, tended their great estates and remained involved in their own region when they could, receiving advantageous royal grants in Derbyshire, Staffordshire and Wales. The fourth earl raised troops for the king against the 1536 northern rebels, support which proved a vital element in the king's victory. The king had taken care to reward his earlier loyalty, hence Shrewsbury used his considerable authority to help the king. The third earl of Derby similarly concentrated on his regional interests, but used his influence to support the king's cause in 1536. Great nobles such as Shrewsbury were consulted by the crown, sat often on the Privy Council, and could hope for grants of land or office when the monarch was generous, or was in need of secure support.

Others fared worse, illustrating the prime role of political success and failure in creating change among those at the top. A stark example of rise to and fall from great power at the king's will was Henry Courtenay. The Courtenays had been earls of Devon since the fourteenth century; Henry Courtenay became one of Henry's closest friends. He was one of the inner group where formality was exchanged for familiarity, sharing in the king's leisure pursuits, and gaining influence at court. Henry VIII created him earl of Exeter in 1525 as a mark of further favour. But Thomas Cromwell managed to poison the king's trust in him. Although he had been so close to the king, suddenly in 1538 Exeter was compelled to forfeit the title, and was executed in January 1539.[3] The Howards also acquired royal favour and patronage, but fell at the king's whim. Henry had raised Thomas Howard to the dukedom of Norfolk in 1514, and his son worked hard as a military commander and Councillor, sometimes among the king's closest advisors, but sometimes eclipsed when opposing court factions had the opportunity to exclude him from the limelight. He was lucky, or clever, to survive the fall and executions of two nieces married to the king, Anne Boleyn in 1536, and Katherine Howard in 1541, still holding on to the offices of Lord Treasurer which he received in 1522, and Earl Marshall which he had received in 1533, and remaining a leading member of the Privy Council. In Norfolk he held sway over local office and local government. All counted for nothing when in December 1546 he was arrested, imprisoned and faced execution with his son, the poet earl of Surrey on suspicion that Surrey's flaunting of royal ancestry meant that he grasped at the throne. Surrey was executed on 21 January 1547, Norfolk saved only because Henry died before his sentence could be carried out.[4] Power was chancy, and could bring the extreme penalty under Henry VIII, as also during the minority reign of his son Edward. But the destruction of Courtenay power in the south-west, and of Howard power in East Anglia, meant that there were no great landowners who might exert local control in those areas, a circumstance which contributed to the uprisings of 1549.

An extraordinary opportunity for exerting power arose when Henry died on 28 January 1547, leaving a nine-year-old successor, Edward VI. The boy's uncle, Edward Seymour, earl of Hertford and one of Henry's executors, became Protector and Governor of the King, with the agreement of the rest of the Council, and acquired the title duke of Somerset. Somerset wielded supreme authority, in effect as regent, and governed not quite as a king, but with more power than any mere noble. Of course, he had to rule under the constraints of all governments, seeking sufficient consent from the realm, and placating the strongest men around the throne. Somerset must have felt secure enough to carry out vigorous policies of change, rather than simply oversee a quiet caretaker government. He pushed economic legislation through parliament, sent out enclosure commissions, and shifted the church in England towards a Protestant liturgy and doctrine. As Protector, Somerset also had charge of the continuing war with Scotland, for which he needed to raise money and troops. Initially he was successful, with the victory at Pinkie, but by mid-1548 he was in trouble. Even his overriding authority did not succeed. How far Somerset had tried to do too much, how far he failed to gain enough support among the rest of the council, how far he alienated the rest of the nobility, are questions which cannot easily be answered. Certainly Somerset failed to comprehend the need for strong support from the nobility. It had to be nurtured in ordinary times, so as to be available to help the regime in emergencies. Somerset did not cultivate the nobility to make them his allies. He frequently ignored the Council, and took advice from a 'kitchen cabinet'. And his actions led to rebellions which threatened property. The rebellions of 1549, which will be discussed more fully in Chapter 10, threw his government into disrepute. The Midlands and East Anglia were stirred to revolt by land questions arising from Somerset's policies, while the protest in the south-west stemmed mainly from hostility to the new Protestant prayer book. Both were put down, but with many deaths. Lack of noble backing forced Somerset out of power in October 1549. With the failure of his policies, a group of nobles, especially John Dudley, earl of Warwick since 1547, withdrew support from the Protector. After intense political manoeuvring, Warwick became Lord President of the Council and took charge of the government. In the absence of an adult king, the selection of the supreme authority was made by a small elite of nobles and court gentry.[5]

Somerset's rise and fall had been swift, yet his successor, too, held power only briefly. By early 1550 Warwick had taken charge of the administration, continuing the push towards Protestantism, but avoiding contentious social policy, and taking care to maintain his alliance with the nobility, as Somerset had not done. He became duke of Northumberland in 1551. He recognised the need to use rewards, grants and especially peerages, to bind men. Lord Russell became first earl of Bedford in 1550. In 1551, William Paulet became marquess of Winchester, William Herbert earl of Pembroke, and Henry Grey, marquess of Dorset, became duke of Suffolk.[6] All might have gone smoothly for Northumberland, had not the young king died in the middle of 1553. In May 1553, the duke had married his own son Guilford to Jane Grey, the grand-daughter of Henry VIII's younger sister, whose descendants were the young king's favoured candidates for the succession, despite statute and Henry's will naming Mary Tudor. On Edward VI's death, Northumberland tried to retain hold on the government, proclaiming Jane as queen. But despite his efforts to secure noble allies, the nobility did not flock to support him. They went over to Mary, rather than fight a civil war against her, and prevailed. Northumberland's failure meant the end of his policies, his life, and eventually the lives of the others involved in the attempt to exclude Mary. He was executed in August 1553, his heir

Guilford, Jane, and Henry Grey, duke of Suffolk the following year. The last decade and a half had seen new nobles made, many only to be unmade within a few years.

Although Mary executed Northumberland and his allies, she favoured noble families, especially sturdily Catholic ones. Of course, like other monarchs, she needed an aristocracy to help in government, court ceremonial, military command, and local pacification, and she could not change every one, even those who had been prominent under the protestantising governments of Edward. William Paulet was the great survivor, with high office under four monarchs: he remained as treasurer throughout Mary's reign and until his death in 1572. Lord Russell, created earl of Bedford by Northumberland's Protestant government, also remained in office in Mary's reign till his death. Religious conservatives received posts, such as the earl of Arundel; Mary restored the Howards to the dukedom of Norfolk, and the earldom of Northumberland and the previously forfeited lands to Thomas Percy in 1557. She made him warden of the East March too, and in 1558 gave him licence to retain 200 gentlemen and yeomen, in addition to household servants.[7] She understood, as Somerset had not, the need to keep a loyal nobility.

When Elizabeth acceded to the throne in 1558 there were 57 nobles. She created few new ones, and those she elevated all had noble ancestry, except William Cecil. She chose carefully which ones to promote to high place, and whom to leave out. Close friendship impelled her grant to Robert Dudley, son of the duke of Northumberland executed by Mary, of the earldom of Leicester, and lands to go with it, in 1564, and his influence derived from the queen's special favour. Because she continued that favour to him, he was one of the most powerful men in England until his death in 1588, a leading member of the Privy Council and a much sought-after patron at court. Leicester was ambitious, and had probably hoped to marry the queen, but he had to work hard in government – he could not just be an ornament of the queen's entourage, and must always remember that she could turn against him (as she briefly did when he married another woman behind her back). Elizabeth's Protestantism, her restoration of Edwardians to high positions in church and state, influenced the political fate of nobles during her reign. She trusted Dudley's brother the earl of Warwick, Thomas Radcliffe earl of Sussex, Henry Hastings earl of Huntingdon, and her cousin Henry Carey Lord Hunsdon, making them Privy Councillors, giving them additional posts and powers and expecting service from them all. Others, including William Herbert second earl of Pembroke and Francis Russell earl of Bedford, also helped to support the crown's authority. Pembroke supervised South Wales and the marches, Russell was a major presence not only in the south-west, but also in the north as Warden of the East Marches and Governor of Berwick, and Lord Lieutenant of Cumberland and Westmorland in 1564, during a time of anxiety over the intentions of the Scots. Walter Devereux earl of Essex soldiered for her in Ireland. But his son

Robert tried to follow a different path at court, exploiting the queen's fondness for him to build up a following, as well as seeking military glory and extending the powers of his post as earl marshall. The younger Essex would not accept the limitations of his place in Elizabeth's scheme, turning to rebellion in 1601. The queen did not always choose well.

She conferred little power on members of the Catholic nobility, with the exception of her former suitor the earl of Arundel at the beginning of her reign and the earl of Worcester at the end. It seems that Elizabeth aimed to reduce the influence of the old regional nobility and create more of a court-based one. Her reasons in the 1560s lay in their history and attitudes and not simply in their Catholicism; the taint of previous rebellion touched many of the old titled families. She removed the earl of Northumberland from the sensitive post of Warden of the Middle March in the north, where border commanders were responsible for defence against the Scots and their allies, but might use their power against the monarch, and appointed the contentious and personally disreputable Sir John Forster instead, since Forster would depend only on her.[8] The role allotted to the Council in the North represents a deliberate reduction of dependence on the northern aristocracy, as much as Tudor centralising, and meant that the earl of Westmorland and Lord Dacre of the North now carried little clout. Later, the third earl of Cumberland, rather than sulking or rebelling, turned his attention outward, equipping fleets for privateering voyages, and spending his time and his money on them, and not on plotting. Elizabeth followed a dangerously firm line in her treatment of those noblemen with pretensions, and perhaps she was lucky to survive.

James I and Charles I rapidly enlarged the nobility.[9] The sudden increase makes comparisons with previous reigns difficult. With 55 nobles in 1603, 81 in 1615, up to 126 in 1628, smaller proportions of them could hold high place and power, although the expansion of the central administration provided office for many. James needed to make up for Elizabeth's shortfall, and Stone believed the new titles were deserved and defensible up to 1615, going to solid gentlemen with sufficient estates. James gave some of these new nobles governmental responsibilities, as Privy Councillors and major office-holders. The Howard family returned to prominence: James created Henry Howard earl of Northampton in 1604 and made him a leading member of the government. Thomas Howard, who had recently become earl of Suffolk, joined Northampton and the earl of Worcester in the Council's inner circle. Suffolk acquired further office as Treasurer in 1614, but besmirched both his title and his office by notorious corruption, and was suspended and temporarily imprisoned in 1618. James increased the size of his Council, compared with that of his predecessor. That was partly because, as well as increasing the number of the nobility, he tended more than Elizabeth had done to make nobles old or new members of the Privy Council. Some remained ineffective in central politics.

James was also more inclined to ennoble his Councillors, or raise them to higher titles. Robert Cecil, who as Elizabeth's hard-working Principal Secretary of State and Master of the Court of Wards had managed the government in her last years, continued in office and became earl of Salisbury, although not until 1605. Perhaps James waited to see how he performed as the king's chief minister. Salisbury became Treasurer as well in 1608, and remained the most important Councillor until his death in 1612. Thomas Egerton, also a very hard-working official as Lord Keeper, became Viscount Ellesmere; as with Cecil, it was a reasonable reward for heavy responsibility and devotion to duty. The Treasurer since 1599, Sir Thomas Sackville, Lord Buckhurst, was raised to become earl of Dorset in 1604. Lionel Cranfield was of merchant not gentry background, and tried hard from 1621 as Treasurer to balance James's budget – perhaps he deserved his earldom of Middlesex for that, if not for marrying a favourite's relation. These titles might be considered as rewards for real service in high office, or encouragements to increased service and loyalty. Other new titles, however, did not reward service or confer power. Conferring the title of Lord Danby on the wealthy Henry Danvers is an example, since Danvers was involved in the murder of Henry Long in 1594 during the Wiltshire faction fights, and had been in exile to avoid trial, returning at the end of Elizabeth's reign.

But it was the exchange of money for titles, and the notorious elevation of James I's boyfriends – Robert Carr as earl of Somerset, and then George Villiers as duke of Buckingham – that tainted the nobility. Neither Carr nor Villiers had displayed any governing talents, merely courtly ones, as the king's favourites. They had no old landed estates or local connections with which to bolster the reputation of the king's court. Yet each in turn gained not only title and wealth from James, but also enormous authority at the king's whim. Somerset ran the crown's patronage from 1612 to 1615. On Somerset's fall from favour after the Overbury murder scandal, another handsome young man, George Villiers, took over the place, the patronage and the power of favourite.[10] His power derived directly from his great personal influence with the king, and not from holding any formal administrative office. Villiers was rapidly promoted in the peerage, as earl, marquess, and then duke of Buckingham. Buckingham gained ever greater influence from 1617 on, so that in the stretch of his authority, he could almost be compared with the Edwardian dukes of Somerset and Northumberland. Perhaps to free himself for running foreign relations, and the Church, James allowed Buckingham to dominate domestic policy, administrative decisions, and all grants of office and title: Buckingham more than the king became the subject of flattery and sycophancy.

Stone notes that between 1615 and 1628, the increase in noble titles from 81 to 126 was due largely to Buckingham's patronage. The favourite's relations particularly benefitted from his control of the surge of new titles, which went to men and women who had offered no notable service to the state which might have justified the honour. Since all who aspired to title or to office in government, central or regional, had to secure his approval, it was almost 'the reign of Buckingham'. Moreover, it continued when Charles I ascended the throne in 1625: the two had become friends after some initial jealousies, and of course by 1625, Buckingham was very experienced in wielding power. Charles, despite his high view of royal perogative, allowed the duke to mishandle the English interventions in the European war, so that both France and Spain were enemies. But Buckingham by his high-handed arrogance and control had alienated many of the nobility and gentry who had been accustomed to sharing in decisions, and upon whom royal power also depended for implementation. By 1626, he seemed to them to be the scourge of the kingdom, and parliament attempted to get rid of him by impeachment; the king chose to support his favourite rather than conciliate the political elite. John Felton assassinated Buckingham in 1628. He had personal grievances against Buckingham's treatment of him in the navy; and he also believed he was ridding the nation of an evil influence. Thereafter no one man, aristocrat or commoner, dominated Charles's government. Ecclesiastical lords, the bishops William Laud, Richard Neile, Matthew Wren, and William Juxon gained influence over crown policies and hence the country, especially Laud, as bishop of London then Archbishop of Canterbury, and a Privy Councillor. Laud briefly, and then Juxon, received secular office as treasurer in the mid-1630s, giving them a powerful voice at the centre. Not all Charles's councillors were ennobled. Although he shared the views of Sir Thomas Wentworth, who was President of the Council in the North and then Lord Deputy of Ireland, he only gave him the title of earl of Strafford in 1640, when the political situation had deteriorated and he desperately needed help.

The nobility who sought influence at the centre, and the office-holders who achieved nobility through their position there, faced serious risks in their pursuit of power. Henry VIII's volatile, suspicious nature destroyed his familiar friend the earl of Exeter. Thomas Cromwell dominated the government and influenced the ongoing Reformation changes of the 1530s. He was rewarded only in 1540 with the earldom of Essex, but died by the executor's axe only three months later when Henry turned against him. The duke of Buckingham died by an assassin's knife when his policies turned out badly. Strafford died on the block only the year after receiving his title, as parliament attainted him when it acted against the supposed instigators of Charles's unpopular policies. But some nobles brought disaster on themselves, in desperate attempts at conspiracy, coup, or rebellion. The duke of Somerset plotted to bring down Northumberland in 1551, and was executed for treason; Northumberland tried to block Mary's succession in 1553 and met the same fate. If other nobles risked outright armed rebellion, knowing the likelihood of penalty for failure, they must have been desperate. In the Pilgrimage of Grace of 1536, the largest uprising from the Tudor reigns to the Civil War, northern nobles faced troubling choices, and it is not always clear how and why each of them decided to act. In the opening stages many were uncertain, facing conflicting aims and loyalties, aware of their duty to the crown but opposing its current policies.[11] For the northern earls in 1569, the hope of freeing Mary Queen of Scots from imprisonment, to secure her succession to the English throne at least after Elizabeth (or perhaps instead of her) combined with their catholic discontent and their exclusion from central power, and led them to rebel. They might press for religious concessions immediately, and expect high office as soon as Mary became queen. Thomas Howard, fourth duke of Norfolk, was different. He was the only duke, with unrivalled domination in East Anglia, a splendid palace, and the loyalty of many tenants. Yet local supremacy and Council membership did not satisfy his pride and ambition. The lure of a royal marriage and the hope that Mary Queen of Scots would either follow, or displace Elizabeth as ruler seemed to promise him dignity and power as king consort, enough to tempt him to take the risk. But such ambition was hard to conceal, and in 1572 another Howard died on the scaffold.

Late in Elizabeth's reign the actions of Robert Devereux second earl of Essex, showed some similarities to Norfolk's. As Elizabeth's favourite and successor to the earl of Leicester, Essex aimed to control patronage via the queen, and his exploits against the Spanish made him a popular figure. Like Norfolk he was earl marshall, he searched out precedents to expand his authority. Essex, like Norfolk, felt insufficiently rewarded, and his military failure in Ireland in 1599 led to the withdrawal of royal favour. In a desperate attempt to retrieve his former position, he destroyed all in a reckless little revolt in January 1601, and was executed. He was the last noble until 1642 to seek political change through armed uprising.

Some nobles jockeyed for political power; some risked their lives for power. But not all nobles even sought it. We cannot assume that because a man held an aristocratic title, he was necessarily ambitious for a role in national politics. Studies of Henry Bourchier earl of Essex, and of the sixth earl of Northumberland in Henry VIII's reign, and of the Talbot sixth and seventh earls of Shrewsbury have shown how little power at the centre a noble might hold, or even desire.[12] Bourchier lived the life of a courtier peer, involved in ceremonial and revelry. He obtained minor office and attendant fees, but never sought much more. By the 1530s he was attending court less often, preferring to concentrate on his Essex lands, his house building, and an impressive household retinue. He also cultivated a following among the local gentry, competing with the de Veres earls of Oxford, but not using his influence to any obvious effect. Bourchier was a run-of-the-mill noble, neither conspicuously elevated, nor notoriously poor, profligate, or treasonous.

Richard Hoyle has investigated Henry Percy sixth earl of Northumberland, who has been seen as weak and incapable, especially on account of his selling and granting away of Percy estates. Northumberland was given responsibilities under the crown for keeping order on the Scottish borders after 1527, and was sheriff of Northumberland in 1534. But in divesting estates, and disinheriting his two brothers in favour of the king, Northumberland apparently ignored his lineage and behaved most unlike other nobles. Hoyle suggests that debt explains some of the sales; and grants to his intimates are interpreted as establishing them as effective forces on the borders, and as personal reward for friendship. It is his willing surrender of his estates to the king that is so odd. We would expect such a noble to seek further power for himself or his family. Hoyle suggests that he did not do so because of chronic illness, from which he died young.

The Talbot sixth and seventh earls of Shrewsbury showed little eagerness for high place at the centre, spending most of their time and energy on their lands and tenants. Neither was much favoured by the crown, especially George, the sixth earl, who was forced into the tedium of guarding Mary Queen of Scots for fourteen years. Other nobles who chose local rather than national authority included the Stanleys, earls of Derby, who were supreme in Lancashire and Cheshire under Elizabeth and James I, but not much interested in court intrigue or in gaining more extensive power.[13] The Clifford second and third earls of Cumberland avoided the court, as noted above. Even the son and heir of Lord Burghley, Elizabeth's chief councillor, was either incapable or uninterested in public office: he served briefly as Lord President of the Council in the North, but it was his younger brother Robert who was trained up to become Principal Secretary, and later Lord Treasurer. There were many nobles who filled their ceremonial and parliamentary roles when it suited them, but preferred the respect, local honour or local quarrelling, hunting, and the comfort of their great houses to the hard grind, the excitement and fears of involvement in national politics. And after 1603, and especially after 1615, there were simply more nobles, but not more places at the top, so a larger proportion had to be content with county politics and country life.

In the counties as at the centre, nobles varied greatly in the degree of authority they could gain. There, too, they experienced sudden rises and falls. It is often said that the nobility ran the localities for the crown, but this needs qualification. Some did, sometimes. Partly because of the upsets they brought on themselves, or because of their economic failures, or changes of monarch, of allies and enemies, very few families managed an unbroken hegemony in their county. Turbulence often characterised county politics, as it did central. Limitations stemming from the crown's disapproval, or from rivalries with office-holders or with other noble families could stand in the way of local dominance.[14] The successful nobles owed much to chance: the crown's attitude, demographic factors, the strength of competition, or temperament. The Russells could thank Henry VIII's sudden destruction of the earl of Exeter, as well as the king's friendship with Lord Russell, for establishing them with grants and office in the south-west. Lord Russell was a Councillor, and was made Lord President of the short-lived regional council of Devon, Dorset, Cornwall and Somerset, in a deliberate royal move to place a trustworthy leader in the west. His son Francis, earl of Bedford, was a leading Privy Councillor under Elizabeth, and maintained the family's power in the south-west; he was chosen as Lord Lieutenant in 1558. Henry VIII similarly built up the duke of Suffolk's land and authority, first in East Anglia and then in Lincolnshire, but failure of immediate heirs made it short-lived. Wales received the attention of the Herberts, created earls of Pembroke in 1551: the first and second earls kept a great house and hospitality at Cardiff Castle, then at Ludlow Castle too, and supervised the governing of Wales, not always smoothly. Local gentry complained that they had no need of 'a great and mighty lord to terrify' them; and the Herberts were humiliated in Star Chamber in 1598.[15] They also established a base at Wilton in Wiltshire, but did not control that county.

A noble who could make himself an effective conduit for royal patronage, for the rewards the gentry sought, could control a county. Success could result from royal favour, from the absence of rival channels, or from a noble's skills as an intermediary between centre and locality. Influencing appointment to a host of royal offices could place a noble's allies in positions of power, while obtaining posts for aspirant gentlemen could buy new loyalties. A noble with extensive estates appointed his own stewards, bailiffs and household officers from among the gentry, and built a following in county government. Yet although the successful manipulation of patronage could make a nobleman great, relatively few succeeded. Elizabeth, like her father, supported, or at least did not challenge noble rule over some counties. For over ten years the fourth duke of Norfolk, despite challenges from Lord Keeper Bacon and Bishop Parkhurst, dominated his county completely. East Anglia did what he ordered – till his execution in 1572. The queen encouraged the rule of Henry Hastings, earl of Huntingdon, over Leicestershire, where he controlled the choice of members of parliament and of the county government. William Cecil, Lord Burghley, and his son Robert till late in his life, had little trouble managing Hertfordshire local governors. Any who dared to oppose them lost hope of future office or aid.

Among the most successful regional magnates were the Stanley earls of Derby. They were by far the most influential family in the north-west: there was no-one else to whom the crown could turn for effective local government, and no-one else to whom the local gentry could turn for support. They held huge estates in the north-west, in Cheshire and Lancashire, and much patronage to reward followers. They chose the deputy lieutenants and JPs, and apparently directed their activities without heavy-handed interference, and so without much complaint, despite the volatile mixture of Catholic and Protestant gentry in Lancashire. There was some trouble around 1601, when 23 JPs were excluded, but the trouble soon passed. In 1612 John Ogle confirmed that for seventeen years he had been 'towards the Right Honourable and Earls of Derby at all times upon command request or warning'.[16] Many other nobles could find some supporters to speak of them with this degree of loyalty – but most nobles also excited more opposition than did the earls of Derby.

The Talbot earls of Shrewsbury held wide estates in Derbyshire and Nottinghamshire, and managed to exert their authority, in Derbyshire at least, over a long period. During the Pilgrimage of Grace in 1536 the fourth earl gathered his tenants to support the king, and his influence was decisive in containing the spread of rebellion. George Talbot, the sixth earl faced different problems, as he unwillingly wasted years of local activity when Queen Elizabeth sent him to guard the captive Queen of Scots, mostly at Tutbury. His son Gilbert, the seventh earl, was more successful and controlled Derbyshire for over 25 years, up to 1616, despite Queen Elizabeth's dislike of him; with James I he managed a better relationship. He exercised a degree of authority over county politics which most other nobles might have envied, ensuring that the vital posts of deputy lieutenant and JP went to his own supporters and relatives who would do his bidding.

Most of the nobles had to make do with more limited power in the counties, and faced challenges from other aristocratic aspirants, obstructive gentry, and disobedient tenants. Constant fluctuations in the personnel and political success of the nobility, and upper gentry, meant that a man or a family might gain, and then lose, the strongest positions locally as well as at the centre. The first earl of Cumberland had been a well-rewarded friend of Henry VIII, but he had difficulties in the north. He angered his tenantry by oppressive use of his powers for profit, and in the Pilgrimage of Grace they did not look to him for leadership but rather rebelled against him and his Clifford kin. Whereas the local power of the earls of Derby and Shrewsbury contained the rising, the unpopularity of the earl of Cumberland helped provoke it. Cumberland's local weakness had been exposed, and in 1537 he had to decline the post of Warden of the West March.

William Paulet, marquess of Winchester, wily political survivor and Lord Treasurer though he was, could not control Hampshire in the early 1560s. A group of gentlemen, with the help of the bishop of Winchester succeeded in engineering the dismissals and exclusions from county office of Paulet's allies, so that he could not even determine who would be JPs in his own county, and he would not be able to control the decisions of local government. Similarly in Nottinghamshire, by at least the 1590s, a group of determined gentry led by Sir John Stanhope vigorously resisted the pretensions to power of Gilbert Talbot, seventh earl of Shrewsbury, who struggled vainly to control them. His is an interesting case, since he succeeded in dominating Derbyshire, but could not overcome a determined opposition in Nottinghamshire with independent access to court favour under both Elizabeth and James I. On Gilbert's death in 1616 however, the Cavendish family, which received the earldom of Devonshire in 1618, and Newcastle in 1628, had more success than the Talbots had, partly because they had never aroused royal suspicions. The Cavendishes were new men, dependent on court favour rather than on old regional pretension, so the earl of Devonshire was able to offer that access to patronage which encouraged the gentry to co-operate rather than contest with him.

Wiltshire provides examples of nobles who might have wished to control the county gentry and government, but frequently failed to do so. The records of its local government are among the fullest for the period, and they show the factious nature of a large and populous county. William Herbert, the first earl of Pembroke gained his Wiltshire lands in 1542–4, and the earldom in 1551 after the fall of Protector Somerset. His desertion of Somerset brought him into conflict with Somerset's surviving supporters, especially Sir John Thynne of Longleat. But he acquired some allies in the county, even as an 'upstart' there, and a continuing if uneasy relationship with Thynne and other gentlemen. The second earl nominated many members of parliament including those for Wilton and Great Bedwyn, but almost none were from the county gentry, and his relationship with the Thynnes was tense and changeable. Pembroke was *custos* of the commission of the peace, had one of its 'divisions' named after him, and very occasionally attended quarter sessions. But he did not make much effort to run the county, and when he was Lord Lieutenant he left the deputies to organise military matters. 'By reason of his far absence' from the county, he avoided conflict: he restored Cardiff Castle, and was much at Ludlow Castle, as an active president of the Council in the Marches of Wales. The third earl, who succeeded to the title in 1601 at the age of 21, was a dedicated courtier, who despised local rule and the factious gentry struggles for influence. He failed to get the Wiltshire lord lieutenancy in 1601, and remained a courtier peer and companion of James I. Edward Seymour, earl of Hertford, son of the Protector, tried to gain control of Wiltshire when the second earl of Pembroke died in 1601. He managed to become Lord Lieutenant, but could not secure obedience from his deputies or the gentry. Rather they all combined against him, made a great fuss over his choice of muster master and refused to pay the man's wages. The gentry received Hertford's orders over military matters unwillingly, acting on them late, or not at all. Hertford's obvious lack of favour with the crown, due to his Seymour heritage and his unsanctioned and dangerous marriage to Catherine Grey, sister of Jane Grey who had claimed the throne in 1553, combined with his unappealing personality and manner to weaken his authority in Wiltshire.[17]

Similar problems confronted Henry, earl of Lincoln, who faced violent opposition from Sir Edward Dymock in Jacobean Lincolnshire. Dymock had support from some JPs, and Lincoln could not simply overrule the whole of the next layer of county government in order to crush Dymock. Questions of authority arose explicity in the disputes, especially over the earl's efforts to exert influence over lesser officials. For instance, in 1604 Lincoln's allies summoned a court sitting, and the undersheriff accepted Lincoln's demands, allowing the earl himself to select the jury in an attempt to prosecute Dymock's men. But the earl's actions were challenged, and the authority of quarter sessions was undermined when a riot erupted between justices of the rival factions. Further trouble arose concerning the Lincolnshire waterways in 1609, with disputes over management and the raising of local taxes between Lincoln and his supporters, and the earl of Exeter and his – controversies which continued for the following two decades.[18]

In Leicestershire, the easy hegemony of the Hastings earls of Huntingdon during the sixteenth century and in James I's reign gave way to challenge and disruption for the fifth earl during the reign of Charles I. Hastings tried stoically to run the country in the face of complaint and criticism from the gentry who should have supported him. He was severely hampered by the king's demands to build up an adequate military force, and the effort to raise the necessary funds from the county. Although there was no parliamentary subsidy in the 1630s, the demands after 1535 for coat and conduct money and for military equipment, men, and training amounted to substantial hidden burdens on the people, and they contested with the earl in his efforts to provide what the king demanded. In Somerset, too, in Charles's reign, Lord Poulett failed to achieve that control which he sought. Although he received his peerage in 1627, and could influence appointments in Somerset, due in part to his contact with Buckingham, he was always challenged by Sir Robert Phelips, and the allies which Phelips successfully promoted in the county administration.[19]

For most of the period, effective and unopposed noble rule was the exception, and even those who managed to achieve it often had to overcome occasional challenges by gentry questioning their authority, or rival nobles advancing their own. Crown office could certainly enhance the chances of successful rule, but not guarantee it, as we saw in the case of the earl of Hertford. The most important additional and formal power given to nobles (and sometimes to gentry) was the lord lieutenancy, but it was not continuous. Lord lieutenants were appointed in Edward's reign to lead local forces against the rebels of 1549, and their major duty was to organise and command county militias if required. Elizabeth chose lord lieutenants at the start of her reign in case of a military challenge, and again in 1569, but only for emergency where needed, and for a limited time: she terminated the 1569 commissions a year later. From 1585 to 1590 lord lieutenants were chosen for every shire during the war with Spain, at least temporarily. From 1590 to the early years of James I's reign, a number of counties had no lieutenant, and there was often no replacement on the death of a lieutenant. From 1607 on, all counties except four had lieutenants appointed, and it became a more continuous office; by the reign of Charles most held it until death. Of 131 persons appointed as lord lieutenants between 1585 and 1642, 103 were peers when they were appointed. Another 13 were the eldest sons of peers, usually appointed along with their father, and succeeded to his title while holding the office. A few prominent commoners served, notably Knollys, Hatton, and Raleigh. Elizabeth appointed more commoners to the lieutenancy than did James I; but then she created fewer peers than did James: nearly all early Stuart lieutenants were nobles. Many of the lieutenants were Privy Councillors, and even Lord Burghley had added the lieutenancy of Hertfordshire to his huge official load, so they were often too busy to do more than oversee military organisation from a distance. Some lieutenants were put over two counties at once, and one or two, like Lord Hunsdon, had no local connections or allegiance in Norfolk where he was lieutenant, so their formal military authority was the only local power they had.[20]

Until the end of Elizabeth's reign and into that of James the central government appointed the lieutenant's deputies, if any. But increasingly after that the lord lieutenants chose their deputy lieutenants from among the gentry, which provided patronage and delegated authority, while the lord lieutenant himself might keep an intermittent managing eye on the equipping and mustering of the citizen-soldiers. Some lieutenants, notably the fifth earl of Huntingdon, worked hard themselves in the role. Pressures of war in Ireland, France and the Netherlands, and the threat of invasions from Spain impelled a slightly more professional approach, with the appointment of captains and muster-masters, over which the lord lieutenant nominally presided – when he found time. In theory a noble who was also lieutenant had considerable power, though in practice it was often left to the deputies to make the decisions on raising money and troops. Lieutenants often exercised a more general supervisory role in their county, but it is unclear how much this derived from their lieutenancy, how much from the fact that many of them were Privy Councillors, and how much from their personal and family prestige: so much depended on the specific political conditions of the man, and of the county or counties at any given time.

As well as having the official military power of the lord lieutenancy, many nobles kept followers who could, if required, appear armed and on horseback ready to fight. The nobles' leadership was vital in war, especially in the earlier sixteenth century, when their private armed retainers and tenants, many of them gentry, followed them into Henry VIII's wars in France. Successful soldiers like the dukes of Norfolk advanced in the king's estimation and received rewards. Licences to retain show that nobles could keep large numbers of followers: from 1541, thirteen individuals received such licences, for a total of 560 men. In 1542, the earl of Rutland's provision of 90 men included 13 of his household; the remainder came from the places in Leicestershire and Lincolnshire where the earl was the chief landholder; in 1544 the earl of Huntingdon was ordered to bring 150 foot soldiers and 70 horse for the French war. For the crown's defence against the Pilgrimage of Grace, the duke of Norfolk had provided 600 men, Lord Ferrers 1,000. The earl of Shrewsbury however had troubles with his men, who sympathised with the rebels, and he had to impose an oath of loyalty; Cumberland's own men deserted him. The Stanleys had a significant armed following, and in the Pilgrimage, Derby raised troops in Lancashire, although at first it was feared none would stick with him – except for his household servants. The funeral of the third earl in 1572 was attended by 80 of his gentlemen, 50 knights and esquires, and his household officers.[21]

Whether or not a nobleman was an experienced soldier or had a crowd of armed retainers, the monarchs chose nobles to quell challenges to the crown in all the serious risings of the period. For such urgent tasks a noble's high status made him more likely to be obeyed, and outsiders as well as regional nobles helped to support the royal authority. In 1536 those loyal to the crown included Derby and Shrewsbury, who helped to contain the rebels in Lancashire. By contrast, in Yorkshire the Percies failed to act for the government – and rebellion flared. In 1549 Lord Grey, as a soldier noble, was sent to quieten the unrest in the Midlands; the Western rebels at Exeter were defeated by Lord Russell and Herbert, with Grey adding assistance at the end. The earl of Warwick suppressed Kett's rebellion in Norfolk. In 1569 the earl of Sussex, a Privy Councillor, led the hastily recruited force which moved north toward the army of the rebellious earls. The news of his advance was enough to persuade the insurgents to turn back and avoid a direct battle; Sussex soon returned to his court life.

Several historians have discussed the military decline of the aristocracy and the development of the Elizabethan militia as a more official force.[22] These changes did not entirely eliminate noble fighting strength, at least in the sixteenth century. Notably, when Queen Mary reinstated Thomas Percy to the Northumberland inheritance in 1557, she gave him licence for 200 retainers. Mary and Elizabeth continued to grant such licences, perhaps allowing 60–100 retainers for a peer. Despite the crown's efforts to reduce such potentially threatening forces, the earl of Shrewsbury in 1592 made a request to give his livery and badge to other gentlemen and yeomen, besides his household and estate officers. Even a courtier peer like the earl of Leicester modernised and fortified Kenilworth Castle, equipping it to withstand a siege, with artillery and arms, for nearly 200 horse and 500 foot soldiers. Nobles provided contingents for the Armada defence in 1588, and in the 1599 invasion scare Elizabeth requested the lords each to provide 100 horsemen as her personal bodyguard. Pembroke replied from Wales that he could come with 300 horse and 500 foot, all armed by himself! However, this kind of personal force was already fading by then, partly through cost and partly through royal suspicion, and it was soon to disappear. Such forces had often been used for selfish ends in private quarrels, as when the seventh earl of Shrewsbury sent 120 armed men to arrest an opponent in 1598. Yet the problems Shrewsbury and Cumberland had in 1536 show that a noble's armed might depended on the willingness of his men – tenants, household servants and other retainers – to act as instructed. There was no blind obedience to the nobility, and their power depended on how their men reacted to the issues, and also on how the nobleman had behaved as a landlord. Cumberland, a harsh landlord, was besieged by his own men.

Land and rural tenant relationships formed a crucial element in noble authority. The nobles were by far the greatest landholders, even if there were variations in their wealth and some suffered indebtedness due to over-lavish building or buying. The administration necessary to supervise a great estate employed local gentry and a host of lesser functionaries. Certainly in the first half of the sixteenth century and perhaps later, the great territorial lords had their own councils of chief officers. The noble chose his stewards of lands and household, treasurers, receiver-generals, bailiffs and so on from the locality. The offices brought rewards for the holders – and obedient supporters to the nobleman. The new earl of Derby in 1572 appointed heads of two prominent county families, Sir Richard Shireburne and Edward Scarisbrick, to important offices in his financial administration. Noble households had gentlemen in service more generally: in the mid-sixteenth century the marquess of Northampton had 34 gentlemen and 13 yeomen in his household, the earl of Huntingdon 10 gentlemen and 25 yeomen, and although the number of such attendants was decreasing, they and their kin owed allegiance to the nobleman. The lord had great influence over his tenants, for he or his bailiffs controlled the details of their leases and rents, and his will, if he wished to trouble himself, could prevail in the manor courts. The deference they were expected to show was provided when they turned out on ceremonial occasions, as when the earl of Derby travelled to Knowsley in 1597. Five hundred Cheshire horsemen turned out to greet him near Nantwich, and 700 from Lancashire when he reached Warrington.[23] Although rent had replaced obligations of military service by James I's reign, some peers still raised their tenants in the Civil War.

The nobility cultivated the appearance of importance. Their grand houses and ancestral castles, surrounded by formal gardens and parks, proclaimed their greatness to those living locally and to visitors. The great wealth of the earls of Shrewsbury meant that they maintained Sheffield Castle as their principal grand residence, but they possessed other houses and castles as well. The Percy earls of Northumberland had Alnwick Castle, the earls of Cumberland had medieval Skipton Castle and grand palaces; the Berkeleys had their twelfth-century stronghold of Berkeley Castle, and so on down a long list. Some spent too much on building or rebuilding, investing heavily in demonstrations of grandeur and raising troublesome debts. Lord Burghley had two palaces: Burghley House and Theobalds. His son built Hatfield House. The many aristocratic builders of great houses in the reign of James included the earls of Suffolk, Northumberland, Northampton, Dorset and Westmorland. Their sumptuous surroundings were intended to overawe lesser neighbours and impress them with the power of the nobleman within. These houses also served to provide hospitality for local gentry, occasions on which suggestions could be pressed about ruling the county. Here too nobles entertained visiting courtiers, sometimes, indeed, the monarch accompanied by a vast household. Nobles commissioned formal portraits which depict the elaborate and richly decorated clothes by which court and even country nobles signalled their significance. They dressed their servants in livery in the colours of the family, and rode with a troop of uniformed retainers to create a spectacular public appearance. Lawrence Stone, Mark Girouard, and others have well described this self-advertising of status and wealth by the nobility, and by the gentry who emulated them. Display had a serious political purpose, emphasising the high place and great wealth of such men to all who saw them.

The monarchs could make new nobles, and unmake old ones if they chose, but they depended on the nobles to help them govern. All monarchs needed counsel, and put nobles on the Privy Council even if they had no national significance – men such as the earls of Derby and Shrewsbury in Elizabeth's reign. The monarch needed great men whose own prestige and magnificence could add to the lustre of the crown, and impress the people. They chose nobles to command armed forces in foreign expeditions or to combat internal challenge, even courtiers with no recent military experience, as with the earl of Sussex in 1569, and the earl of Leicester in 1585. Nobles appeared to have great power, and many did, in county and in court. But these were relatively few: they could lead, but their ability to govern depended on the gentry and lesser officials. The gentry, the subject of the next chapter, were far more numerous, and competed to exercise authority over the people.

3

Gentry

Most people in early modern England never saw a monarch; few met a nobleman. So who seemed to rule over daily life? Secular authority spread from the centre throughout the counties via the justices of the peace, and under them the constables, assisted by lesser officials. In towns, the mayor and borough officers provided control. The justices performed far more than their original legal function of keeping the peace in the localities, dealing with thefts, disputes and other minor lawbreaking. In addition to these duties of keeping order, they actually governed the counties and had a huge range of responsibilities. They controlled wages and labour, licensed alehouses, directed people to repair bridges and highways, kept track of everybody, ordered local drifters to work, vagrants to be investigated, punished, and sent back to their 'home' villages, and parents of illegitimate babies to pay maintenance, as part of the schemes to supervise and help the poor. Reading William Lambarde's instruction handbook for justices, we might suppose that no-one would wish to take on the burdens of administering 'not loads, but stacks of statutes', many of them involving long hours of evidence of neighbours' quarrels and crimes.[1] Justices often had to deal with such matters at home; one justice could make orders for certain recognizances or binding over to appear at quarter sessions, other problems required two justices acting together. A conscientious JP was a busy one. Moreover, the office carried no salary, only a notional expenses payment that the JPs put towards their dinner at meetings. But, surprisingly, many among the landed gentry did serve. We might ask who among the gentry became JPs, and why they chose to do so?

Historians generally assume that all of the major gentry, or all members of parliament, were JPs. It is also thought that once a man was appointed, he remained in the office for life.[2] But neither of these assumptions is correct. Despite the increasing 'stacks of statutes' to administer, members of the gentry competed vigorously to become JPs, and in most counties more desired office than the central administration would appoint. The government had to select from among the hopeful aspirants, theoretically choosing the most able. However, other factors intervened: the gentry who ruled the provinces were not only men such as Sir John Newdigate who believed that wealth and leisure implied a duty to public service. Political ambition spurred gentlemen to seek a place – for honour and status, and also for power. A man's standing in the locality increased if he were a JP. The people living around respected him more, and knew they could go to him to request action. At quarter sessions court days, he appeared formally on the bench of justices as the local face of government. The quarterly sessions of each county's justices were impressive occasions for both participants and onlookers, and many turned out to watch or take part. The commission listing the JP's names was read, and they sat in order of precedence; the *custos rotulorum* or a deputy read the official charge, or exhortation, specifying the court's duties and the problems needing attention. Around the JPs thronged men and women – jurymen, high and petty constables reporting on every part of the county, and all those with business for the sessions: those indicted for theft or other small crimes, alehouse-keepers, neighbours in dispute, men appearing as sureties sometimes, and lots of witnesses. Women as well as men appeared as complainants or those complained against, and as witnesses. In Essex in the 1550s and 1560s, writs to the sheriff to bring in people to the quarter sessions list astonishing numbers of names, sometimes hundreds. Even if not all of them appeared, it made quite a crowd. The public arena for the JP was extensive, and he could feel important there. He could participate in decision-making, exert control, be seen to do so, and earn respect.

Status within the county elite mattered even more than increased standing among social inferiors, and beckoned gentlemen to strive eagerly for a place on the bench and the influence it brought. A JP could gain prestige and alliance among nobles and gentlemen in his county, and opportunities to lobby at the centre for offices and rewards: a place on the commission was a means of advancement, and well worth the struggle. There was vigorous competition for places, and both local and central influences worked to produce frequent changes to the commissions, with new appointments and dismissals. Initial appointment stemmed in theory from the Lord Chancellor (or Lord Keeper). But a prospective JP needed to be brought to the Lord Chancellor's attention, by visibility at court or in the country, and a recommendation from a prominent person such as a Privy Councillor or a courtier, one of the assize judges who travelled on circuit twice a year and reported on JPs, a bishop or (from the 1570s) a Lord Lieutenant. Relatively little direct information remains about such recommendations to the Lord Chancellor, even in the voluminous papers of Sir Thomas Egerton, later Lord Ellesmere, who held the office from 1596 to 1617, but there is enough evidence to demonstrate the insecurity of office, and the influences which operated. A new commission was issued every time a justice was appointed, dismissed, or even repositioned in the order of names after a change of status, such as being knighted (although not for a death).

Details of new commissions show far more extensive change than is suggested by the annual Patent Rolls lists which historians generally use. But even the patents for new commissions of the peace in Henry VIII's reign show many changes year by year. For example the Warwickshire commission for February 1531 listed the names of 22 local men. By a year later, 27 sat, including seven new ones: quite a high proportion over twelve months. The Shropshire commission issued in March 1531 listed 19 local JPs. In December 1536 a longer list of 26 had only eight of those men, plus one from the family of his 1531 predecessor. So 17 were new compared with five years earlier, nearly two-thirds of the bench. It was similar in other counties in the 1530s, even those not connected with the Pilgrimage of Grace in the north, where major changes could be expected after the rebellion. Some counties were altered more often than others in those years, including those just mentioned and Dorset, Northamptonshire, Sussex, and Wiltshire.[3]

We have much more detailed evidence of the changes for certain periods in the Crown Office working docket books, which survive for the years 1595–1603, and 1616–29, registering the issue of every new commission of the peace for each county, with the names of the JPs to be inserted or removed.[4] The docket book for 1595–1603 lists hundreds of revised county commissions. In 1595 the alterations responded to a general 'reformation'. In 1596, over 100 new commissions were issued, most giving the names of one, two or more new, or dismissed, justices, and sometimes a reason. From late November 1596 to a year later, Kent had ten new commissions, three of them in February alone; there were 45 revisions noted for the county between 1595 and 1603. Over the same period at least 21 new commissions were issued for Wiltshire, 36 for Essex, 30 for the West Riding of Yorkshire, 24 for Dorset, and so on. For many counties the revolt of the earl of Essex in 1601 led to a great crop of revised commissions in order to remove all his supporters. Unfortunately the next docket book is missing, but the one beginning in 1616 continues to register frequent alterations. In one year from late March 1618, 160 new commissions were issued. A few of the bigger counties had frequent changes, while there were hardly any for some counties. Occasionally the clerk noted a reason for the new issue: in the Wiltshire renewal for 20 December 1616, John Hall was left out for non-attendance, and Sir Giles Wroughton for outlawry. That was the fifth revised commission for Wiltshire in that year alone. (There is a rare request from a gentleman to be left out: Peter Warburton in Cheshire in 1623). For the twelve months March 1622–3, there were 125 new commissions made out for the counties. As Charles I's reign commenced, the dry docket books reflect turmoil as sudden turnover occurred – numbers of JPs dismissed, or as in early 1626, restored. In October 1626 a whole batch of dismissals, to be discussed below, removed prominent county governors, including Sir Richard Grosvenor, Henry Sherfield and Oliver St John. By 1629, revisions were being made in sets of several counties at a time, for adding new men, for restoring some to their former place, and for dismissals. In 1630, 133

Fig. 2: JPs found guilty of misdeeds were dismissed. Sir Francis Michell was a busy Middlesex JP, but in 1621 was dismissed and degraded from knighthood for bribery and oppression as JP and monopoly commissioner. A ballad described his fall. (Pepys Ballads, I, 143, Pepys Library, Magdalene College, Cambridge with permission).

revised commissions were issued. The commission of the peace was not a stable body, and comings and goings were frequent. What lay behind such frequent alteration among the gentry who held local power?

Since the government depended so heavily on the JPs to supervise policies throughout the realm, royal ministers compiled detailed lists of gentry in each county, showing great concern over who might be made JPs. William Cecil (later Lord Burghley) made many such lists, methodically annotated: in 1562 he catalogued gentry approved by the justices of assize to be added, and others to be dismissed. However, the assize judges bi-annual visits to a county cannot have made them experts on all its gentry.[5] The choice of men to be put on to the commission, dismissed, or ignored, altered with political change. A new monarch, or a new minister, changes in policy and the shifting religious requirements of the Tudor reformations all led to alterations in the counties as at the centre. Some wholesale purges occurred, with many justices dismissed at once. Henry VIII, with first Wolsey and then Thomas Cromwell, sought to create a loyal group of county gentry by giving them honorific court posts as knights and esquires of the body, registering their names by county. By the mid 1520s over 200 county gentry appeared in this book of the king's 'affinity', by 1535 there were 263. Some of them, especially the most prominent, were put into local commissions of the peace, but not all: in Surrey, Suffolk and Kent, half of these men were JPs under Wolsey, in Norfolk a third, though fewer in Somerset, Buckinghamshire and Oxfordshire. Wolsey also reduced the number of local JPs in Kent and Gloucestershire and the north, and put in men who would implement crown policy reliably. In the 1530s, especially after the Pilgrimage of Grace gave the gravest threat to Tudor government, Cromwell organised a much greater turnover in the commissions. From a total of 547 JPs on the commissions issued between 1536 and 1539, nearly a third – 172 – were completely new appointments, perhaps 10 per cent of them directly linked to Cromwell. Moreover, Cromwell issued frequent letters and circulars to encourage compliance. But other influences, including local ones, always worked against total crown control, so that some prominent men who opposed Wolsey or Cromwell nevertheless retained office; only the most active opponents were purged.[6]

A change of monarch and of policy could bring sudden upheaval to county commissions. At the beginning of Elizabeth's reign, half the justices for Norfolk were dismissed and replaced, and the same happened in Sussex and Northamptonshire certainly, and probably elsewhere. One would expect these changes to reflect the new Elizabethan Protestant Church and loyalty to the queen. Yet Catholic JPs remained, some in Norfolk because of their loyalty to the duke, and in other counties through the influence of Catholic nobles – or, as in the north, because not enough gentry were Protestant. But because of doubts about the reliability of some, the government soon sought to remodel the commissions.[7]

On 17 October 1564 the Privy Council wrote to the bishops demanding full reports on the gentry's and JPs' attitudes to official religion, for suggestions of those who should be dismissed for opposition to it, and of others, not currently JPs, who were fit for appointment.[8] Religious loyalty was used as a test of support for the regime, and the government aimed to purge suspect gentry from the commissions of the peace. Each bishop reported on prominent gentlemen, with notes on whether each man was a 'furtherer' of Elizabeth's Protestant church, a 'furtherer earnest', or conversely a hinderer, and probably Catholic. Overall the bishops reported 431 JPs as favourable to the Church settlement, 264 as neutral, and 157 as hinderers of the newly established Church. They also reported that most of the towns mentioned were hostile. In Worcestershire, Edwin Sandys reported many adversaries, including five resident JPs, and he also found strong adversaries in Warwickshire, including Sir Robert Throckmorton. By contrast, in Wiltshire nearly all were 'furtherers earnest' or not hinderers. Some of the bishops in the 1564 enquiry mentioned attributes besides religious loyalty for selection of gentry to be JPs. The bishop of Salisbury noted that George Ludlow, Lawrence Hyde and Henry Clifford could be added: they were 'furtherers' of religion, and also 'wise and politick and able to serve'; Hyde was appointed and later became very prominent on the Wiltshire commission, possibly the other two were also added.

Other bishops used the term 'to be trusted'. In Essex Edward Bocking and George Christmas were not: Bishop Grindal claimed that in their words they seemed to favour the new religion, but were not favourable to its ministers. Worse, they governed 'undiscreetly' and used their office for gain, as Grindal was informed by 'grave and godly persons'. Despite this, Bocking certainly was not permanently dismissed: he attended quarter sessions very assiduously during the following years, and petty sessions as well, and gave much time to out-of-sessions work, dealing with local people and the problems of disputes, alehouses, bridges and suchlike. On 25 November 1569 Bocking subscribed, along with other Essex justices, to the Act of Uniformity, and promised to observe the established religion. Bocking may have worked so hard in order to overcome official doubts about his suitability. The uncertain tenure of office is underlined by the comment on Thomas Frank, who had denied a report that he was a hinderer. Grindal suggested that Frank only be allowed to hold office on trial, until the truth about his attitude was known. He seems to have become acceptable: he attended quarter and petty sessions, and he worked out of sessions, sending in recognizances, though less frequently than Bocking. Probably he was still anxious about his position in 1566, for he notified that his absence from the Easter quarter sessions was due to illness. George Christmas, in contrast, did not succeed, and disappeared from the commission's records.

In Somerset, the Bishop of Bath and Wells reported that 'every justice do diligently (as they say) execute their office'. That somewhat subtle requirement, reputation, commended two new men to be put in: William Hill who was 'well esteemed among his neighbours' and well known as favourer of the Gospel, while John Sydenham was known to be wise, sober and discreet, well affected to religion, and also well esteemed. Of course, the bishops were influenced by whoever gave them advice, and, as Archbishop Parker warned, 'sometime informers serve their own turn and gratify their friends'.[9] Although the advice of the bishops was not followed in all cases, the commissions of the peace in some counties were remodelled. In Sussex, a quarter of the justices were dismissed, and new ones appointed. But elsewhere there was little change, and in Lancashire so many of the gentry remained conservative in religion through most of Elizabeth's reign that it was not possible to secure a totally Protestant bench of magistrates. There, Burghley's continuing efforts concentrated on making sure the conservatives who were JPs were generally peaceable, did not make a fuss over their Catholicism, and were otherwise loyal.

Foreign relations could also affect whether or not specific members of the gentry could hold the office. In 1587 the threat of invasion by Spain led to a major purge of the commissions of the peace, with many justices dismissed in efforts to secure a reliable, non-Catholic commission. Assize judges were asked to list justices for dismissal: men from outside the county, those unlearned or not conforming to the minimum wealth, as well as Catholics. The dismissals which followed did not fulfil these criteria, however, and showed that the visiting assize judges were often misinformed, so Burghley requested the bishops to advise again on a new reorganisation of personnel. In Norfolk nearly half the justices suffered dismissal during 1587–8. Even in Wiltshire, where most of the gentry were firmly Protestant by 1587, an official list shows that twelve men suffered the shame of dismissal, although not for Catholicism. Another purge followed in 1593, probably to eliminate men missed before for their non-residence or inadequate wealth. Eleven Wiltshire JPs were dismissed, some relatively poor; but even three wealthy and soundly Protestant local gentlemen – Walter Long, John Dauntsey and Henry Baynton – were left out for a year or two, for unknown reasons. Catholic sympathies were not the only religious opinions which could affect the selection and removal of the provincial governors. In 1607, Dudley Carleton reported that puritan members of parliament were dismissed from the commission of the peace, though it is not clear how far this actually occurred. In 1622 again rumour circulated that all puritan JPs would be removed.[10]

Clearly the government did try hard to make an informed choice from among the gentry. The Privy Council planned dismissals of the 'unmeet' in 1572, 1580 and 1582, the last commanded by the queen, for removal of papists and base men. John Hawarde described hearing the Lord Keeper's complaints in 1595 about unlearned and negligent justices. Thereupon, wrote Hawarde, the queen herself took the list of JPs and noted ones she wanted to remain, those she thought should be dismissed, and demanded the rest be scrutinised. The queen did not want any JPs who were retainers to great men, who did not live within the county they served, or who were not 'of sufficient living and countenance' (that is, were poorer and less estimable, lacking an imposing manor house and troops of servants and retainers). She told the assize judges to enquire carefully and remove those who failed to meet her conditions.[11] Burghley's annotated list marked justices assessed at under £20 in the subsidy, those suspected of Catholic recusancy, and those who were retainers of other men. The docket book noted that commissions for all the shires were renewed according to the latest 'reformation of Justices'. But again, the dismissals did not entirely follow these rules, and some men were restored within months. Hawarde commented on similar complaints made by Thomas Egerton, Lord Keeper (Lord Chancellor from 1603) in 1602, 1604 and 1608. In the 1621 parliament, Secretary Calvert reported the king had ordered unworthy JPs to be dismissed, but compliance did not follow. One problem was that there was no clear definition, and no suitable test. Choices involved subtle social gradations, with wide variations between the wealth of poorer northern gentry, and gentlemen in the richer south. A gentleman's personality and dependability affected the Privy Council's judgement about a JP, but these are now very hard to recover.

The key issue was connection, and the influence of patrons often explains why the Lord Keeper's outbursts and the plans of Elizabeth and James did not really achieve their aims. The earl of Derby's friends were soon back on the Lancashire commission after the purge of 1587. Many JPs lost their places in national purges supervised by the Council; others were dismissed for more personal reasons – and often we do not know why individuals were removed. Edmund Ludlow was a very active Wiltshire justice, as shown by the quarter sessions minute book starting in 1574: he attended sessions regularly and made orders between them. Yet Ludlow was dismissed from the Wiltshire commission five times. Between 1596 and 1601 his removal may have been due to the Attorney-General's suit against him for land-use offences, possibly on the information of political enemies in the county. Between 1605 and 1607 he was fined for riots and an alleged assault, and again dismissed as JP – but he managed to return in 1608. Since a new commission was issued for every slight change, gentlemen riding to sessions could not even be certain that they were still included, until they heard the names on the commission read out at the quarter sessions meeting. Sir Arthur Heveningham arrived at the Epiphany session for Norfolk in 1583, only to discover that in full view of the assembled crowd, he must endure the shame of being left out. Worse for Sir Thomas Wentworth in 1626, he was actually presiding at quarter sessions as *custos rotulorum* when the warrant for his dismissal arrived, creating an appalling public disgrace.[12]

A gentleman's hold on the office, or his place in the order of precedence, was very uncertain. Bishop Freke of Norwich moaned that he was not sure who was or was not a justice 'for that the commission of the peace is so often altered and daily renewed'.[13] And he was right. Half of all Elizabethan justices for Norfolk were put out at least once. For late Elizabethan Norfolk there were at least six new commissions issued every year to omit or put in names, or both. In Wiltshire between 1590 and 1620, a third of JPs suffered dismissal at least once, and some several times. Although some exclusions were temporary, others were permanent. In one year, 1616, for instance, six new commissions for Wiltshire appeared. In Somerset in 1625 there were eight revisions, in 1629, six, and sometimes two came out in very quick succession. For all the counties in 1630, the Crown Office issued 133 revised commissions. Each fresh commission put one or several men out, or new men in: gentlemen did not hold their power with any security.

Official purges and random decisions about the suitability of individuals brought instability to county commissions, and so did the machinations of county politics – especially through faction and patronage. Both affected the selection of the men to rule the counties, and both contributed to instability. Gentlemen vigorously sought appointment for themselves and for their allies; they often also succeeded in removing rivals. Once appointed, they frequently had to strive hard to retain the place. Many counties saw severe conflict over local office in struggles for prestige and power. Hampshire,

Herefordshire, Kent, Lincolnshire, Norfolk, Northumberland, Nottinghamshire, Wiltshire, Worcestershire and Yorkshire were factious counties where the gentry divided in bitter disputes affecting appointment and dismissal of local governors.[14] Late Elizabethan Wiltshire was especially disrupted by faction amongst many ambitious men. One gentleman complained in 1589: 'Mr Wroughton hath gotten together other of the like faction, and he and his accomplices hath done acts of great force.'[15] Wroughton's faction included John Thynne, Henry Knyvet, and Walter Long; their opponents were James Marvin, John Danvers, Edmund Ludlow, Lord Audley and William Darrell. Each side tried to place their friends on the commission of the peace and remove their opponents, sometimes by extreme methods. Darrell tried to have Knyvet removed by accusing him of using the office to protect murderers. But Knyvet triumphed over Darrell by spreading an allegation that Darrell had organised the murder of a newborn baby in his mansion at Littlecote. Darrell was disgraced and imprisoned, while Knyvet retained his place as a JP, adding to it the offices of deputy lieutenant and subsidy commissioner.

The bitter contention between Thynne and Marvin, and between the Longs and Danvers in the late 1580s and 1590s, saw arguments at quarter sessions descend to street affrays and Henry Danvers' murder of Henry Long during a confrontation in 1594. Accusations of misconduct in office provided a frequent method to seek exclusion of an enemy: Thynne accused Marvin of a whole range of malpractices, as a JP, deputy lieutenant and subsidy commissioner. The allegations included taking bribes from men wishing to avoid militia service, altering tax assessments, appointing an inadequate collector, and even of causing riots at quarter sessions and assizes in 1589. Yet both men retained office, although in 1595 John Thynne's name was lowered to almost the bottom of the commission list from near the top; the dismissals of Marvin's ally Edmund Ludlow may have been connected with these disputes. Henry Knyvet was also involved in struggles with Henry Poole in 1593 to 1596, as each tried to persuade the Privy Council of the other's unsuitability, and engineer his dismissal. Poole complained that Knyvet pretended that he was reforming misdemeanours in the county, and had great integrity in the service of the county, but rather was merely encouraging people to accuse Poole of misbehaviour and damage his reputation. Each suffered the penalty of a Star Chamber fine in 1596. Poole withstood the onslaught and retained office then, but was dismissed 1607/8.

From 1618, Henry Moody and Thomas Ivy each overtly attempted to discredit the other as a justice, and to claim precedence at the Wiltshire quarter sessions. Ivy accused Moody of misusing his office and behaving disruptively at meetings of JPs. More seriously he said that Moody abused his authority by holding private sessions in his own chamber and took bribes to discharge offenders. However, this attempt to prove that Moody should be dismissed failed. Five years later, Ivy alleged that Moody had snatched up warrants to sign his name before Ivy, despite knowing that Ivy was the 'more ancient knight and Justice of peace', seeking to disgrace Ivy in public. A witness described how during the signing of documents, each kept trying to sign first. They too were sentenced by Star Chamber to pay fines: the judges recognised mere factious allegations.

Elizabethan Norfolk suffered the destabilising effect of competition among gentry for control of office-holding. Every office became a prize to be disputed between the factions, as each tried to promote allies and exclude opponents. Sir Arthur Heveningham and his supporters, including the Lovell family, stood against the Bacon/Gawdy alliance. In 1586 Sir Nathaniel Bacon accused Thomas Lovell of malpractice, but failed to have him dismissed then, although he was removed in the purge of 1587. Bassingbourne Gawdy and his faction campaigned to prevent Lovell's return to office, and were successful for several years. Lovell achieved reappointment after Gawdy senior died, and thereafter contended with Gawdy's heir. Soon Lovell was dismissed, but was reappointed after the Privy Council ordered an enquiry, suspecting the information against Lovell derived from these disputes. Although Lovell paid £240 for reappointment to the commission, the fight was not yet over; it continued in all aspects of local administration including the militia, until Lovell's death.

Norfolk also saw a long dispute in the 1580s between Edward Flowerdew and Arthur Heveningham, in which each sought to achieve his rival's dismissal by alleging misdeeds in office and violent ambush. Here, Flowerdew's disapproval of his rival's whole approach to local administration added fuel to the fire of competition for office. Heveningham was put out of the commission, but retained support among some remaining justices. As in Wiltshire, factional rivalry in Norfolk created instability on the commission of the peace: in the 1590s two justices achieved each other's dismissal; one for two years, the other for life.

In Elizabethan Kent also, powerful factions fought for power and control of local office. The Sidneys, the Sackvilles, the Wottons, Sir Edward Hoby and Sir John Leveson vied with the two successive Lords Cobham over all the major offices. There were conflicts between gentry of east and west Kent, over where the sessions should be held. In 1596 those from the west prevented the holding of alternating sessions at Canterbury, and insisted on meetings only at Maidstone. Sir Edward Wotton the Lord Lieutenant and Leveson as a deputy lieutenant faced opposition early in James I's reign from other JPs in the search for prestige and control. Some of the rivals had powerful allies or held central posts, which helped to make it difficult for any one faction to prevail in Kent. William Lord Cobham was allied with the Cecils, and held central office as Lord Chamberlain. The Sidneys were close to their kinsmen the earls of Leicester and Essex, and Sir Thomas Sackville was Lord Treasurer from 1599, becoming Lord Buckhurst, and then earl of Dorset in 1604. The alternating success and failure of the factions helps to explain the exceptionally frequent revisions of the Kent commission of the peace noted above.

In the 1587 purge of JPs, Yorkshire suffered more dismissals than any other county, reflecting political dissension as well as Burghley's policy of eliminating unsuitable gentlemen and, if possible, reducing the number of Catholics. In the West Riding from 1597 to 1610 a faction led by Sir Stephen Proctor and Sir Timothy Whittingham opposed established neighbours whose recusant sympathies could be used to discredit them as local office-holders: each faction managed to have opponents temporarily imprisoned. A later contest between Sir John Savile and Sir Thomas Wentworth affected local politics from 1614 to the 1630s. Both men were extremely ambitious, and as Savile 'maketh use of his authority to satisfy his own ends', so too did Wentworth.[16] In 1617 Savile tried to dislodge Wentworth from the *custos*-ship for Yorkshire, procuring a letter from court telling Wentworth the king wanted him to resign it. But Wentworth protested, stressing his honour, his gratitude to the king and his lack of personal ambition! He insisted that if Savile should replace him, 'it might justly be taken as the greatest disgrace that could be done unto me'. Savile and Wentworth argued over resistance to the war taxation of the 1620s, and over the treatment of Catholics, and used these issues in their struggle; both pestered the duke of Buckingham for support. In 1626 Savile seemed to be winning, when he finally achieved Wentworth's humiliating public removal from the leadership of the commission, and the dismissal of three Wentworth allies from it. But Savile lost a patron with Buckingham's assassination, while Wentworth revenged the disgraces when he became Lord President of the Council of the North in December 1628.

Even counties with resident aristocratic claimants to authority experienced contention for local power which affected the choice of local governors. At the start of Elizabeth's reign, old William Paulet, marquess of Winchester, tried to rule Hampshire with his conservative faction. But the zealous Protestant gentry faction worked hard to seize control, succeeding by the end of the decade. In 1564 the Winchester supporters were dismissed from the commission; in 1569 others were refused appointment. Nottinghamshire likewise saw bitter resentment from leading county families opposing a noble seeking supremacy there. Here too, the religious conservatism of the earl of Shrewsbury's faction provided a spur for the zealous Protestants, led by Sir John Stanhope. The Stanhopes used all the county offices in their struggles to thwart the earl, leading to disorder at the 1593 parliamentary election. The disruptions in county government became notorious, and during the troubles in Kent in the 1590s one gentleman complained 'I fear we shall soon see it worse than Nottinghamshire'.[17]

County gentlemen struggled to promote themselves and their allies and to defeat and disgrace their enemies. They often sought to do so by enlisting the help of influential patrons, Councillors, or powerful provincial nobles. In Norfolk, the Howard dukes of Norfolk long dominated the choice of local governors, even retaining their supporters in office in the face of official disapproval, as in 1564 when the bishop recommended removal of Catholics. But after the fourth duke's execution in 1572, the Norfolk gentry had to seek new patrons at court. Edward Flowerdew, then a junior member of a lesser gentry family, succeeded in gaining appointment to the bench with Leicester's help. Secretary Walsingham's and Lord Hunsdon's relative Wimond Carey secured a place; Walsingham and Sir Thomas Mildmay put in Thomas Sidney. Thomas Lovell was dismissed from office through the efforts of enemies in 1592; seven years later he secured the help of Lord North, through astute persuasion and financial 'gifts', and returned to play his part in local government. These new men gained authority through patronage, not ability. Since the powerful put in their clients, the loss of a patron could mean rapid loss of office, as the Norfolk Knyvets discovered when their patron the Lord Chancellor Sir Thomas Bromley died in 1587. Suddenly, moaned Sir Henry Knyvet, those who had been friendly now seemed strangers when asked for help, and soon Thomas Knyvet was out of the commission of the peace and the deputy lieutenancy.

In Wiltshire, the earl of Leicester promised his good will to Sir John Thynne in 1570; Leicester's support probably helped Thynne to retain his place on the commission for the rest of his life, to become *custos* and to appoint his own nominee, Walter Berington, as clerk of the peace. After Thynne's death in 1580, the earl of Pembroke was appointed *custos* with Leicester's backing and Berington lost his office when Pembroke put in a different clerk. Perhaps Pembroke was suspected of undue partiality in appointments, protesting in 1590 that 'if it fall out that I prefer them nearest in blood, kindred, alliance, or in other respects, yet I assure your Lordship that my commendation proceeds of sufficiency in them, not of partial affection in me'.[18] Well, he would say that, wouldn't he?

Thynne's son John used intensive and widespread lobbying to establish a position in local government after his father's death. The family's London agent Maurice Browne, one of Walsingham's men, helped and advised on dealings with the great. 'Cousin' Reynold Williams, a servant of the Lord Chancellor, promised 'to use all means and expedition he could': in April 1580 Thynne's place on the bench was promised for the end of the next law term, 'and what may be done in the meantime shall not be omitted'. However, that was not enough. Browne told Thynne to cultivate his court contacts, especially the earl of Leicester 'whom you have vowed to follow and have required his countenance and friendship in all your just causes'. But Brown warned Thynne of adversaries aplenty 'to dissuade him and others against you', which he should counter 'by coming to my Lord often and using his countenance with familiarity' and by seeking the help of other courtiers at the same time, including Christopher Hatton. Brown even advised Thynne to dress better, with investment in a new suit of apparel 'to gain you far more than that expense, beside the credit and estimation it would bring you both in Court and in the country'.[19] Despite all this effort,

Thynne had to wait another three years to overcome the Lord Chancellor's objections to his appointment. Perhaps the Chancellor doubted Thynne's interest in doing the work on the commission; if so the suspicion was justified, for after appointment Thynne did little work as a JP, and involved himself in many disputes. Thynne's unusually well-documented campaign was probably typical of the tactics used to gain office. The Gawdy family likewise kept a contact at court to advance their interests, and Philip Gawdy reported on his efforts to help his brother Bassingbourne become a deputy lieutenant for Norfolk. Philip Gawdy lobbied three peers, and claimed that he also had a special friend on the Privy Council in Lord Zouche 'by whom I dare undertake at all times to do you a good turn'.[20] In 1605 Bassingbourne succeeded after two years of lobbying, probably through his brother's cultivation of the Howards. Sir Dru Drury was a gentleman usher of the Privy Chamber and *custos* in Norfolk, and used his court position to help Nathaniel Bacon and Bassingbourne Gawdy.

Late in Elizabeth's reign, ambitious men in many counties appealed to the earl of Essex, who was himself seeking to build a clientage, and he became one of the major influences on local office-holding. Essex directly requested the Lord Keeper to put two men into the commission in Carmarthen. And in 1599 he told Egerton 'as your Lordship hath heretofore made me beholden unto you for many others by placing them in the commission of the peace at my request' so he now requested the Lord Keeper to put in an uncle who wished to be on the Carmarthen and Pembroke commissions. All the leaders in the Wiltshire factional struggles appealed to Essex for aid, and the earl suggested quite explicitly that gentlemen should seek their advancement through him. In 1596 he asked John Thynne for help in raising men for the militia, for by doing so, Thynne would 'declare your good affection to myself'.[21] Essex's execution in February 1601 meant that there had been only a few years in which he could try to establish a wide influence over selection of county governors. He could not entirely dominate the choice, for gentlemen worked through other patrons too, such as the earl of Dorset in Sussex, and the Howards, including the earl of Northampton. Courtiers like Sir John Stanhope, Treasurer of the Chamber to James I, provided another of the many channels to the centre which affected the choice of office-holders.

The strongest regional nobles were effective patrons for gentry seeking office. The Stanley earls of Derby were exceptionally successful for most of the late sixteenth and early seventeenth centuries in determining who held office. The earls recognised that some Catholics should remain JPs, because the gentlemen were needed to provide local control, prosecute petty thefts, and to help inhabitants, who could not travel to distant JPs, with problems in disputes. But even in Stanley Lancashire, conflict with a strong new Protestant group around 1600 was followed by twenty-three dismissals of JPs in only five years: although some of these men reappeared, not all did. In Leicestershire, the earls of Huntingdon expected to nominate local governors and often succeeded. In 1623, the fifth earl wrote to the Lord Chancellor, suggesting one JP be omitted because he had left the county, and requesting inclusion of three new ones. Huntingdon favoured two of these, George Ashby and Roger Smith, as very religious men and of very good estate.[22] Gentlemen who owed their places on the bench to recommendation from very powerful local figures needed to do as their patron wished, if they were to remain in office.

Bishops also tried to influence appointments of magistrates, often to strengthen their own position in their dioceses. Bishop Parkhurst of Norwich wanted more Protestant support: his recommendations for three new justices in Norfolk in 1571 mentioned local need, and stressed William Blennerhassett's godly zeal. But his effort failed, although after another plea a year later, one of Parkhurst's candidates became a justice. In the late 1570s Bishop Freke of Norwich procured places for his allies to counter puritan opposition to him, and thus helped to polarise politics in Norfolk and Suffolk. In 1587 Bishop Edmund Scambler recommended dismissal of ten Norfolk JPs reputed backward in religion; in the 1590s he brought in outsiders to the commission as allies during his conflicts over church property.[23] Henry Cotton, Bishop of Salisbury from 1598 to 1615, fought vigorously against the local secular authority, the godly magistrates. One of his weapons seems to have been the appointment of cathedral personnel to the Wiltshire commission – John Bridges (briefly) and William Tooker, and probably the registrar Thomas Sadler, who first became a JP in 1608.

The number of patrons for aspiring gentlemen to approach reduced after 1617, with the growing power of the duke of Buckingham. As the king's favourite, Buckingham aimed to dominate and make himself the sole source of power over office-holding. Where he chose to intervene, his voice prevailed, and he could exert pressure on the Lord Keeper's decisions while the office was held in turn by Sir Francis Bacon, Bishop Williams, and Sir Thomas Coventry. During the long contention for county leadership in Somerset in the 1620s and 1630s between Lord Poulett and Sir Robert Phelips, Buckingham's influence was crucial. Poulett gained positions on the bench for Sir Francis Rogers and George Poulett through Buckingham. The favourite had Hugh Pyne removed as deputy-*custos* in 1626, and almost certainly organised the dismissals of Pyne and John Symes from the bench along with Thomas Light in September 1626. Phelips wrote to Buckingham as his faithful servant, but soon fell completely out of favour after Phelips failed to follow Buckingham's wishes in Parliament.[24] In Yorkshire, Savile triumphed over Wentworth only while he had the support of the duke. Buckingham's determination to dominate not only the personnel but the policies of government, and his insistence that suitors rely solely on him, meant that only those he supported could be sure of gaining or holding posts. In 1624, the earl of Worcester told John Castle that the king had ordered Privy Councillors not to make recommendations over appointments; Buckingham was allowed to decide.

The hold of gentlemen over their positions on the bench grew even more fragile as Buckingham, with the support of King Charles I from 1625, refused to tolerate political opposition in parliament or criticism outside it. Widespread opposition to the conduct and financing of the war, and the refusal to grant customary financial levies for life to the new king in Charles's first parliament, led to the dismissal of 15 leading Somerset gentlemen from the commission. Opponents in many counties were made sheriffs so that they could not attend parliament, including Phelips in Somerset, and Henry Sherfield in Wiltshire. But Buckingham's death ended the attempt to create a government run by his sycophants. Contention continued bitterly in Somerset, for example, but reverted to the use of various patrons.

Another reason for striving so hard to gain a place, and to remain on the commission of the peace was to use that important and highly visible post to impress the government and so secure further posts, even though most were intermittent or short-lived. Influential roles in county rule included that of subsidy commissioner to assess tax rates, at variable intervals when a parliament granted a subsidy; or a place on local *ad hoc* commissions, especially that for sewers in counties such as Essex and Lincolnshire, where river and drainage schemes created opposing interests. A deputy lieutenancy gave greater powers. When lord lieutenants were appointed to organise the militia, gentry in each county contended to become one of the small number of deputy lieutenants, giving them influence over the selection of men to serve in the trained bands of citizens, and over training and equipment. From 1585 to 1590, increasingly in James's reign, and continuously in the 1630s, leading JPs were chosen as deputy lieutenants. At first the government selected them: in 1602 Sir John Stafford pleaded with Cecil to make him a deputy lieutenant, to further the service, and desiring 'nothing but grace and credit among my neighbours' in order to do so.[25] James allowed some lord lieutenants to choose their own, but Charles conceded the lieutenants the right to choose their deputies. Some served briefly, others for long periods. The numbers per county rose slowly: during the Spanish threat late in Elizabeth's reign two to four was common. Norfolk had three in 1588, six in 1615, and eight in 1626. The deputies had more to do in the 1630s as Charles insisted on military preparedness, and by 1638 the trained bands of England numbered 73,000 foot and nearly 5,000 horse. Although the deputy's work could be onerous, especially under an assiduous lord lieutenant who pressed for mustering and training, the gentry sought the place as a further mark of their ability to rule, in addition to their powers as JP.

While gentlemen had to strive for a place in county government, and patrons used their influence to secure appointments and dismissals, each government sought some control on the choice of men to implement its will. Strong ministers with controversial policies, such as Wolsey and Thomas Cromwell, had succeeded in remodelling the commissions, as we saw, even if they could not remove all who did not support new policies. From the beginning of Elizabeth's reign William Cecil, later Lord Burghley, tried very hard to contain mere ambition among aspiring gentry, and to create sound and hard-working benches of JPs, with the purges and enquiries which led to sudden falls followed by rises in the size of each commission. His son Robert Cecil, earl of Salisbury became the chief but not the only patron; he too tried to keep the numbers of JPs down to a reasonable level, and to maintain benches of assiduous and estimable men until his death in 1612. Both Cecils received requests from the hopeful, but resisted some, and both ministers helped to contain the pressure of patrons to put gentlemen on simply out of a desire to have the honour. Salisbury maintained good, flexible, working relationships with many potential patrons, which helped him to keep some control. A further check came from the rigorous attitude of Egerton (Lord Ellesmere from 1603) as head of the Chancery from 1596 to 1617. He held a very stern view of the qualities and diligence needed in gentry to become JPs or to remain in office, and he too acted as a restraint on unbridled gentry ambition. He recognised the ill effects of patronage and faction. He complained in 1602 that some JPs were in office by countenance. In 1608 he stressed that they should be 'men of best desert, who study to execute justice and to maintain peace but they rather make war'. Ellesmere tried to direct matters, stating that he put few into the commission except with recommendation from 'the lords or Judges', who should recommend according to their own knowledge. He was reported to require a recommendation for a new JP to be made by the assize judges and two current JPs for the county concerned. His notes on proceedings in Star Chamber sometimes mention gentlemen who had acted improperly and who were to be dismissed from the commission of the peace. Serious crime or misbehaviour obviously meant dismissal, as in 1621 when the Middlesex JP Sir Francis Michell was dismissed as a JP and degraded of his knighthood for corrupt and harsh acts as a monopolies commissioner, giving rise to ballads warning against ill use of office.[26]

During the Buckingham decade from 1618, selection of gentry to rule the counties changed. The search by central government ministers for worthy local governors had always been partly negated by the influences of faction and patronage, but the pressure for more appointments had been contained. Buckingham's criterion was reliance on him, combined with full acceptance of his policies – divergence of opinion made gentlemen fit for dismissal. The numbers of aspiring gentlemen had been rising, and the numbers allowed to become JPs expanded too, with sons sometimes serving at the same time as their fathers. In most years, new men were appointed while fewer were dismissed. In Buckinghamshire about 36 local gentlemen had been JPs in 1585, and roughly 45 in 1625. Norfolk had approximately 36 in 1584, and 52 in 1626 and 1636. The increases were very uneven, because there were still dismissals through factional manoeuvring, and batches of them due to Buckingham's disapproval. After Buckingham's death, Charles's efforts to dragoon local government by the Book of Orders in 1631, and his demands for deputy lieutenants to raise money and troops, led to some unwillingness among gentlemen to coerce their neighbours. In Buckinghamshire only four of the eleven surviving gentry families who had served in local government since late in Elizabeth's reign had a member serving in 1637. In Cheshire a whole group played no part in county government in the 1630s, and in Somerset Sir Robert Phelips was lukewarm in support of the king's policies. Perhaps the duke and Charles had lost sight of the need not simply to control but also to conciliate the gentry. By the end of the 1630s it was apparent that neglecting the gentlemen who were potential local officials had been a fatal error of policy.

4

Towns

The gentry exercised authority over the villages and hamlets of the rural majority. Small numbers of settled inhabitants, with parish officers and accustomed ways of ordering life, helped the maintenance of peace, as we shall see in later chapters. But towns were the exception. With people crowded together in poverty, travellers and traders passing through, 'masterless men' and women flocking to them, all likely to cause trouble, the potential for unrest was much greater than in the scattered rural communities. We would expect the urban centres to have seen constant disturbance during this turbulent period of recurring economic difficulties and religious change. Yet there was less trouble than in many European towns, somehow the rulers managed to avert massive urban disorders. But potential sources of disorder did pose threats. Strong and effective government which could procure popular acceptance was an even more urgent goal in the towns than the counties, because of the increased dangers facing towns. The 800 or so county and market towns were small, with populations under 15,000 in the largest, Norwich, York, and Bristol, and only a few thousand or even a few hundred in the others. Somerset had 39 towns with markets, Gloucestershire had 34, Devonshire 45, while in the north Yorkshire had 54: most of these were in very small towns, but some stood on main routes and formed important centres for surrounding areas. The county towns, those where quarter sessions or assizes were held, attracted very large numbers of visitors when the courts were sitting, many bringing quarrels and grievances with them. London of course was different – by far the biggest city, growing fast from perhaps 60,000 in 1520 to 200,000 by 1603, and with greater potential dangers to order than other urban centres.

Towns generally were built of adjoining houses within a very compact area, many retaining their defensive city walls and shutting their gates at night. With population growth, many towns spread into overflow suburban housing beyond the walls, but still all the people lived very close together. Streets were few, narrow and busy; buying and selling was a chatty business, so rumour and grievances over prices, policy or religion easily gathered groups of talkers. Crowded alehouses and inns in the towns provided centres for news and gossip as travellers passed through gathering opinions as they went, and doubtless distorting facts as well. Locals were always eager to hear of events in the capital and other centres. Market and fair days saw crowded trading, and brought countryfolk to town as farmers and their wives brought animals and produce for sale, and purchased town-made goods if they could afford them. Drinking in the taverns led to arguments and fights on fair days. Such conditions might easily lead to stored anger and urban uprisings, which both central and local authorities dreaded throughout our period, and beyond.

They had only to look to European towns for frequent examples of citizens on the rampage, impelled by social or religious demands. During the German reformation conflicts erupted in many German towns: bands of townsmen met and rushed to the churches to tear down images, and instal Lutheran services (or conversely, to force a return to Catholic services and images). Street violence and brutality often accompanied the actions. The mobs in Paris and at least eight other French cities massacring Protestants on St Bartholomew's Day in 1572 were only the worst of urban horrors during the religious civil wars in France during the second half of the sixteenth century. And in the Netherlands, towns saw much of the conflict during the long revolt against Spanish rule and the period of civil war, partially fuelled by convinced Calvinists among the citizens, seeking to impose the new religion. A combination of religious and economic grievances produced widespread urban rioting and iconoclasm, in 1566–7 for example. It was a frightening array of comparisons for English urban authorities.

Nationwide difficulties of all kinds might create worse reactions in towns than in the countryside. Severe social distress always brought a risk of disorder, but in towns riots could easily be organised. This ever-present danger was exacerbated by extensive migration from the countryside to the towns from the mid-sixteenth century, as rural people sought to improve their prospects in trade and crafts, or by apprenticeship, or, for girls, in service in artisan or shopkeeping households, or making lace, clothing, hats and other such products. Towns grew bigger, despite high death rates, with inward 'betterment' migration of this type. Not all incomers were successful, however, in finding sufficient work to live reasonably. Many crowded uncomfortably into mean tenement rooms; some tried begging, despite the efforts of town authorities to prevent street begging. The rapid growth in English population from 1530 to 1640, with a near doubling of the total number of people, certainly contributed to problems of urban poverty, and created hard choices for local officials and inhabitants in coping with them.

Poverty was a real worry for town authorities, not just a nuisance. They feared the consequences of serious poverty, for disorders of the poor or homeless in the more confined and crowded arena of a town could quickly engulf it in disorder, where it was more dangerous than in a small rural village. The rulers needed to cope with the widespread fear that the very poor and destitute, whether local or stranger, would cause trouble; on a small scale by thieving, or more seriously, by mob protest, looting and destruction. Bad weather meant danger. In the 1520s, late 1550s, 1586–7, and most severely in 1594–7 there were harvest failures, and again in 1622–3. Many town-dwellers had to purchase all their food. Times of low-yield harvest and high prices for basic foods meant real misery, pushing some towards death – the mortality figures rose after harvest failures, notably in 1586, 1596–7, and 1622. In the 1590s the mortality rate in poorer areas of Bristol and Exeter was nearly double the normal rate; in Reading the mortality rate was almost four times the normal level.[1]

Shortage and the high price of food hit town-dwellers fiercely. To add to that problem, unemployment of many rural labourers, who normally depended on work in the fields, brought influxes of really poor men and women into the towns. They might hope, in vain, for urban employment; they might seek better begging returns in the streets where tradesmen and merchants passed; women might turn to prostitution since towns held a concentration of potential customers; and all the homeless incomers supposed that town governors would have more organised programmes than their villages to help the poor. But these 'strangers' found little welcome and much fear: in 1598, 96 men and women were whipped out of the town of Salisbury, most of them having moved in from nearby rural areas.[2] They were seen by the town-dwellers simply as a threat to the quiet of the town, and as being likely to steal, or even to riot. Food rioting occurred in towns during all the worst harvests, usually trying to secure grain supplies which were in transit. To take just a few examples, riots occurred in Norwich in 1533, Taunton in 1536, Gloucester in 1586, Basingstoke in 1595, Canterbury in 1596, Southampton in 1608, Leicester in 1618, and Newbury in 1630. Unrest was most likely in towns close to the capital, as governments anxious to prevent problems in London emptied the granaries of the home counties to ensure the capital had sufficient food.

During times of harvest-related economic distress especially, but even in relatively good times, the towns included many poor people, and rulers worried about keeping them quiet. Although many town houses had some garden space for perhaps some hens and vegetables, or crops, and pigs or cows might be kept outside the gates, there were fewer opportunities than in the country for residents to supplement their food supplies. Thus townspeople were much more dependent on buying, and were vulnerable to high prices, which had to be paid out of their often meagre earnings. Decay of a town's enterprises, especially variations of demand and price in the textile trades, could take craftsmen and women from self-sufficiency into destitution without warning. Censuses of the poor were made in many towns, indicating high anxiety. Comparison of six censuses between 1557 and 1635, each made during harsh times, shows variations in the proportion of poor from around 20 per cent in three towns, down to only 5 per cent in Salisbury. The

Norwich census of the poor in 1570 showed 22 per cent of the people suffering poverty, while many could just subsist but were too poor to contribute to help the worse-off. Paul Slack suggests that urban areas suffered a continuous 5 per cent level of poverty, rising to 20 per cent in times of food shortage and high prices. These figures relate to the destitute poor. In addition, relative poverty existed everywhere, comprising people who normally managed at a pretty low level of comfort, but could fall into real trouble from sudden sickness or disappearance of their source of income. The problem of poverty never went away completely.[3]

Threats to urban peace came partly from the very make-up of many towns, with their concentrations of specialist workers and artisans. This was particularly the case with woollen cloth weaving and its associated trades, in the dockyard or metal-work centres, and for all the basic urban trades – food and other household provision, clothing, building, cart-making, leather goods (shoes and saddles) and transport. If anything upset the cloth market, a whole range of people suffered. Disruptions of the overseas trade severely affected cloth workers: this occurred in the 1520s, 1550s and 1620s due to international conflict, and in 1615 because of the king's interference. The disastrous Cockayne project, which not only failed in its aim to improve the English cloth industry but actually damaged the market with Europe, made textile workers destitute. Any reduction of the demand for cloth, by war, plague, currency fluctuations or economic crisis abroad, brought unemployment, distress, social friction and the threat of disorder.

Influxes of poor led to overcrowding, with cottages being squeezed in between other houses and tenements being subdivided to hold more people. Complaints about overcrowding troubled Worcester, York and, especially, London. Even a small town like Cambridge, with less than 3,000 inhabitants, petitioned in 1584 against overcrowding, and in 1619–23 the danger of newcomers and subdivision had still not been solved. This, then, was another headache for town authorities as they tried helplessly to stem the flow, fearing that the newcomers were adding to the problems, and costs, of the poor within the towns. At Chester in the early seventeenth century there were three surveys of the poor and vagrants, with attempts to stop inhabitants accepting lodgers because the newcomers might become a burden to the city.[4] Vagrants, the wandering vagabonds and sturdy rogues, are the most studied of the early modern English poor. They worried village and county officials, but they caused even greater concern in towns. In popular opinion, they wandered in large and threatening groups of young males who would be difficult to confront, especially in a town where they could whip up the urban poor to disorder. Not all migrants counted as rogues, but vagrants were defined by law as unworthy and potentially dangerous. They were idle, and – worst of all in a hierarchical society as Tudor and Stuart England tried to be – outside all control by landlords, employers, parents or other authority. The aim was to force them back under control by whipping and sending them back to their parish of birth or last residence. This may have been a reasonable theoretical solution, but it was unlikely to cure the problem, since they presumably had no 'master' or employment there either, and the inhabitants were not overjoyed at their return! Vagrants were the suffering victims of the effort to impose hierarchical order throughout English society. Vagrants and the really poor were certainly liable to commit crime – it could well be their only method of survival. Opportunistic theft could provide food, or objects to sell for food: the crime records are full of thefts of clothes stolen from hedges and fences, where they had been spread to dry, of cheeses, bacon and grain stolen from houses, dairies and stores. Animals such as pigs, geese, hens, and ducks were taken from gardens, some to be slaughtered and immediately eaten. The true rate of crime cannot be known from prosecutions, but many people were indicted for petty theft and the numbers of such indictments rose in hard times, for example, in the 1590s. The figures from assize court records and those from the lesser courts suggest a wide range of small thefts: theft formed 74 per cent of crimes prosecuted at Sussex assizes 1559–1625, and 98 per cent at the more urban Middlesex sessions 1550–1625. Since the poorest stole mostly from poor inhabitants, the theft could impel the victim into destitution too, as happened to a Stratford man who claimed that theft of the wares from his business had forced him into vagrancy too.[5]

Since urban rulers observed the dangerous effects of poverty and resulting crime at close hand, they made efforts to help those who suffered most. Schemes to raise money from the wealthier inhabitants in order to assist the poorest developed during the sixteenth century, increasing in complexity and compulsion. York started compulsory contributions toward relief of the poor in 1538, as a temporary solution, making them permanent in 1550. Other large towns, notably Norwich, also began to seek a comprehensive approach to helping those who could not survive otherwise, taking a census of those who needed help, those who could contribute, and those who were too poor to pay out for any poor relief. Recognition by urban authorities of the plight of the 'deserving' poor within their towns, and serious efforts to help them, made it easier to keep order. Local poor relief rating and distribution schemes, and the poor relief laws of 1572 and 1598, made the destitute or inadequately paid inhabitants aware that the town rulers would try to assist them if they could, and lessened the likelihood of rioting and looting.

While poverty and the influx of strangers and vagrants created the toughest challenges for town authorities and the strongest impulses to impose effective rule, there were occasional additional threats which needed well-organised responses from above. Plague struck without warning and was a scourge of early modern towns, where it spread much more quickly than in the country farms and villages. Its deadly progress could rapidly disrupt the normal functioning of the interdependent production and trades of a town, and lead to poverty as well as sickness and death. Although the role of rats and fleas was not understood, it was clearly recognised that plague was an infection which spread in crowded areas: often the poorest suburbs saw most victims. This was true in York in the 1604 epidemic of bubonic plague, with a very heavy death rate among the poor. The communities simply could not wring their hands and do nothing. Richer families fled to relatives in the country, if they could, or away to other towns. But someone had to order isolation of infected households, pay watchmen to stand at the doors, and organise payment for food while the inhabitants stayed indoors – or, until they died. In Salisbury in 1604 about a sixth of the population died. But the costs of those who were quarantined created a terrible burden for the town's governors, and possible opposition from those surviving: £598 had to be found over a year when several houses were shut up for nearly six months. Moreover, cloth workers and other tradesmen who survived often found they had no employment. By the 1620s the combination of these factors with depression of the Salisbury cloth production meant that almost half the people there needed some help to survive![6] Urban authority had to be strong, to surmount such crises.

Fire was a disaster which struck even more suddenly than plague, and in towns could spread fast between the buildings. With much wooden building, and many thatched roofs, fire could be impossible to halt. The best remedy was prevention. Occasionally rivals threatened to burn down an enemy's house, a threat which posed a danger to the entire town and so met with severe treatment. In Tudor York there were 265 sets of recognizances to prevent arson in the quarter sessions records between 1571–5, and 198 in 1591–5; and neighbours demanded that the authorities take action over a man 'for keeping a fire in his house, without a chimney'. David Underdown has studied the far-reaching effect of fire in the small town of Dorchester, where about 170 houses, about half the total, burnt down in August 1613. The fire forced a total rethinking in the town. Due partly to the influence of its preacher John White, who interpreted the 'fire from heaven' as a punishment and sign, Dorchester was propelled into a very tightly ruled polity endeavouring to live up to a radical Protestant ideal. Its governors began to interfere even more strenuously than elsewhere, and punished all disorder, drunkenness, brawlers, masterless men and vagrants. In this case a much more cohesive town government tried to create a disciplined population, not just for order, but as a divine duty. Dorchester's leaders saw themselves as God's elect trying to bring about a completely reformed community in time for 'the last days'.[7]

Practical problems needed both ideological solutions and the power to carry them to action. But ideology itself could create conflicts, when from 1532 on religious changes were demanded or desired by rulers or the people. Members of town governments could not agree what stand to take. Urban turmoil stemmed often from the alterations in the Church and its worship, from Henry VIII's first tentative moves away from the pope right through to Charles I's Laudian policies. Lay people disputed with their clergy over ceremonies, services, sermons, tithes, clerical dress, church discipline or lack of it; some wished for more reformed practice, others resisted, or refused to go to church. Overtly religious disputes could create or worsen political relationships within towns. In York the early Reformation met with fairly united hostility. The Pilgrimage of Grace in 1536 gained support from the citizens, and the mayor and aldermen allowed the rebels to occupy the city for two months. Under Edward VI, the citizens resisted the new emphasis on sermons and stayed away from church. But attachment to the old Catholic ways began to break down, and there were struggles over traditional pageants. When Mayor William Alleyn staged one in 1572, two Protestant aldermen were imprisoned for their opposition by the other aldermen. One of Alleyn's opponents became the next mayor, other Protestants became aldermen, and the archbishop banned the Corpus Christi and other such traditional plays in York. The increasing official pressure to punish recusants also created problems, since even a mayor's wife and the wives of some aldermen faced persecution. There was real division within the city government. The conservative Mayor Criplyng opposed sermons and the Protestant clergy, in which he had the support of humbler citizens. But when he was imprisoned by the Council in the North, his corporation decided to deprive him. The executions of twenty Catholics at York in the 1580s also exposed major differences within the city's governing groups.[8]

York's dissension arose chiefly from a small but increasing number of committed Protestants among its citizens and governors, who wished to challenge the prevailing Catholic survivalism. The Reformation, and divisions of opinion which followed, created differing views of how to run towns. Some towns faced conflict because firm Protestant notions among leading citizens conflicted with less enthusiastic or downright hostile views. In the late sixteenth and early seventeenth centuries, strong-minded Protestant councillors formed tight groups and tried to impose godly solutions to town problems and to control town government. But the authority of the 'chosen few' could not achieve total moral reform; instead it often angered those inhabitants who could not agree and considered the campaign illegitimate, and divided rather than united the community. In Salisbury in the late 1620s the efforts of Henry Sherfield, George Ivie, and other godly officials to solve some of the city's poverty by establishing a communal brewhouse became only a short-lived experiment in social engineering, because others within the elite opposed such an approach. Gloucester suffered long-term economic decline with escalating poverty and population, and with fears of conflict which proved accurate in 1586, in 1604 and, most seriously, in 1638. The increasingly puritan elite of the town sought to create a godly civic commonwealth from the 1590s, increasing their efforts even more strenuously in the 1620s and 1630s. Their religious principles led them to promote church-going and stricter control measures: on alehouses, poor relief, and the reorganisation and control of hospitals and almshouses. Not all the citizens accepted the actions of the elite, and their resentment led to complaints of corruption – of fraud over grain stocks for the poor, abuses in leases of land, and of contracts awarded to fellow aldermen. Nevertheless the radical ruling elite retained command of the city, despite massive social problems, and some criticism.[9]

Towns which had a cathedral, a bishop and an ecclesiastical establishment experienced an extra level of urban relationships, which could produce religious conflict or disputes over jurisdiction. After the Reformation, there were ideological conflicts between bishops and city rulers. Norwich contained many enthusiastic Protestants who increasingly favoured a puritan approach to policy. Edmund Freke, bishop of Norwich from 1575 to 1584 was more conservative, and vigorously opposed the godly leadership in the city as he did the county gentry who were more radical Protestants. Samuel Harsnett, bishop there from 1619 until 1629, when he became archbishop of York, also provoked disputes, as he sought to impose an Arminian discipline on Norwich.[10] Salisbury suffered severe conflicts while John Coldwell held the see during the 1590s, and while Henry Cotton was bishop from 1598 to 1615. Such friction was not new; Salisbury had developed its own governing institutions and mayoral office from the twelfth century onwards despite recurring conflicts with bishops. Coldwell and Cotton involved themselves in outright disputes over the episcopal jurisdiction in the city. Coldwell tried to maintain or increase his powers over office, against the mayor and citizens. He was *custos* of the Salisbury borough commission of the peace, and that too brought trouble, when the earl of Pembroke attempted to dislodge him. Cotton also held a strong view of his own powers in the city government. He bitterly attacked efforts by the mayor and the city rulers to stop him controlling appointments to office, and wrote vitriolically about Giles Tooker who was legal counsel to the mayor. Cotton alleged that they contravened the authority of the bishop's ancient charters and opposed his rights. The conflicts with the bishop when the citizens moved to obtain new charters for the city did not make for peaceful relations between the rival authorities. The Lord Keeper's prediction when Cotton became bishop of Salisbury that Cotton would have wars, before he had peace, was amply justified. Moreover, Salisbury contained a core of puritans among the ruling elite, while Cotton opposed such views, intensifying the friction. Perhaps, though, the long dispute between city government and bishops in Salisbury made the urban authority more united against outside interference from episcopal power. In places with very strong doctrinal divisions, the stance of a bishop could serve to exacerbate those divisions within the urban government.[11]

Religious conflict often led to splits within the ruling groups of towns, and made it much harder to impose order and uniformity on the citizens. But other urban difficulties, perhaps paradoxically, could strengthen town rule. Individual townsmen could not deal with poverty, plague, flood and fire, and effective communal responses were necessary. Someone must enforce rates for poor relief, plague restrictions and support for surviving victims, and organise rebuilding after fire or flood. While none wished to pay up, townsmen generally accepted the apparent urgent necessity and the authority of the councillors to organise civic solutions and to deal with crises. Although not all town rule ran smoothly, the potential for serious dispute was very much greater than the number of disruptions which actually occurred. Why was urban government relatively effective?

One reason for townspeople's acceptance of authority was their participation in electing and in holding municipal office. While many studies of towns have emphasised increasing oligarchy in town governments during the sixteenth and seventeenth centuries, it was not necessarily rigid and narrowly confined to specific families, excluding and alienating most freemen. If wealthier men predominated in holding the most onerous offices, that owed much to the expenses which some offices entailed, and which few towns ever recompensed sufficiently. In the city of York, the 225 men who were aldermen and members of the 'Twenty-four' between 1500 and 1600 included most of the wealthiest citizens, men who could advance money to the city when necessary. But the 225 councillors came from at least 168 families, while the mayoralty was similarly shared around. Chester and Winchester were like this too, more so than Exeter or Norwich. Craftsmen as well as merchants participated as aldermen of York, and many lesser men served as members of the 'Twenty-four', providing half the mayors, although fewer craftsmen reached that honour in Norwich, Bristol or Exeter.[12]

Oxford's ruling group was surprisingly open in the sixteenth century. To participate, men had to belong to the guild of the merchants, but a third or even half the male population were freemen, who could elect to the major offices of constable, chamberlain, bailiff, aldermen, and mayor. Moreover, since so many offices needed to be filled, and few were held repeatedly by the same person, a substantial proportion of men experienced civic office at least once, while a recognised path from lower to the higher offices existed. So the office-holders changed often, with new recruits coming in. Even the lowliest, the Common Council of 24 freemen, shared in voting with the Town Council, which together with the large Mayor's Council spread political authority among a high proportion of the adult male population. Holding office if only briefly gave these men experience of administration. Even if the wealthier dominated the top offices, in towns like Oxford and York, many levels of the (male) urban economy had some representation. With friends in the Council, and some hope of serving, inhabitants had more reason to accept and not to frustrate the exercise of power in the town.[13]

Some towns maintained a much narrower ruling group. The small trading centre of Lewes in Sussex was, by the end of the sixteenth century, ruled by a small, self-perpetuating oligarchy, the 'Twelve' and the 'Twenty-four'; the members selected each other without popular consent, in contrast to procedure in the more 'open' town governments like York and Oxford. This provoked troubles: to avoid disorder, it became necessary to move the choosing of the Twenty-Four from the publicly accessible Castle, to the closed Town House. Other small towns, such as Hastings, followed this pattern, and larger ones like Gloucester did too. From the late Tudor period, and probably earlier, a restricted set of Gloucester men, often with family ties to other members of the corporation, dominated civic leadership. In this declining clothing town, the traders took the largest share of offices, while the less esteemed workers had far less part in governing than the craftsmen in Oxford.[14] Gloucester councillors lacked sufficient wealth to avoid the lure of profiteering from office. Additionally, factional conflicts from the 1580s demonstrate that such narrow government was not entirely successful; more 'populist' aldermen had the support of freemen and discontented inhabitants against a self-seeking old guard. Arbitrary government for selfish ends met opposition, and led to reform – with more co-operative efforts to improve control of the community and maintain obedience.

Such pressures occurred within a context of major changes in control over towns following the Reformation. Urban leaders coping with increasing social problems and the Tudor regulatory legislation wished to free their towns from control by ecclesiastical or lay landlords, to gain greater self-government and enforce solutions. They did so by requesting charters of incorporation from the crown. Since charters also increased royal control over towns, queens and kings could readily be persuaded to grant them. The crown already had extensive control over government of the shires, with the appointment and dismissal of members of the county commissions of the peace, the sheriffs and deputy lieutenants, even if faction and patronage played a part. But royal influence over towns had been less direct, in contrast. Towns varied in their political make-up, with overlapping and uncertain jurisdictions. Many towns had been under the heavy seigneurial influence of monastic lordships, who had authority, for instance, over the local courts leet. The dissolution of the monasteries transferred them into the hands of new secular landlords. In other boroughs local manorial lords traditionally exercised rule in urban affairs. Towns had a strong communal identity, but self-government was often limited. Nevertheless, certain older towns had long enjoyed some autonomy, such as Exeter which had received a royal charter from Henry II and operated as a civic entity with its mayor and stewards. York, Bristol and Norwich also possessed established structures of urban government.

From 1540, leaders of many other towns hastened to increase their self-governing powers under the crown: the number of incorporated boroughs increased dramatically – 24 boroughs gained charters under Mary, 53 under Elizabeth (plus 17 reincorporations) and 51 from 1603–40, plus 54 renewed charters. By 1640 well over 200 were incorporated. A royal charter defined the borough's authority, prescibed the institutions of rule, and guaranteed its political, legal and economic privileges. Most charters established a borough court, and even named officers. It thus protected the town from other authorities, such as county JPs, perhaps the bishop in cathedral cities, and made it responsible to the crown directly, while the crown was to protect its rights, when requested. Moreover, the mayor and bailiffs were officers of the crown. The crown had expectations of urban officers: co-operation in raising taxes, purveyance, and military service, which might be easier to enforce over its chartered boroughs. But a town gained greater control: the right to issue bye-laws was vital in keeping order and dealing with the problems outlined earlier in this chapter. Crucially, it gained control over who held authority as mayor, member of common council or alderman, and other official posts.[15]

Sometimes new charters narrowed the selection of people who governed towns, especially in the case of towns which gained self-government as a result of the displacement of monastic and other ecclesiastical seigneurs in the Reformation. Lichfield's new charter of 1553 gave it higher status and more extensive rights, although the bishop retained some; its ruling elite was to be dominated by a small number of families for two centuries thereafter. Even more dramatic was the limitation of office-holders in the 1590 incorporation of Newcastle-under-Lyme. For the first time, all officials there could be selected by co-option. The 1573 charter of Beverley, Yorkshire, also changed the town government's methods of selection. Until then, the burgesses in general had annually elected a governing Council of Twelve, with retiring governors ineligible for re-election. The new charter reversed this, with a mayor and twelve governors making up the common council; the governors serving for life. They were to be replaced on death, by co-option. What is not clear is whether the citizens opposed that move. Those in Stafford did try to stop such restriction in 1614, but they failed. With or without complaint, some sixty-five boroughs sought re-incorporation between 1590 and 1640; these were the ones tending to narrow their ruling elites. Narrow or not, most needed to heed the demands of the people.

Bigger towns may have experienced more conflicts over who exercised power than did smaller ones, since more was at stake. The civic conflicts in early seventeenth century Norwich show how vitally power of mayors and aldermen depended on pleasing at least the more vocal men of the city. When they did not, the citizens demanded more choice over who might be mayor. After some discontents from 1610 on, the freemen electors in 1618 abandoned the custom of choosing the mayor by selecting from among the aldermen who had been longest in office. Instead they began to pick younger more controversial figures who had only recently become aldermen. But this provoked opposition from the senior aldermen, and the threat of election disorders. The senior aldermen in 1619 determined to maintain their chance of higher office, and not to give in to the risks of freer choice by the citizens. The aldermen managed to persuade King James that younger men should not be promoted to any major offices over the longer-serving ones, and the king confirmed this by a letter which was proclaimed throughout the city before the mayoral election day. Antagonism from the common council and disturbances among the freemen simmered along for years, with further interventions from the crown and the Privy Council. In 1627/8 a new byelaw on elections restricted who might be elected to the Court of Aldermen, but did not remove wider electoral influence nor impose a tight oligarchy of self-selection by the corporation. Those who had been in the governing group probably wished to create an oligarchy, but the disturbances seem to have made them realise that order would become impossible if they removed all electoral voice away from the citizens.[16]

The involvement of a significant proportion of the citizens in selecting the personnel of town government was one of the elements which made authority possible in towns, despite intermittent local difficulties. Political participation could reach quite far through the social levels: the range of urban offices, the opportunity to rise through them, and the turnover in office enabled many to wield authority at least briefly, and to experience the need to impose order. Corporations promoted the town's interest and alleviated daily problems as well as major disasters. The most powerful urban official, the mayor or bailiff, held office for one year only – a mighty incentive to tread warily in case an opponent should become mayor the next year and be able to retaliate. In Worcester and elsewhere the bailiff, as the chief executive officer, also served one year at a time, with his responsibility for order, control of markets, and economic regulation giving wide power. Again overuse was limited by his need for co-operation. Increased urban oligarchy has been noted by some historians, and perhaps that started to undermine acceptance of the officeholder's authority. Reduced political involvement by the citizens, together with the government's high financial demands in the 1550s, 1590s, the 1620s and 1630s, and the economic uncertainties of cloth towns, all created stress for urban populations. But while major disorders did occur at times – riots in York in 1529, 1536, 1539, 1546 and 1550, for example – they only temporarily disrupted a more normal pattern of relative obedience of town-dwellers.

If the wealthiest families increasingly dominated many town governments, their responsibilities grew more extensive than those of the past. Tudor social and economic legislation, especially the requirements to deal with poverty and vagrancy, made great demands on town governments for enforcement, and populations in towns increased just when conditions were worst, making the task harder. In addition, functions which before the Reformation had belonged to ecclesiastical authorities, guilds, or manorial lords now also fell upon mayors and aldermen. The resulting proliferation of offices to deal with growing civic jurisdiction extended the number of people with a stake, however small, in managing towns. New posts went to residents, although not all were freemen. Civic maintenance required officers: men responsible for hall and market keeping, and sweepers. The new town halls and market halls needed care, as did gaols and houses of correction, almshouses, quays and customs houses, armouries and animal pounds. In 1559, the small town of Boston in Lincolnshire added a Town Husband, a public works foreman, to tend the civic property. Then there were inspectors of food quality and ale-conners, and the officials directly concerned with order: watchmen, town waits, and toll gatherers paid by the borough. And as civic ceremony grew, the attendants required increased in number – sword- and mace-bearers, waits and trumpeters. The sergeant-at-mace, the mayor's aide, had to attend the mayor at all times, and at Reading and doubtless elsewhere, attend the meetings, summon the borough court to session and give service afterwards by proclaiming the decisions and conducting the guilty to gaol. Other officials dealt with finances. The expansion of numbers and authority in urban government gave more duties to the town clerk, who sometimes had legal training and became a full-time official, as in Ipswich in 1572. More and more towns also appointed a Recorder to serve as a fully qualified legal advisor to the officials; a necessary precaution to deal with the mass of Tudor legislation affecting local administration. Civic officials were not only more numerous, but more visible.

Urban authority had impressive props to encourage acceptance. Ritual and spectacle provided a highly colourful representation of civic power in the streets. Pageantry and processions displayed the current mayor and office-holders to the whole town, and involved members of the organised crafts and trades in preparation and performance. The traditional Corpus Christi Day processions emphasised both the common unity of a town and the hierarchy of its various crafts and occupations, with their play cycles in which each guild mounted a pageant. The guilds in their uniforms marched in order, then the aldermen, councillors and sheriffs, and last and most prominent, the mayor, with the consecrated host, and the clergy. Processing in order of precedence, with the humbler crafts first, then the wealthier, followed by the civic officers in their finery, showed vividly the structure of authority in a town, while emphasising social cohesion. Even after the Corpus Christi Day religious celebrations ended, the plays continued until closed down by government and bishop's orders, in 1574 in Chester, and 1579 in York. They had brought in visitors for the spectacle – the plays were acted in rich ornate costumes and accompanied in York, and probably elsewhere, by displays of the town's gold and silver. But they had also been communal occasions where various occupations could project their own honour and identity, and those who could not join in could at least gather in the street to watch.

The Reformation, and the economic decline of many crafts and guilds, killed much urban ritual, but ceremonies relating to the most important urban ruler, the mayor, remained elaborate. Towns varied in the method of electing a new mayor, but solemnity always helped to instil his authority. Oath-taking ceremonies marked many steps in the progress of a successful citizen, when he pledged himself to city, craft, or guild, or civic office, including the highest if he made it. The oath entailed a sacred as well as a civic commitment of loyal duty, and violation was a legal offence as well as a broken secular compact. It served as a mark of accession to office. The newly-chosen mayor's inauguration day centred on a formal public oath-taking: in Coventry all the incoming officers processed into St Mary's Hall, where the new mayor doffed his hat in deference to the out-going mayor and aldermen, entreated assistance from sheriffs and coroner, and required the junior officers to do their duties. Solemn ceremony helped to underline the temporary majesty of the new mayor, in order to encourage responsibility and obedience.

On the election, or usually the inauguration of the mayor, he gave a dinner, the mayoral banquet, as a way of adding significance to the day and persuading the town, or at least its civic leaders, to co-operate with him during the year to come. Maidstone and many other towns recognised the importance of the dinner for the Mayor's election, and set out regulations on payment for the costs. For instance, at the dinner in April 1601 wine was to be provided for 21 commoners. If most of a town's population missed out on the dinner, at least they saw the processions. A contemporary was impressed in 1565: 'the Estate that the mayor of Chester keepeth is great. For he hath both Swordbearer, Macebearer, Sergeants with their Silver Maces', walking before him. The sheriffs and the mayor on workdays 'do go in fair long gowns, welted with velvet, and white staves in their hands'. That was just for the ordinary daily walk. For festival days they had 'Violet and Scarlet also'.[17] Ceremony provided citizens with constant reminders of who held authority. The Maidstone orders stipulated that the mayor was to go to the town courts accompanied by two of the jurats, 'with one mace born before him, and so to dinner and from thence to his house, as also to every Sessions, Leet, and sitting as Clerk of the market'. On Easter Sunday, Whitsunday and Christmas the mayor was to process to and from church, as on election day, with both the maces. Moreover, every Sunday, two or more of the jurats living nearest the mayor were to walk with him to the church in their gowns, and all jurats were to sit in church in their gowns. Even for the mayor's routine work of surveying markets, checking weights of bread, and so on, he was to be accompanied by town officers in their gowns. The Sergeants of the Mace needed extra money allocated by order in 1629 yearly to provide themselves with cloaks 'trimmed alike' for attending the mayor.[18]

Civic ceremonial aimed to instil honour and respect for the mayor and corporation. And the governors demanded deference. In York, for instance, citizens must doff their caps to the mayor and aldermen, and address them formally as 'Master'. Insubordination could be punished with imprisonment at the mayor's pleasure, even for a draper who insulted a sheriff, or a constable offending the Lord Lieutenant's officer. Insults to the mayors in King's Lynn, Guildford, Hull, Boston, and Norwich brought fines or prison. We cannot know the scale of such disaffection, but it obviously worried civic leaders. The need for occasional imprisonment demonstrates how important deference was for the men holding office for the time being. To recognise and underline municipal authority, monarchs sometimes knighted mayors during royal visits to York and other towns, as Elizabeth did for the mayor of Norwich in 1569. If towns were reducing or narrowing participation in community events and in corporations, perhaps insistence on due ceremony and on deference became essential in the attempt to maintain stable town government. The effort was more successful in some towns (e.g. York and Worcester) than in others (e.g. Norwich, Gloucester and Dorchester).

Robert Tittler has argued that more towns were building town halls, and more elaborate ones, during our period and especially in the 1560s and 1570s, to symbolise administrative reality and emphasise the trappings of hierarchy.[19] This may have become desirable in order to counter the ending of hierarchy-defining processions and plays of Corpus Christi and other pre-Reformation traditions. The town hall could become the focus of civil authority. It created a dedicated space to dignify the urban government, especially the mayor, as well as the standing of the town. The ceremonial at the mayoral election could centre on the town hall, as well as (or instead of) the church. The other annual ceremonies also moved to town halls, with banquets for Ash Wednesday with homage to the mayor. In Chester on Easter Monday archery contests were followed by a walk to the guildhall by the mayor and other dignitaries for a celebratory breakfast. In Norwich the St George's Day festivities involved a sermon, then a feast in the guildhall. All these included some of the craftsmen and other more important urban dwellers, but excluded women and the poor, a tendency which grew in the early seventeenth century. It seems that some towns were moving from an inclusive political culture of involvement and intimacy to an exclusive one of deference and distance. Exclusion and greater pomp increased as the town halls began to set aside a 'Mayor's Parlour', where the mayor could confer privately. Formal mayor's seats, imposing and decoratively carved, moved the mayor from his former place on the bench with his brother aldermen to a solitary throne. This too tended to exalt his status, and hopefully his ability to demand co-operation and obedience.

All the problems of towns large and small affected London. It was by far the biggest town, a major city, the capital, seat of national administration, parliament and the central law courts, and home of the leading merchants and traders, who catered for the increasing market for luxury goods and books. London divided into its parishes for many administrative purposes, but the City of London with its Lord Mayor was the grandest town and outdid all others in the magnificence of its civic ceremonial. London's government and governors have been exhaustively studied by recent historians, and here we need only refer briefly to some of their conclusions. Not surprisingly, the elite of the capital – the men of merchant wealth, and members of the great livery companies – monopolised political power there. Participation in selection involved relatively few of the population. Aldermen controlled recruitment, and frequently nominated the common councillors as well, even though in principle freemen had a vote. Presumably contests to serve occurred fairly often within this elite, but the surprising feature, as Ian Archer shows, is that the bulk of Londoners accepted their governors quite readily through the Elizabethan period. Both he and Jeremy Boulton discuss the importance of involvement by many people in various spheres of rule – parish officers, down to humble street cleaners. Visible attempts by the rulers to deal with crises of poverty, plague and unrest also helped to maintain stability, as in the towns.[20] So although potentially London threatened greater disorder, generally only minor instances occurred, as will be discussed in later chapters.

All the early modern towns experienced problems. Poverty was more concentrated and more visible than in rural areas, especially because so many out-of-work rural labourers and craftsmen and women flocked to nearby towns in hard times. It is not surprising that some of the earliest efforts to organise municipal schemes for assisting the poor occurred in the larger towns, notably Norwich and York. The towns had much to offer their residents: domestic servants, artisans and cloth-workers, traders, brewers, innkeepers, lawyers, and in larger cathedral towns, ecclesiastical officials too – but disorder threatened when the poorer townsmen suffered from low wages or high food prices. If controlling their inhabitants was not always easy, there was an impressive range of ceremonial to impress citizens with the power of civic authority, and to make town governments more acceptable to their inhabitants.

PART II

5

The family

Patriarchal maxims defined clear lines of authority within the early modern family. They described the power of every husband to rule over his wife, and over children and servants. Biblical sources underlay them: Eve's role in the fall proved that women must be ruled, and St Paul's Epistles justified male headship over the family as a godly duty. In sermons, ministers explained to their parishioners that these duties were required by God. Patriarchal theory was spread in other ways too. Clergy and laymen published books expanding on those Biblical texts which emphasised the superior place of the male head of household and the duty of obedience by wives and children. These conduct books owed much to the Swiss Protestant Bullinger's text on matrimony, translated into English in 1541 and again in 1542; Henry Bullinger knew many English Protestants, corresponding with them until his death in 1575. Among English writers, Edmund Tilney in his treatise on duties in marriage, first published in 1568, emphasised that 'divine and human laws . . . giveth the man absolute authority over the woman in all places' and a husband's edicts must never be questioned.[1] Andrew Kingsmill's tract published in 1574, advising his widowed sister about her remarriage, insisted that wives should submit themselves to their husbands. Dudley Fenner's 1584 book on the government of the family likewise stressed female submission, and lamented men who could not maintain their authority but allowed women to usurp part of it, meddling in matters not fit for them. Robert Cleaver's manual, revised by John Dod and reprinted several times, required that women be silent as well as submissive. Henry Smith in 1591 demanded that women should never even examine whether their husbands were wise or simple, but simply obey without question. Thomas Salter, William Perkins and Thomas Bentley also published exhortations on family duties; Philip Stubbes, William Harrison, John Mayer and others printed funeral eulogies of dead wives who been models of submission.[2]

Since the male head of the household must be obeyed by all within it – women, children, servants and apprentices – any who resisted might be made to conform. For some of those explaining power in the family, husbands might use violence to secure conformity to their rule. Most of the prescriptive books in their discussion of gender roles considered the troubling question of whether or not men might beat disobedient wives to make them obey. Some believed that they could if it was necessary to achieve adherence to male rule. Thomas Bentley's 1582 book sympathised with the plight of husbands who suffered taunts from their wives, and the issue was debated publicly in Oxford in 1608: William Gager argued in favour of husbands' legal right to beat wives who were not submissive. A wedding sermon, preached by William Whately and published in 1619, castigated female viragos who wanted to be governors and strove to break the yoke of obedience. 'If she will rail upon him with most reproachful terms, if she will affront him with bold and impudent resistances', that was just cause for correcting her forcefully. ''Tis true, that no man in scripture hath so cudgelled his wife . . . [unless she] offended him in such kinds and degrees, as might reasonably call for such severity'.[3] It cannot have been a jolly wedding. Some historians believe these books were written to combat a sixteenth century shift in marital behaviour: a reduction in women's obedience to men, and widespread male anxiety about it. Patriarchal texts and the punishment of scolds by ducking have been seen as reactions to a 'crisis in gender relations'. But women were rarely ducked, and those punished as scolds were sowers of discord in the whole neighbourhood through slander and harassment. Moreover, accusers were not men who had been challenged, but women, or husbands acting on behalf of their own aggrieved wives against the scold. Women were probably no more assertive than they had been before.[4]

The Elizabethan and Jacobean spate of family advice books does not reflect widespread attitudes around England. Most of the books came from a tiny group of godly Protestant academic theologians from Oxford and Cambridge, some of whom left England for more fully reformed centres in Europe; some became puritan parish ministers, trying to impose a 'reformation of manners' upon their congregations. Moreover, these authors were not only zealous Protestants, they were very closely connected with each other. Dudley Fenner had been at Peterhouse, Cambridge; he was a famous preacher but he found the English Church insufficiently reformed and followed the presbyterian Thomas Cartwight to Antwerp; his book was published in Middleburg in 1584. William Perkins was a celibate Cambridge don for most of his life, and probably the most influential English moral theologian of his time up till his death in 1602.

Oxford was the strongest link between the would-be instructors. Kingsmill was at Oxford when he wrote his book in about 1560, aged only 22, and he soon left England to seek a more Protestant life among the Calvinists in Geneva and Lausanne; his book was published posthumously in 1574. Salter was probably at Oxford. William Gager held a doctorate in ecclesiastical law and was a single, college clergyman, for 25 years. Henry

Smith was attached to Lincoln College, and then went to join the famous puritan Richard Greenham, before settling in London as a preacher. Greenham's son-in-law was John Dod who was temporarily suspended by two bishops for his nonconformity. Dod had been a fellow of Jesus College Cambridge, then became a diligent Oxfordshire cleric, preaching often at Banbury for 20 years or more. The vicar of Banbury was William Whately (and a Banbury puritan was satirised by Ben Jonson as Zeal-of-the-Land Busy in *Bartholomew Fair*). These men must often have discussed their ideas about scripture and ways to secure its application in life. Most of them were single when they proposed patterns for husbands and wives to follow, and celibate college communities had provided them with little experience of family life. They wrote because of strong Protestant anxiety about ensuring conformity to Biblical models of behaviour, and perhaps because their friends were writing too. These much quoted treatises did not reflect wide-spread male anxiety about gender relations. They expressed the views of a very small earnest group of puritan men who were determined to change the world: a godly clique.[5]

Other books from beyond that clique expressed less repressive notions of family life and values, and even some of the strongly patriarchal ones allowed some delegation to wives at least. The didactic books varied in their emphasis: the late Elizabethan ones especially stressed male leadership and female meekness in following. Yet some of the men who published instruction manuals knew that a clear pattern of family order might not actually work among real people; though many of the books were written by unmarried men, not all extolled pure male primacy. These authors tempered their general notions of family hierarchy with modifications. The prescribed roles for husband and wife complemented each other, so that indoors, each spouse had some authority. Women might be weak, owing obedience to men, but they were allotted the power to help rule the rest of the household in domestic matters, and much more during a husband's absence. A woman had to juggle conflicting attitudes, finding herself now humbly doing as she was told, now ordering around children, servants, apprentices. Historians of gender relations have often neglected this ambiguity, because the emphasis on subservience and female silence seems so limiting.

Dod and Cleaver expected a husband to follow his business or calling in the world outside the home without any interference from the wife, while the wife could be ruler over both persons and materials of the house, without his meddling, she could buy and sell necessaries as she decided. Women are 'fellow-helpers'. But the effort to define roles in so delicate an arena as family relationships created a real struggle to balance the conflict between the requirements of male authority in general, and female power over the household. Fenner tried to solve this by telling a wife to be the image of the authority and wisdom of her husband in her whole administration, yet to remain meek and quiet. In Henry Smith's *Preparative to Marriage* the wife is an under officer, so she must be obeyed by children and servants.

Moreover, some authors explained that a husband had to butress woman's partial authority, and so he should moderate actual use of his theoretical powers. Gager and Whately may have argued in favour of physical repression, but most did not agree. Henry Smith and Dod and Cleaver recommended husbands should give good instruction, but not lay violent hands upon their wives. Tilney observed that some women took too much upon themselves, but wrote resignedly 'if a woman will not be still with one word of her husband, she will not be quiet with as many words as ever the wise men did write'. William Heale published *An Apology for Women* in 1609, depicting a wife as an 'equal associate' with a husband in rule of the family. He wrote to refute Gager, and argued that men must not beat recalcitrant wives. Moreover, he suggested that a husband might be beaten in return if a couple should fall out, for 'if I should chance to marry with a stout and valiant woman . . . and after a while from Cupid's wars fall unto martial arms . . . my learning would not save me from some unlearned blows'.[6]

Dealing with marital love created even greater problems for the writers in reconciling conflicting requirements of men's rule and women's complementary role; harsh male authority might not mingle well with the intimacy of sharing bed and body. Bullinger had told men to love their wives as their own body, and wrote of mutual conjugal love, and enduring sexual fulfilment, which should get better as years passed, he also praised a uniform agreement of mind between the couple. Dod and Cleaver sixty years later echoed this idea more circumspectly. Edmund Tilney was no godly clergyman but a London courtier, and became Master of the Revels. His view was gentler, and for him love was vital in creating an indissoluble knot between the pair. He painted a happy picture of its expression in bed, and of wives lovingly sharing secret thoughts with husbands on the pillow. His book recommended more love and less fear of husbands, and he added a list of unpleasant behaviour that men must avoid in order to keep their wives's love. Husbands must not brawl, scowl or grudge, nor speak unadvisedly, certainly not indulge in adultery, gaming or drunkenness. And the couple should make allowances for each other. The wife as well as the husband possessed rights to each others' body, for Fenner and others.

William Gouge's precepts were somewhat different from the tough rules of the earlier Protestant zealots discussed at the beginning of this chapter. He wrote a more balanced guide in 1622, revised in two further editions. For Gouge, men and women are equal in 'the power of one another's bodies'. A wife is of all persons on earth the most proper object of a man's love, and that love should keep him from abusing his authority, and encourage him to seek the good of his wife and take greatest care of her. It 'must be annexed to every other duty of a husband, to season and sweeten the same': his affection to his wife cannot be too great. Gouge even counselled his parishioners to read the Song of Songs. Moreover, he advised, love helps a man maintain his authority by being an example to the whole family. Dealing with the sexual union between husband and wife reinforced the inconsistency, however. Gouge restricted the extreme patriarchal model of behaviour, instructing the husband to make his wife 'a joint Governor in the family'. He showed how husbands and wives needed co-operation in daily life, and provided a whole section on husband's and wives' parallel duties. Gouge tried to solve the dilemma of women's ambiguous position by telling wives how to share rule over the rest of the family: children, apprentices and servants: there, she had authority. He assumed that the husband would often be busy elsewhere, and the wife exercise control over domestic life.[7]

Gouge argued much more than other precept books for the duties of husbands toward their families, as well as their right to rule over them. He was more realistic too about family life. Although insisting on male authority, he saw the wife as the nearest possible to the man in equality: they were yoke-fellows and partners, and companions. So a man should kindly accept what his wife can do, rarely command, and when necessary, do so by entreating rather than ordering (though this was partly to reserve the power of command for when he really needed it). Unlike previous manuals, Gouge gave advice to husbands on special care of a pregnant wife: to procure any foods she craved, to hire the midwife she desired even if more costly than the regular one, and to hire a nurse. Gouge had 13 children, which meant he knew a great deal more than most of the male writers about the realities of childbirth and family life. Gouge emphasised the duty of a husband to protect his wife from all sorts of dangers, including those which might arise from unkindness of mothers-in-law, servants, even children. And if he must reprove her, he should do it tactfully when they are alone, so as to maintain her honour before the rest of the household. Although there is some condescension, there is a good deal of interplay in Gouge's ideal household. He gave instructions of the role of children in detail too. Children were subject to the head of the household, but owed duties to both their parents: they should not seek to oppose parental powers. Children must help their parents – and put up with their infirmities as time went on. Gouge's household mingled the authority of its head with reciprocal duties of wife, children and servants.

How widely known were these instructions? Most of the treatises were in small format, easy to carry about, but were printed once only: we do not know how many copies were printed each time, but probably very few. More popular than any of the prescriptive books was Philip Stubbes' praise of a dead wife who had, he insisted, been perfectly obedient and silent: it reached 24 reprintings by 1637, and other funeral eulogies sold well too. Among the advice books, two contrasting texts, Dod and Cleaver's *Godly Form of Household Government* and Tilney's gentler *Brief and Pleasant Discourse of Duties in Marriage* were each reprinted several times, suggesting there was a market. However, the book market was small and centred on London, where most of these were published: books were expensive and few could afford them. Most Englishwomen and a majority of men were illiterate. The godly writers aimed to make people perfect; to persuade them to organise their family lives strictly by scriptural precepts. Those who tried to achieve such a family order through reading these books were zealous gentlemen with access to a bookshop in the capital and godly London laymen with the desire to examine their own lives. The puritan artisan Nehemiah Wallington bought Gouge's book to read aloud to his family to instruct them all on their duties – he was exceptionally devout, going to sermons several times a week, so no wonder he also wanted printed instruction too.[8] But perfection is elusive, and books may not produce it. The books are what remain to us and seem very important, but only a tiny proportion of early modern men and women ever saw one of them or heard it read aloud.

The sermons which some of these had originally been reached more people. Fenner had been a famous preacher in Cambridge in the 1570s before he left for Antwerp; he returned to preach in Kent but was soon suspended for his refusal to conform to the Church's requirements and left again. Dod and Whately were zealous puritan clergymen who worked hard to create godly congregations at Banbury: Whately's gloomy prescripts were wedding sermons. Henry Smith was perhaps the most popular puritan preacher in London. Gouge preached for over 20 years at Blackfriars, a large London parish, and his book derived from his expositions on St Paul's Epistles to the Ephesians which dealt with domestic duties. It was a big book, probably with larger print runs in each of its three editions, since many more examples survive than of others. Gouge was more even-handed than many in his recommendations for the sharing of power in the family. But we know that, even so, not all his listeners agreed with his view. In the preface to the third edition in 1634, he recounted how the women in his parish had complained bitterly to him about his rules which, they asserted, made a husband's exactions too harsh and a wife's yoke too heavy. Gouge was constrained to add an apology, and explain that a husband should not actually use all his authority, and that a wife might have the ordering of many things. Gouge defended himself: he was not a hater of women as his female parishioners had grumbled, and he claimed he had emphasised parallel powers and duties. But he had not convinced the wives in his parish – and they were assertive enough to berate their minister.

Books reached a literate few, puritan sermons were heard by more people, although their hearers may not have agreed with their prescripts, as we know Gouge's did not. But it was the Church's official Homily on Marriage that instructed far more people than the godly preacher or his book.[9] The Homilies were Protestant set sermons to be preached in parishes everywhere in sequence throughout the year, when there was no sermon, or the following Sunday when there was. They were to be delivered by non-preaching ministers, but also by more learned ones, especially earlier in Elizabeth's reign when fewer ministers could preach. So nearly everyone in England would hear the one on marriage from time to time, in the nine and a half thousand parishes across the country. In distant villages and small towns as well as London, that was the message most received, and its message was more realistic than that of the stern godly preachers; it dealt more moderately with patriarchy in practice. Although male authority prevailed – 'Ye wives, be ye in subjection to obey your husbands'- the anonymous author of the Homily on Marriage recognised more clearly than those of the godly treatises the strains and complexity of relationships in the family. It followed St Peter in assuming the weakness of women, but told men to use measurableness, and not tyranny, and never to beat their wives. A man should yield on some things; he should 'be not too stiff, so that he ought to wink at some things'. Marriage should be a perpetual friendly fellowship. The Homily reminded listeners of the difficulties which they would encounter in securing male pre-eminence and marital harmony, and lamented 'For this folly is ever from our tender age grown up with us, to have a desire to rule ... so that none thinketh it meet to give place to another'. It stressed threats (by the devil) to break up the knot of marriage, and the need for concord. Couples will quarrel, but both should sometimes apologise, although women should give in more, and patiently bear the sharpness of their husbands.

The highly ambiguous position of married women was very clearly expressed. A wife should be subject to a husband, and bow to his will, while at the same time wielding authority over children, servants in the household and the direction of daily life: 'to obey is another thing than to control or command, which yet they may do to their children and to their family'. The author of the Homily realised that if women were to rule the rest of the household they needed to be shown respect by their husbands, who were told 'You husbands, deal with your wives according to knowledge, giving honour to the wife', who should respond by doing his will and making home so pleasant that he will delight to return. More surprising was the recognition that single women had power over their own lives, and when they married might find it hard to 'relinquish the liberty of their own rule'. The lesson most people received taught them that making marriage work harmoniously was not always easy, and that both partners must make some allowances, while acknowledging male authority in the family.

How did the messages of obedience to patriarchy work among most people? Did women resist subjection? Did early modern men behave as tyrannically as certain of the books and sermoms seem to suggest? Everyone had to get on with their lives in the daily world beyond theory, where issues of gender power depended on circumstance and personality. Some men did use their place as head of the family stringently to force obedience, a few beat their wives, children or servants within the law, or even beyond it and came before the courts. But across English society, husbands generally wielded lighter authority, and wives more, than the model. Women were not meekly silent, but they contributed much, and men depended on them. Children could be wilful, but often they had left their parents' house to become apprentices or servants, and the upheavals of puberty bore more on employers than parents. For most ordinary families, the careful division of male and female spheres delineated by Cleaver, Smith, or Gouge did not apply. Peasant wives could not simply remain indoors distributing what the husband brought in, and awaiting his direction, they helped in field and forest, and sometimes laboured to earn a little money too. Artisans and cloth workers worked together in cottage manufacture or wool spinning and weaving, and in selling their wares.

Most families lived more complicated lives than the models the logical university-educated preachers laid out for them, and power in the family shifted according to events, and even within days. Sir Thomas Smith observed in 1583 that although the English law seemed somewhat rigorous toward the wives, women had more liberty in practice, and could handle their husbands very well.[10] Among the wealthier literate groups who have left more evidence of their lives than have the poor, most husbands did not domineer totally, and wives were not silent closeted minions. Many men must have followed sage advice to marry a competent woman and not a flighty girl. Among the elite, the parents often chose a partner for their offspring, while allowing a veto for real dislike of the one chosen. In the middling and lower orders, young people had more freedom to select their own spouse, with customary patterns for the stages of courtship and public approval in village or town. Both arranged marriages and those where couples had made their own choice led mostly to more equal partnerships than the books suggested.

In the Lisle family power was shared. Lord Lisle was governor of Calais during the dangerous 1530s, during which the Lisle correspondence survives in extraordinary quantity, including many letters to Lady Lisle.[11] From

Fig 3: Women and men were expected to work together, as in this early seventeenth-century illustration. (*Roxborough Ballads*, I (1871), p. 547)

it we gain an exceptional insight into how the family operated. Lord Lisle was gentle in nature, while his wife Honor was a capable, energetic, organising woman determined to protect the estates, even if that involved legal tussles. In 1536 she was busily involved in tactics to secure grants of monastic lands, and offering gifts to sweeten those who might help. She also took responsibility for organising the education and the advancement of the children by well-chosen marriages, sending gifts of game and garments during such negotiations. The people entrusted with the children's care wrote to Lady Lisle, not to her husband, about the sons as well as the daughters. And people who wanted Lord Lisle to do something often took the precaution of writing first to Lady Lisle, asking her to persuade her husband. Correspondents recognised her power and her influence over him. Some of her vigour in worldly and political matters may have been because she had been a widow with young children when she married Lisle, not an inexperienced girl. But most was because she was a powerful personality with ideas about what needed doing and how to achieve it, and he accepted her authority in doing that.

John Thynne and his wife Joan never fitted the published pattern of gender powers.[12] From the time of their marriage in 1576, the sixteen-year-old Joan, youngest daughter of a London merchant, wrote peremptory letters and instructions to her husband, claiming the right to instruct him on how to behave to other members of the family, including her father. After 1580 when they held Longleat House, and later Caus Castle, she told him how to manage estate business in London, how he should operate politically at the court to obtain a knighthood, and what supplies to buy for the great house. And he allowed her, and trusted her, to manage the estates, the cattle, the tradesmen and building repairs, the employment of servants – and the manipulation of lawsuits and local juries – while he simply chose to stay in London although he had no need to do so. Although she included some of the language of deference in letters to him, the dominant characteristic was partnership in the management of a large estate, with a strong capable woman taking charge of very complex responsibilities, not mere indoor household ones.

Sir Robert Sidney's very frequent letters to his wife Barbara, most of them commencing 'Sweetheart', amply demonstrate his warm affection and intimacy, and the attitude of partnership between them. Sidney's tone is certainly not one of patriarchal condescension to his wife. He tells her what is happening, since his duties keep him away, but adds 'Think no unkindness I pray you at my long stay from you': he was often absent on official duty in the Netherlands or in London.[13] He wrote constantly about how anxious he was to return to her, and to make arrangements for her to come to be near him when possible. And he respected her competence even in a normally male sphere: in 1594 he wrote that he trusted her with the progress of the building work, which she was supervising in his absence. It is impossible to gauge how many spouses shared the responsibilities to this extent. The evidence for such trust in well-documented marriages shows that it was possible: these partners recognised the abilities of wife as well as of husband to exercise power in the family interests. People at other levels of English society did too.

One way to discover more about how far men permitted the authority of their wives is to consider what they decided to do about land and possessions at death. Sir Thomas Smith's description of England noted that most men made their wives sole or chief executrix of their will. Smith assumed men had trust in the competence of wives to deal with something so vital as the family's assets.[14] And Smith was correct that husbands very frequently demonstrated trust and affection by choosing their wives to execute wills. This shows that the widow was expected to understand the family's material position and be able to handle the land, goods, and animals, to pay debts and receive those due. Of course, the wife might already have died; some men chose children, or other close kin, and the wealthier gentry with extensive lands usually named more than one executor. Many husbands included warm praise of a wife in their wills, praise which was more than formulaic. Men expressing this deep affection after a marital life together *may* have been authoritarian tyrants, but that is not the impression which strikes the reader: the words suggest more equal relationships. This kind of evidence is not available from the very poorest, who had nothing much to leave and made no wills. However, fairly modest tradesmen, farmers and merchants did make wills, so did virtually all of the landed gentry. The newly widowed woman certainly would be operating in the world, even if a small one, rather than simply staying indoors minding the housework and children.

A brief survey of several hundred wills suggests that wives were named to execute wills much more often than not. Many wills made a wife sole executrix, while a large proportion shared the duty with sons, or daughters. Many quite humble men made such wills, such as the farmers and tradesmen whose wills were proved in the manor courts of Yorkshire, and in local ecclesiastical registries. Even an illiterate wife could administer the goods, as did Anne Bland in 1613 – she could only sign with a cross. Lancashire farmer John Fawcett made his wife Margaret his 'whole executrix', and she was to keep his farm. In 1536 Richard Tolnson's will said that his wife Anne should have his whole farmhold while she lived, and she and two daughters were named executrices. Ralph Guy, a Yorkshire yeoman, willed in 1550 that his wife should have his lease, which must have been substantial, for she was to use it to keep all their children at school till they could read and write and reached the age of 15, when they were to be sent to London to merchants 'or other sciences'. Those merchants too, whose business dealings were rather complex, chose their wives. George Matheson a Hull merchant, obviously respected his wife's ability to manage, and expressed it more clearly than some men. In 1540 he gave to his wife a mill and house, all his lands and buildings etc, 'to give and to sell at her pleasure', plus all moveable goods and debts, and made her executrix. A Bristol merchant setting off to sea, and fearing the dangers of the voyage, made his will in 1529, giving all to his wife, the sole executrix. Sadly his fears were realised for by the following year he was dead.[15]

Perhaps it is not surprising that farmers and tradesmen trusted their wives with managing the property or goods; they had probably worked closely together. But so too did a significant proportion of wealthier men, gentry and townsmen. Sir William Newenham, who was departing from Nottinghamshire in 1544 to the French wars, made his 'well beloved' wife sole executix. In some 65 wills of gentry connected with Wiltshire in the late Elizabethan and Jacobean period, some chose male executors, but many made their wife sole executrix, others chose a wife together with a son. For example, Thomas Harrison, a very substantial landowner, with manors, farms, houses and woods in Berkshire and Wiltshire named his wife Elizabeth sole executrix in 1602. The wealthier gentry with extensive lands tended to name more than one executor, often sons or other male kin as well as the wife. Henry Sadler esquire trusted his wife Ursula and wrote movingly of his singular and most unfeigned love for her in his 1617 will.[16]

Men also gave power to women in their families other than wives to manage probate. Of course, not everyone had a wife when they approached death: earlier in our period many clergy were celibate, well into Elizabeth's reign for the ones who remained Catholic outwardly or in their hearts. And some men were widowers, or bachelors. Still they often chose women. Sir John Lowther's will in 1554 made his brother and Jane Carlyle joint executors, and upheld Jane's rights by stipulating that his brother was to take nothing beyond his necessary expense from Jane. Richard Farrow, a northern parson, made his unmarried niece and his brother executors. In 1584 Thomas Middleton also chose a niece, alone this time; some chose a mixture of brothers and in-laws, occasionally cousins. James Nelson of Ryton in 1596 chose his wife and the child with which she was pregnant, but if they did not survive, then his wife's sister was to be executrix. Aunts too, as well as sisters appeared in the recorded wills. Robert Booth, of Dunham Massey, Cheshire, a gentleman (apparently unmarried) chose his sister, and another woman who was probably a relation, plus three male executors. The choice partly depended on what family members were available at the time of will making – but the number of women is startling. Wills from a very wide range of people in the sixteenth and early seventeenth centuries confirm that men were willing to give such authority to women, including daughters, despite the supposed limitations on female authority.[17]

Women shared in family decisions and were chosen to execute wills, they were not simply silent and powerless under the command of their menfolk. And wives and children did actively contest the command of the head of the household. They resisted it for differing reasons, ranging from strong temperament to rejection of male domination or cruelty. We have assumed that patriarchy equalled tyranny, because the conflict-ridden families have left more striking evidence than the peaceful ones. For the aristocracy and gentry, the stakes were high in disputes, producing angry letters between the contestants, reports to their relatives and friends, and attempts to mediate or to inflame. Some led to lawsuits, even among poorer people. Such quarrels involved not simply wilful resistance to the head of the household, but divisive family issues: incompatible temperaments made worse by property disputes, differing plans for the marriage of the children, especially the heir, or drunkenness or infidelity. In the 1580s Lady Margaret Stanhope berated her husband Sir Thomas for such wickedness, seizing a rod with which he threatened to beat her and tearing off his ruff and part of his beard. Informal separation followed, not surprisingly. Stanhope also fell out with his sons, and his pugnacious character made him unpopular locally, so his wife had reasons for her resistance to him. Elizabeth Cavendish, the wife of George Talbot, sixth earl of Shrewsbury, battled so bitterly with the earl, her fourth husband, that Queen Elizabeth intervened, and eventually 'Bess of Hardwick' was licensed to live apart from him, supervising the building of her great manor house in Derbyshire. They were fortunate to have the means to resolve their differences in that way.[18]

Anne Clifford was another forceful woman contesting the power of men, and she recorded her efforts to secure the inherited property she believed was rightfully hers, a struggle lasting decades in the early seventeenth century. She defied her menfolk: her uncle, her first husband, and even King James I, who advised her to give up and stop agitating. Despite Anne's active role opposing the men in her family, her first husband, the earl of Dorset, wrote to her in 1617 that he loved her in all things: he considered her a good wife – except for her persistence in trying to get the lands. And despite their contention, she defended him to her mother, calling him 'the best and most worthiest man that ever breathed'.[19] She did not 'take rule' over him in other matters. In her old age, she reflected on this marriage and the memory of her defiance as a young wife was still important to her. Some wives refused submission at times, but not continuously. Alterations in the delicate interaction of couples during their lives together could change harmony into contest, or vice versa. Sir Francis Willoughby and his wife Elizabeth did have 12 children, but they quarrelled seriously, and she refused her husband's rule, moving back to her own family after years of marriage, and conducting a bitter correspondence with her husband. This was not just temperament. Sir Francis felt justified in his angry behaviour because her father had failed to pay over her dowry, while she wanted support to live separately. Even when Willoughby refused and tried to make her return and apologise 'in such humility as is meet and convenient for the recovering of my good will' she refused 'hard conditions'.[20] But she had to give in, eventually, despite her resistance. Contest had limits.

William Gouge may have been thinking of these notorious marital contests when he wrote that some wives would not obey, but must have their own rule, and make a hurly-burly in the house if the husband tried to maintain his authority.[21] Or perhaps his Blackfriars parishioners also failed to fit the patriarchal model. With Gouge, we have rare insight into the people's reception of the doctrine of patriarchy, because of the women's objections to his preaching of the limitations on them, objections which persuaded him to insist that husbands must co-operate and not demand harsh things of their wives. No doubt women everywhere at times resisted both reasonable and unreasonable orders, in the contests which the Homily foresaw, but generally they co-operated well enough to keep out of the records of the courts. But there were some extreme cases in which marital relationships deteriorated very badly: a very small number of disobedient wives died from beatings – which were legal if they could be defended as 'reasonable chastisement'. The evidence of neighbours in these cases often told of a history of previous quarrels and violence. Some did involve the question of authority, but personality and drunkenness complicated it. Passions which led to such an extreme action must generally have built up over time, not from just one reported quarrel over command and obedience. Edith Jagger's husband assaulted her over a string of minor 'failures' – when walking along together she was too slow; she could not lift a sack of corn onto his back as he required; she asked him for a smock. But he was found not guilty when she died, because he had not intended to kill her. John Holden's wife refused to give him money to buy more ale when he was drunk; he struck her and she soon died. Robert Maude told his wife to prepare some meat for him, but she did it too slowly, so he hit her with a stick.[22]

However, we need to see these terrible examples in perspective. Domestic homicide was unusual and formed a much smaller proportion of all homicides than today. Murder of any kind per head of population was rare in early modern England: across the several London jurisdictions, between 1550 and 1625, murder and manslaughter formed only 4 per cent of serious crimes prosecuted at assizes. In the counties for which assize records survive, the murders involving family members averaged around 12 per cent out of the small total of murders. For instance, in 140 years from 1559–1700, the Home counties assizes dealt with 70 men accused of murdering their wives, and 32 wives accused of murdering their husbands. Nearly half were acquitted, although some of the husbands were only acquitted because they claimed they had merely intended to give 'reasonable chastisement' for disobedience, and had not intended to kill their wives. Some of them had maltreated their wives on other occasions before the fatal blow. But the evidence given before Northern and Home counties assizes by neighbours who had been confidants of the victims showed that the community did not condone such beatings. Sometimes, neighbours themselves took action to stop the violence. In 1612, Christopher Lewis was bound over by the Kent quarter sessions to keep the peace towards his wife, and ordered not to beat her as he had been doing. But three village women had also tried to control Lewis's violence – by going to his house and beating him, so that he was forced to flee upstairs. Their action showed that wife beating would not be tolerated by the villagers.[23]

Probably a minority of couples faced really serious conflict or power struggles; most had too much to do facing the challenges of providing for themselves, or keeping up with trade, or running their estate. But as parents they encountered more problems. Among landed families, parents assumed that they should arrange marriages for their offspring, but they could meet problems in imposing their authority over older children. For sons, fathers and mothers sought wives who would bring maximum dowry, and for their daughters, men with rich lands who allowed favourable conditions. While sons and daughters often fell in with such plans, many refused. Examples include Stephen Drury in 1575: he and his prospective bride agreed to marry, but her mother objected to the match because they were not of the same social level. Drury found scriptural backing for the couple to make their own decision. Anthony Mildmay, son of an Elizabethan Chancellor of the Exchequer, refused the bride his father selected for him, until the threat that he would not be allowed to marry anyone else brought obedience. Thomas Thynne, heir to Longleat, went further in rebellion against his parents. He was 16 when he secretly married Maria Audley in 1594, without his family's permission or even knowledge. But he knew they would be furious, since she was the offspring of the Thynne family's greatest political opponents. Then he defied his parents during a long lawsuit to decide the validity of the marriage, and eventually settled down happily with Maria in 1601. William Tooker, canon of Salisbury, tried to prevent his son from defying his wishes: in 1619 Tooker's will stipulated that his son would be disinherited if he married Maria Baylie.[24]

Fathers frequently countered 'unsuitable' marriage choices with the threat of disinheritance – sometimes the son or daughter obeyed, sometimes the parents eventually accepted, and belatedly made financial arrangements, as in the cases of William Lowther, Anne Townshend and others. Thomas Thynne's hasty marriage meant the family received no dowry, but later negotiations aimed to redress this. The most extreme resistance was shown by Peter Coryton in Cornwall, an eldest son who wanted to marry against his father's wishes. The father threatened to disinherit him, and the young man allegedly murdered his father. Parents often did allow a veto, however, if their son or daughter really could not stand the prospective spouse. The minister Ralph Josselin's diary shows the control he expected to wield over his family. Yet a son married without any consultation, and a daughter refused Josselin's choice, though she persuaded her father to give in to her decision.[25] Well might William Cecil warn parents to marry their daughters before they marry themselves, if parents were determined to make the decisions for the family interest, on grounds of financial advantage, amalgamation of lands, and political alliance. Among the middling and lesser classes, young people had much more freedom to select their own partner, and then consult parents and kin. Yet the agreement of the families remained very important, and only a few married if their parents and relations really disapproved.

Gentry parents often failed to obtain the obedience of older sons in financial matters. Heirs like Sir Henry Slingsby spent too much money in London, his father complained. John Phelips, heir to Montacute in Somerset, ran up impossible debts, so much so that his father made a grant of the estate to a younger son.[26] And some parents disapproved of their older childrens' choices of companions and diversions. Sir John Thynne moaned that his son John enjoyed the delights of Oxford life more than the study of books.

Choice of employment also ranged offspring against their parents. Farmers often needed their sons to stay and help, while the young men wished to try more adventurous paths. However ambitious they may have been, most farmer's sons ended up working on other farms or becoming apprentices; a few served in war or at sea. Fathers wishing to decide their child's future often arranged apprenticeship in a trade. The child did not always agree – though necessity meant eventual submission. Since the majority of young people left home in their mid-teens, the master (or mistress) took on the powers over them that their parents relinquished. However, parents did not simply abandon their offspring; some took action against the employer when the young person was not treated correctly, or received inadequate instruction in an apprenticeship. Girls worked in agriculture, or found apprenticeships in textiles, or garment-making. But many opposed their parents' plans by going to seek work in the capital, as did Jane Martindale in 1625 when she decided to leave Lancashire for service in London.[27] For some young people there was no work, especially in the hard years of the 1550s, 1590s, and 1620s. They became the wandering 'masterless' vagabonds who were not under the authority of parent or household head. They were not really rebels against parents and masters, but economic victims, and would have preferred work, even with the duty of obedience.

For the majority of people in rural and artisan families, work defined how they lived, and the joint struggle to survive by sharing tasks outweighed any rigid theory of patriarchy. Fire was essential to cooking and to survival in cold winter: men could chop down trees while women gathered smaller wood. Men did the heaviest tasks in agriculture, but women helped with urgent labour in the harvest. Women, in addition to childcare and household, did other work, as did children – care of hens, feeding pigs, milking cows, collecting eggs, making cheese and butter, and picking fruit and berries. In crafts, both worked together part or all the time, or the husband made, and wife sold. Artisans in London and other towns depended on a wife's participation in their work: artisans whose wives died usually remarried very speedily, often to someone familiar with the family's craft, a woman of the household. Dod and Cleaver's tidy pattern of men going out to seek a living, while women stayed within the house could not apply to the majority of English families; they just managed their lives together as best they could, and women frequently did not bow to male authority within or outside the home.

Successful family power relationships worked through a wide range of different strategies. Wives, children and servants often could accept the pattern of the Homily on marriage, and internalise habits of deference to the household head. As long as the particular personalities fitted in, making the arrangement of daily tasks and decisions satisfactory to them all, the family co-operated without much strife. Husbands did not need to domineer, or wives to resist them, and married women expected some freedom of action. Ordinary women maintained control over major family events. When giving birth, men were excluded and women gathered to help the mother, to join in female festivity when all went well, or in mourning if not. The mother's traditional month of lying-in gave her an agreed respite from some duties. Wives rather than husbands or clergymen wanted the religious ceremony of churching to give thanks afterwards – and organised the celebratory partying to mark the mother's return to normal village life. Relatively poor couples, giving evidence to the church courts when the legality of their marriages were challenged by parents, or disappointed suitors, described gift-giving and joint activities which demonstrate co-operation during courting and after the wedding, rather than a condescending patriarchy from the men. The love and respect of spouses mattered to people at all levels of society. Richard Napier's patients suffered when their emotional life went wrong, because they normally expected co-operative and loving marriages. Richard Rogers' diary gives a rare insight, as he thought about the possible death of his wife when she was about to give birth in 1588. Rogers feared 'Forgoing so fit a companion for religion, housewifery and other comforts' – and it is the word companion which he puts first. If some men tried to insist on strict patriarchal values at home, for most families companionship and sharing in the struggles of life were more important than rigid patterns of obedience.[28]

PART III

6

The practice of authority

In July 1561 the Privy Council sent a digest of essential statutes to the sheriff and JPs of Wiltshire, and doubtless other counties, pressing them to work hard and report monthly on the state of the county. The letter reminded the justices to remember the purpose for which every one of them had been appointed by the queen: 'not to exercise authority for your singular credit and reputation, nor to colour and shadow your own causes', but to be worthy to govern and punish.[1] It was one of many such reminders to those who were responsible in practice for ruling the counties. Each monarch needed to impose their will, but had to rely on selected subjects to transmit it to the people – and these subjects had their own agendas, as the central government recognised. Nobles, gentry and townsmen intrigued to gain the positions of power – partly to acquire status and partly to protect their private interests, it was suggested by leading Councillors and successive Lord Chancellors. Once achieved, how did local men wield authority? Was it all as lackadaisical and erratic as central officials complained? Since the system relied mainly on intangible rewards of honour, respect and patronage to gain co-operation, the men exercising power at any level needed to accept policy if they were to enforce it; but they also needed to overcome natural human indolence and greed.

For the central government there was a delicate balance between harrying and encouraging the men who must implement decisions, especially difficult during controversial shifts of policy. Early in 1538 Thomas Cromwell noted that the Lord Chancellor was to call all the justices of the peace to the Star Chamber, specially to press them to deal with vagabonds, unlawful games, and with people spreading rumours against the current policies.[2] The various changes of religious policy in the 1530s created severe problems of enforcement. Cromwell supervised prosecution of serious opposition through the central law courts, but also demanded that local authority remain vigilant; he sent frequent circulars to local governors demanding effort: to implement the new social legislation and to find and punish opposers of the religious changes or the Boleyn marriage. He succeeded more than might be expected in achieving action. Cromwell's correspondence shows that many justices tried to fulfil the Council's demands, seeking out obstinate papists and reporting them to the centre – though in religiously conservative regions, such as the area of the Pilgrimage of Grace, little was done in response to the circulars. Cromwell believed in frequent pressure, with occasional encouragement – as in the circular late in 1538 thanking JPs for their work to support the royal supremacy and punish sedition. A memorandum of 1539 noted that Cromwell intended to send letters to all JPs specifically telling them to carry out the latest policy. A long draft government circular to JPs in 1541 illustrates the dilemmas in achieving the practice of new or controversial policy. It expressed surprise that notwithstanding 'sundry advertisements lately made', they were not being carried out, and there was danger through negligence. In particular, the JPs must watch diligently for supporters of the pope, and, once again, for rumours against the king or the laws (meaning the new ones): the government feared serious disturbance. Beside the exhortation to action, the circular ended with the threat that if the JPs did not act, there might be sharp punishment of the negligent.[3]

Careful supervision continued after Cromwell's execution had removed his guiding hand, and the Privy Council and secretaries sent out streams of instructions on matters large and small. In 1569, during the scare over the northern rising, a letter to the sheriff and JPs of Wiltshire exhorted them to silence all seditious rumours and ensure quietness, especially as their Lord Lieutenant, the earl of Pembroke, was under suspicion of collusion with the disgraced duke of Norfolk. The order insisted on how well governed the realm was, and anyone seeking to alter things was not worthy to be a member of the realm: it contained a clear call for local governors actively to support the Elizabethan regime, but betrayed anxiety about their willingness to do so. Sir Henry Whithed thought Council instructions sufficiently important to make copies of those received between 1601 and 1624 when he served as a Hampshire JP. They ranged from a letter from the Council to suppress rumours about the queen's illness in 1602, to one of 1608 requesting aid to Bury St Edmunds after a disastrous fire. And he and his felllow JPs responded quickly: very soon after noting Council letters which had arrived, Whithed recorded the despatch of instructions to constables to carry out the necessary actions.[4]

Frequent, anxious exhortations to vigilance went around the shires. If the Privy Council continually feared that chaos was just around the corner, did the county governors think so too? Did they do the onerous, unpaid, business out of a sense of duty to hold at bay disorders which constantly threatened? The 1580 notes by Sir John Thynne for a charge at the Wiltshire quarter sessions dwelt heavily on how local authority must take care of national issues – the need for religious unity, and the danger of false rumours creating discord between the queen and her people, or concerning prelates, nobles and officers of state. Then he outlined the staple local issues.[5] But Thynne's notes, though providing very detailed instructions, lacked the emotional thrust of William Lambarde's rhetoric. Lambarde, a Kent JP and author of manuals of instruction for justices and constables, was in real fear of anarchy. He warned mournfully at Kent quarter sessions in 1583 of the struggles required to combat disorder, and of the unruliness of the people. He feared miseries 'if every man breaketh loose without fear of God, restraint of conscience, estimation of law, or regard of charity'. A huge range of problems must be contained: religious dissension, food shortages by unlawful buying and selling, retainers of greater men vexing neighbours, lusty youth producing illegitimate babies, thieves and rogues who swarmed in the highways. Action was needed too against card-playing and unlawful games, alehouses which were the 'nurseries of naughtiness', unseemly apparel, oppression and deceit, unlawful trades, evaders of tax or military musters, and public officers not content with their fees.[6]

Lambarde expounded these dangers again in 1587, for 'in so working a sea of sin and wretchedness as this age is, the ship of commonwealth shall be in peril'; and in 1596 he lamented 'the infinite swarms of evil that of latter years (more than in former ages) have invaded the realm and overrun it'. So, he asked, 'Shall we not unsheathe the sword of authority and use it against offenders?' The unruly people must be made to obey, for, as he had claimed earlier, 'obedience is the life and safety of the commonwealth'. Lambarde's gloomy view of ever-present threats to order meant that dutiful men were required to control them, and he was one of those fitted and chosen to do so. He illustrated the threats as persuasively as he could at quarter sessions, to fire up the constables to report all dangers, and the jurors to indict and prosecute offenders. In these addresses he frequently worried about these local officials turning blind eyes to the misdeeds of their neighbours, which is why he sought strong rhetorical descriptions to jolt them out of their complacency – or their inactivity for fear of local retribution.[7]

Lambarde was not alone, although he expressed his fears more colourfully than many others. Michael Dalton referred to the risk of chaos in his preface in 1619 to *The Country Justice*, and emphasised the need to maintain order firmly 'to the honour and safety of the King's Majesty, and the good and peacable government of all his subjects'. Dalton dwelt on the laws for controlling alehouses, 'to prevent the mischiefs and great disorders happening daily' from abuses in unruly or unlicensed establishments. He was echoing King James's speech in the Star Chamber in 1616 against alehouses as haunts for robbers, thieves and vagabonds – a plaint recurring in all the prescripts against disorderly alehouses throughout the period and beyond.[8]

Monarchs and their Privy Councils feared breakdown of obedience, and demanded a great deal from the local enforcers. In every reign special problems needed action from local authority. Henry VIII and Cromwell tried to force JPs to work hard to search out opposition, and the justices had more work imposed on them than ever before. Each reign brought increased responsibilities, as the crown sought to impose solutions for economic and social problems as well as the customary administrative and legal tasks. Much of the enforcement involved forms of social control – over alehouses, as we have seen, and over games such as bowling, which seem harmless but might incite disturbance. Statutes laid down procedures to deal with poverty and to control begging, while helping those most in need. These were finally codified in the poor laws of 1598 and 1601. Taxing and distributing relief for the incapable poor was always difficult and time-consuming, since many villagers resisted payment. Bastard babies were to be provided for, and their parents punished, more severely after the statute of 1607. Employment problems, especially with labourers and apprentices, required action, and maximum wages had to be set. JPs also made orders for maintenance of roads and bridges. Various commissions, and most onerously the ones to assess for subsidies, depended on those JPs appointed to them. Besides all this day-to-day oversight of the shire, there was the constant effort to enforce order in private disputes, by sureties to keep the peace, and the extensive list of crimes to punish. If the Book of Orders of 1631 seemed too heavy a weight to place on the JPs, it built on a long tradition of tasks allotted to them.

It is not surprising that Lambarde complained in 1599 of 'the loads of statutes that continually are increased and for execution laid upon our shoulders'. Reading his *Eirenarcha or of the Office of Justice of Peace*, or Dalton's *The Country Justice* or his *The Office and Authoritie of Sheriffs* astonishes the modern reader with the range of responsibilities imposed on those voluntary working gentry who sat on the commission of the peace or acted for a year as sheriff in their counties. These men really needed the instruction books of Lambarde and Dalton, and no wonder the latter were reprinted frequently. A Bodleian Library copy of Dalton's *Country Justice*, 1619, is annotated, summarised and cross-referenced in the margins in a contemporary hand, obviously for rapid reference on many tasks, especially to do with settling labour problems, and weirs and fishing disputes. Dalton, like Lambarde, referred to the burdens – the 'wearying of ourselves, the spending of our time, wits, and estates . . . and requited many times . . . with much evil will'.[9]

Evil will seemed to come from the central government, too, despite the many tasks entrusted to these men. Circulars, and Lord Chancellors' speeches to them continually complained of slackness. An order of 1561 threatened the JPs who did not try: 'with which sort of men we mean not so long to bear, as perchance they think we will'. Particular justices were dismissed, as we saw in Chapter 3, and there were wider purges, notably on Elizabeth's accession, probably in 1564, and again in the later years of the reign when Lord Burghley sought tighter control. Reports from the bishops in 1587 castigated the justices brought into the commissions by faction, who were 'unworthy to govern, being so far out of order themselves'. Nathaniel Bacon kept a long letter from the Privy Council in 1609 complaining that JPs failed to act on orders and carried out their public service so confusedly or remissly that the vulgar sort of would get habits of disobedience. In addition, the Council admonished the sheriff for selecting dishonest or inadequate juries – another frequent complaint. But worse, he was accused of negligence in publishing the king's proclamations, not conveying such orders into the hearts of the king's subjects.[10]

Remonstrances in writing were not enough. Periodically the Lord Chancellor or Lord Keeper called the JPs into the Star Chamber to remind them of particularly urgent tasks, but also to complain about their performance; assize judges before going on their circuits were instructed on how to lecture local JPs. This practice had certainly commenced under Henry VIII, and probably before. In 1565, Lord Keeper Nicholas Bacon described idle justices as drones among bees. In June 1595, Lord Keeper Puckering alleged that the number of justices had grown almost infinite, many of them insufficient, unlearned, negligent and indiscreet: the queen herself looked through the list and noted some she thought should be dismissed. While Thomas Egerton, later Lord Ellesmere, held the office from 1596 to 1617, he made many such speeches to harry the local governors. In 1605 he complained that there were too many justices that did no good and too few that executed the duty of their place, preferring to live in London most of the year.[11]

The central government frequently railed against the provincial holders of authority and chivvied them with sharp letters, but did they deserve the complaints? Thomas Cromwell's correspondence shows that many justices felt a strong sense of duty, and an anxiety to do what the king or his ministers required. The implementation of policy provoked questions from those responsible for it in the localities: in 1538 the duke of Norfolk and Sir Roger Towneshend wrote on behalf of the Norfolk justices to ask Cromwell if a Catholic friar who was to be executed should first be sent to the Tower for torture. In 1539 two Oxfordshire JPs, Sir Walter Stonor and Thomas Carter, wrote to tell Cromwell that as soon as they received the king's letters (on observance of religious injunctions), they had summoned the other justices to meet in three days, and they reported on the subsequent investigations.[12] Such alacrity suggests eager co-operation, even if tainted by ambition and fear. From the later sixteenth century on, there is much more evidence of the local governors' attitudes. As the variety of tasks increased, gentry thought and wrote more reflectively about them, and perhaps took them more seriously. They also acted to preserve a written record of what they did. Details of their activity survive in document files prepared for quarter sessions in Essex continuously from 1556, and in some records for Middlesex, Norfolk, Cheshire and Staffordshire – with materials for more counties from the end of Elizabeth's reign. Wiltshire has the earliest record of the decisions JPs made, starting in 1574, meticulously written in Latin minute books, with the working files as well from 1603. The Wiltshire JPs ordered a new chest in which to preserve the documents, and their orders to their assiduous clerks of the peace (Walter Berington, 1567–80, and John Kent, who was clerk for three decades) ensured that we now have a full view of local authority in action.

Some justices had a marked sense of their duty as local governors. William Lambarde's charge to the Kent quarter sessions jury in 1582 expressed his concern for the common good. He spoke of how they were all there 'for the glory of God and the service of our prince, but also the common benefit of this our country [county] and the particular good of us all'. The next year he outlined what was important: to secure the quiet of the good and the correction of the bad, the advancement of public profit and the restraint of injurious and private gain. Michael Dalton explained that he had written his book of instruction partly as response to the king's speech in 1616 praising the system of JPs, a view which, Dalton explained, had given him new vigour and encouragement. Dalton hoped 'we may courageously and constantly undergo the charge imposed upon us'. He wrote of the business 'wherewith myself and many others are daily employed and set on work, without yielding any pleasure or profit at all to us, otherwise than for the public good'.[13]

Sir John Newdigate was one of the godly magistrates, and he put his position clearly in 1606. He felt a duty to his inferiors to fulfil the office conscientiously, for 'as obedience is due to us, so is our study, our labour, and our industry, with virtuous example, due to them that be subject to our authority. A governor must be painful [i.e. take pains] in his own person'. Speaking to the Warwickshire grand jury, he insisted that both JP and juror had to act 'not to be lookers on but actors in this public service. For our pre-eminence over men, it is but for the benefit of men'. Most of Sir Nathaniel Bacon's papers about his official duties in Norfolk contain the details of what was done. But they also show that he was thinking about the best ways to get the work done, and cared about doing it well. The military tasks over musters, arms, and money led him to prepare notes about the best way to proceed – in 1605 to make rules on how to deal with difficulties and defaulters; in 1615 an agenda for a meeting of deputy lieutenants. In 1617 he formulated a careful set of rules for better organising the overseers of the poor and the accounting for Easter 1618, which demonstrates his concern for the efficient use of authority. The Wiltshire and Salisbury city JP Henry Sherfield considered that God had called him and his allies to bring about reformation of abuses and to bring order. Sir Richard Grosvenor's Cheshire charges and letters extolled a view of local authority integrated into central, with firm duties for JPs. In their care for the poor and weak, he wrote, justices should 'neither triumph over nor trample upon' them. In explaining the aims of local government he wished to emphasise the paternal nature of social authority.[14]

When Grosvenor encouraged the grand jury, he stressed the benefits to the community if they performed their duties, and spied out those who needed punishment – for jurors were better acquainted with the common grievances of the county than justices themselves were. But they should be sure not to yield to the wishes of great men or their neighbours, an obvious danger in authority which was localised. Grosvenor was proud of his image as a godly local governor, a 'chief pillar in the public affaire of this kingdom'. He saw public service to the commonwealth as the first duty of a gentleman, who should seek the common good and serve it unselfishly, not withdraw to his own interests. For the honest man, the public interest should be stronger than the private, which might be selfish or corrupt. It was also the service of God to fight sin, and in the mid-1620s Grosvenor wanted attention to witchcraft and to ecclesiastical offences, such as disturbing preachers, swearing and cursing. He was concerned to detect papists who 'eat up and devour the seeds of loyalty and religion'. Grosvenor regarded his own service as his godly calling, to which 'we are all born' – meaning such gentlemen as himself, and he wrote to his son extolling it. Grosvenor was accepted as an honest, learned, godly 'father of the country', and had a trusted role in arbitrating local disputes. He also spoke on broader issues such as the defence of Protestantism, the liberties of the subject, and the bond between centre and localities. Ironically, his adherence to these same virtues brought him into conflict with the government when he opposed Buckingham's recusant clients, and he was dismissed from the bench in 1626. Grosvenor's concern for what he saw as the public good led him to oppose Buckingham, government policies and the Forced Loan, and to speak against them in parliament in 1628. Conscience, virtue and the service of the commonwealth mattered most to him. Like others in the 1620s and 1630s, he maintained his own interpretation of duty in serving the public, even when that brought him into collision with the crown. Sir Henry Poole of Okesey, Wiltshire made his will on 17 March 1630: he warned his son not to be carried away with idle sports and the vain delights of the world, but first to apply himself to the service of God and next to the good of his country.[15]

Some men may have desired public authority selfishly for status, for advancing their own interests and harassing their rivals, as successive Lord Chancellors complained. However the private diaries and letters of JPs, and the surviving quarter sessions archives, demonstrate astonishing devotion to duty by many gentry while they held local office. The attitudes of men like Nathaniel Bacon, the elder John Thynne, William Lambarde, Henry Whithed, John Newdigate and Richard Grosvenor suggest that accusations of slothfulness were unjustified. While the most committed were probably more likely to keep diaries, which show us their hard work, the quarter sessions files reveal that a great many others also tried to exercise their power properly. In Elizabethan and Jacobean Norfolk, the JPs worked very conscientiously to administer the county and resolve disputes; they certainly did not fit the idle image of Lord Keeper Nicholas Bacon's harangues. Of 38 men who were local justices in 1595 and who could have attended quarter sessions, 34 were there for at least two days, and nearly half of them attended more – varying from eight to twenty days sitting. Of the total 70 JPs resident at some time between 1590 and 1600, only five missed attending at least a few days in most years. Moreover, they devised a complicated system of quarter sessions adjournments, which meant travelling to more places, for the convenience of those with business at quarter sessions. On meeting, the justices had to deal with much criminal and administrative work: the most difficult duties included selecting high constables for each hundred, and auditing the constables' accounts every Easter, to check on the collection and handling of county taxes and to stop corruption. Tax rates had to be set for bridge or highway repair, and for the annual grants for the destitute poor, maimed soldiers and so on. Each JP argued to keep the rate low for his own area, so prolonging the discussion and provoking dissension.[16]

Attendance at quarter sessions was only part of the duty. A huge range of problems required attention between meetings, and most justices in Norfolk governed their localities vigorously, seeing complainants and taking large numbers of recognizances from quarrelling or criminal inhabitants. Norfolk founded 'Bridewells', institutions to provide correction and work for the poor, the first in 1574; and the justices had to supervise them by monthly meetings. At these times, they also dealt with misdemeanours or disorders, and tried to mediate controversies. The Norfolk justices had effectively run petty sessions from Henry's reign onwards, and divisional meetings regularly met six-weekly by 1600. So the Privy Council order of 1605 prescribing such six-weekly division meetings simply confirmed existing procedure in Norfolk. Essex and Wiltshire also held petty sessions: the Essex petty sessions meetings reported very regularly to quarter sessions from 1565 to at least the 1580s, naming one or two high constables as present, and usually one or two JPs as well. In Wiltshire petty sessions left fewer specific records but they were active: a minute book records a petty session in December 1592. In April 1615 a hundred jury informed the Justices that they had presented all their problems 'at the last petty sessions'. In 1616 it was agreed that the justices at their next petty sessions within their divisions would arrange to carry out orders of the previous quarter sessions; the wording shows clearly that the petty sessions were regular.

The licensing of alehouses and supervision of poor law regulations involved most working JPs in constant labour. They had to decide who should keep alehouses and hear complaints, approve the overseers of the poor chosen for each parish and check the accounts of money collected and spent. Investigations into would-be settlers, into passing vagabonds, and into who was responsible for and should maintain bastard babies meant tedious interviews to elicit the facts from not necessarily truthful people. At home, justices were always on call to deal with a wide variety of urgent tasks relating to poverty, crime, and disputes. The out-of-sessions work of organising and training the able-bodied men of each county for military service increasingly devolved on three or four of the justices chosen to be deputy lieutenants. The group of justices who did all this, and also served on subsidy commissions, worked fairly constantly on county business, even in mid-winter. Bassingbourne Gawdy kept detailed notes showing that, for instance, in January 1600 he was riding about Norfolk attending many separate meetings: for the recusancy commission, for quarter sessions of four days, then for muster administration, and others for Bridewell supervision. The following month he was just as busy. Nathaniel Bacon's official notebook for the years 1584–91 recorded 185 people he had bound over: some to appear at quarter sessions, some to prosecute or to act as witness, others to keep the peace, and ale-house keepers to keep good order in their ale-houses. In 1615–16 he checked overseers accounts 1615–16, with lists of sums collected for 14 parishes, plus another set of accounts for 24 parishes together. This represents much time and trouble, seeing so many people, but is only a small sample of Bacon's activity.[17]

Norfolk justices worked hard, and so did the Jacobean Somerset ones, with generally about 20 of them present at each quarter sessions meeting, and only six who never appeared.[18] Most Wiltshire JPs also appeared regularly, although a few merited the Lord Chancellor's strictures against idleness. The hardworking Wiltshire core was about 25, with attendance at each quarter sessions numbering around 20, up to 29 in 1618 during a controversy among the justices. Some gentlemen tended to ride mostly to the sessions nearest home: the distance from Salisbury to Marlborough sessions was, as was noted in 1618, around 40 miles 'over very deep and foul ways' – a powerful disincentive to attendance. Yet William Blacker and Giles Tooker, Salisbury lawyers, attended most of the sessions every year. In 1605 a government order tried to ensure full attendances and to check on what services the justices had performed, with the clerks of the peace to certify which resident justices had been absent. In Essex there were occasional efforts to list those absent through sickness. But attendance depended not on coercion but on notions of duty and the hope of making a favourable impression on the Privy Council.

The correspondence of Sir John Thynne of Longleat shows that he was an assiduous and trusted local governor right up to his death in 1580; he was *custos* from 1562. He carefully kept sets of instructions from Privy Councillors and the queen, and, as a 1561 missive exhorted, he surely did set aside slothfulness, and was careful of his charge to govern worthily. From April 1570 to 1571, for instance, he was very busy dealing with the assessment and collection of Privy Seal loans, and Cecil gave him discretion to spare some people from being pressed to pay up. Making up the detailed lists of all those people who had been asked, twice, to contribute, with the dates on which each paid, and of refusers, meant tedious time and effort for Thynne. He also kept copies of letters from the JPs about their work, for example one of 1568 about purveyance when the JPs had a special meeting during the assizes: after long debate, they settled on limits for wheat for the queen's household, which was all they could persuade their poor neighbours to accept. Although his son, also John, was far less hardworking in the county administration, the correspondence of these gentlemen with other JPs demonstrates much effort in governing Wiltshire.[19]

Sir James Marvin, who had a division of the county named after him by the quarter sessions, was another hardworking justice: from 1576 till just before he died in 1611 he attended nearly every quarter sessions meeting – 35 years of effort. And between those sessions he usually dealt with at least two local problems; often six or more, and before the Michaelmas sessions in 1606 he sent in 31 recognizances, which meant he had interviewed many people. He insisted that he made decisions for the good of the inhabitants, when justifying his choice of men for military service. He made up the book of musters, as he asserted, by his own effort, noting that other justices had done so too, and emphasised that he attended quarter sessions out of duty. Sir Henry Knyvett also exercised county authority continually, especially during the Armada scare of 1588, and considered the sessions so important that he arranged his travel accordingly: in September 1590 he wrote of what he planned, 'some time after our next quarter session'.[20] Sir William Eyre contributed three decades of hard work from 1586, as did Sir Henry Poole from 1590. Many others, Sir William Brouncker, and the Penruddocks among the Elizabethan appointments, John Hungerford, John Dauntsey and Henry Martyn through James's reign, also laboured for the county.

The Surrey JP Bostock Fuller kept a diary which shows how continuous the administering of a county could be. Fuller worked at his own house or nearby, noting his settling of disputes, and the suspects he interviewed, making recognizances for their appearance at sessions, as well as attending the sessions, and petty sessions. In April 1608 he noted that in riding along he and another JP had arrested four rogues who had stolen ducks; he saw them whipped, and made out their passports for travel to Devon and Somerset. The next month he dealt with a man suspected of stealing James Knolden's lambs: the suspect confessed and was gaoled. Fuller copied down the entire recognizance he had made, and noted how the prosecution was to be organised, with Knolden to put in a bill of indictment and to give evidence. These local problems could linger on and increase the JP's work. Fuller notes that on 26 May 1608 a Mister Day of Bletchingley complained of an assault on his maidservant by Richard Plant, so Fuller sent a warrant for Plant. It was three days before Plant came, and he then complained of an assault that day on him by a third man. On 30 May, at the house of another JP, the three trouble-makers appeared, and all three confessed to the two justices, who ordered that they pay five shillings each to the poor, and Plant also a small fine. It was a pretty minor matter, typical of the kind that JPs saw all the time, but it had taken time and effort on three separate occasions, including a journey. In that May, Fuller travelled somewhere or took action as a JP on at least twelve days, on some of them more than one task needed attention. The chief impression from his diary is of continuous careful work, and close attention to the people with whom he dealt.[21]

The Dorset JP Sir Francis Ashley kept a casebook from 1614 to 1635, noting people bound over and the amounts of sureties, and he included some detailed examinations of local men and women. In July 1615 he noted 19 separate issues on which he acted: he dealt with quarrels, and with men and women whom he ordered not to keep alehouses without licence; he took evidence about thefts of sheep and of a little box containing money. Ashley noted that he committed Gilbert Reason to the gaol for two days, for impudence to the chief bailiff, and to Ashley himself: 'for daring me often to lay him by the heels, with other foul language'.[22] Three vagrants were brought to him 'by strength' after resisting lesser officers. He questioned them about their way of life, decided that their answers were unsatisfactory and therefore sent them to the house of correction. Over the years he copied a great many statements and actions into his casebook, giving a clear picture of a JP's busy activity even out of sessions. Some JPs employed a clerk to help: they certainly needed assistance. At least 12 Norfolk JPs in our period had clerks, and 22 in Caroline Somerset. The clerk could write out statements as the JP interviewed people, and attend quarter sessions even if his master was absent, to deliver documents to the clerk of the peace, and report back.

The justices worked at home and rode about their counties, they interviewed many people who came to them with disputes, complaints of thefts and assaults, and other problems. They spent much time on efforts to reconcile quarrels among the poor, and the rich too. Some disputes which arose within families went to the JPs for arbitration. Every file for the Essex quarter sessions contains a great many recognizances and other items, each one representing such work by one or two justices; so do the Wiltshire ones. A recognizance required the person to swear (a) to keep the peace toward specified persons, or (b) to be of good behaviour and not cause disorder, and usually to appear at the next quarter sessions (or assizes for serious crimes). Both types were on pain of a financial penalty for disobedience, set by the JP. Two people acting as sureties also had to promise to pay if the principal person 'bound over' failed to do as ordered. Often the documents bear later note by the clerk that the principal appeared, as was then free.[23] The roll prepared for the Michaelmas sessions of 1606 in Wiltshire contained 111 recognizances, each signed by one, two or occasionally three justices; in some rolls there are even more. Every sessions dealt with quarrels, alehouses, highways and bridges, clearing trees and ditches, treasurers for the poor and decisions about who should receive help, and purveyance – as well as theft and other petty crime.

Sometimes the quarter sessions deputed JPs to go off and make special arrangements or inspections: in July 1628 in response to a petition for help in repairing bridges in Lacock, Wiltshire, four JPs were ordered to go and view them; by early September they produced their detailed recommendations of the sums needed for each bridge. Charles I's 1631 Book of Orders tried to reform the whole organisation of local government by much stricter control of the JPs, and demanded reports to the Privy Council centre. The policy sought to command a co-ordinated response to recent problems in the cloth trade and manufacture, and bad harvests which brought the threat of famine: food thefts had risen far above normal levels. The Book required tighter supervision of the poor law with relief for the needy, masters were to be compelled to take apprentices, vagrants to be punished rigorously, and grain markets regulated. The repairs of highways and bridges, the closing of alehouses, and the provision of houses of correction were all to be more strictly managed. More pressing still were the provisions for organising the justices' own work. Each county had to formalise their divisional meetings once a month to enforce the Book of Orders: this made the petty sessions a more frequent, mandatory and permanent task – and since justices had to report not just to quarter sessions but also to the Privy Council, it also attempted to make them accountable and enforce national policies uniformly.

Local responses varied, as might be expected, with some areas sending in detailed reports of what they had achieved in their regular meetings, with attention to poverty and other problems. Compliance depended on JPs, but also on constables, overseers of the poor, and other lesser officials having time and enthusiasm to attend to the issues – but clearly many did try at first.[24] Later in the 1630s, however, constables met increasing resistance from their neighbours when the king's policies demanded levies such as Ship Money, and the recruitment and equipping of soldiers to fight the Scots. Then, if not before, the Book of Orders failed. Before that, and even before the Book of Orders, most JPs did what they saw as their duty, and many constables followed.

Occasionally among the formal recognizances, examinations, certificates and so on there is a glimpse of how they did that duty and the reasons for an action. Arthur Herris wrote a letter to the deputy clerk of peace for Essex in February 1590, which shows how a JP could take account of the circumstances of the people with whom he dealt.[25] The letter concerned a plot for Rowland Griffiths to kill a man, allegedly hatched by the intended victim's wife with another man, Chandler. Herris explained that he had already given an order for her to appear at quarter sessions, but she could not because she was then about to give birth, and she remained too weak to attend the subsequent sessions; while Chandler had defaulted. Griffiths was still in gaol, and having remained there all winter was very weak. Herris recommended that he be freed immediately, since the plot was never carried out, and Griffiths was the only one who had been punished.

Another example from Essex occurred in July 1617, showing the JPs taking account of practicalities. They decided that a seaman who had been bound to the peace and to appear in court should after all have his recognizance discharged, because he continually went on voyages, departing for the next as soon as he returned – a simpler solution than continuously chasing him would have been.

Some gentlemen appealed to reality, others employed the rhetoric of responsibility when they disagreed about the correct action to take. For Sir John Newdigate, the JP was the 'champion of justice, the patron of peace, the father of thy country and as it were as other God on earth'. One example of a JP's stern view of what was right occurred in 1577, when Lord Morley had sought to avoid the usual investigation for one of his tenants who had made a girl pregnant. Morley intended that the couple would not be punished, and a private financial settlement would meet the costs of mother and baby. But the Hertfordshire JP Thomas Leventhorpe believed that this evasion was wrong: the financial arrangement must be public 'as the statute doth appoint', and the pair whipped as they were supposed to be. Morley was horrified by this 'cruelty', but Leventhorpe insisted that 'the law of the prince and God's law upon which the prince's law is grounded' must be obeyed. Morley's reaction showed more compassion, and he reviled the sanctimonious magistrate with his array of punishments – whippings, mutilations – employed against the poor, who were, Morley claimed, 'often times . . . more honest a great deal than the justices' who terrorised them.[26]

Morley may have favoured leniency, but other JPs did believe that terrorising miscreants was necessary, and could improve their behaviour. For the Hilary sessions 1617, the Wiltshire JP John Hungerford sent the clerk of the peace some recognizances with a letter which showed how well he knew the people involved, and what he thought should be done. Various witness statements described how a wedding party on the way to Richard Thomas and Frances Synott's marriage saw on the church gateposts a buck's horn and a chalk drawing of 'a woman's privities': rude symbols of cuckoldry. They also described how Richard Truman, son of the blacksmith, made two horns with his fingers towards the groom and others near the gateposts, crying 'look ye, look ye, look ye'; he was also seen with a buck's horn, and allegedly indulged in lascivious boasts and gestures towards a maidservant the same morning while he was chopping wood.

Hungerford's letter discussed what might be done about Truman, who was under 18, but had been accused by witnesses on oath of the 'foul matters' which he completely denied. The justice thought it probable that the victims of Truman's insult would not appear at the next sessions to testify because of the distance involved. But he considered Truman a problem adolescent, who was 'otherwise lewdly given, and works a fear and terror in young fellows in our parts': he must have been big and rowdy for his age. Hungerford recommended that if the court should find him guilty, Truman was too poor to pay any fine, and if found guilty should be committed [to either gaol or house of correction] 'which I hope will work a reformation in him'.[27] No doubt many other JPs had a close knowledge similar to Hungerford's of their 'constituency', but only rarely do we have such clear glimpses of how they used their authority over them. Clearly Hungerford spent much time on his duty as a JP attending three of the four annual sessions every year for over two decades from 1602, and nearly always contributing items for attention. At Michaelmas 1605 he sent in 22 items to the sessions, some prepared by his clerk, but he signed them all, and wrote some himself.

The Privy Council provided overall instructions for county commissions of the peace, and sought to supervise some of their work, but could do so only spasmodically and on specific issues of concern. Nobles (especially lords lieutenant) – some of them Councillors, some not – could take an interest in such work and give directions to JPs. But more widely it was the JPs who took active responsibility for local decisions in ruling the country; they displayed their concerted power formally when they assembled at quarter sessions and assizes. Those who also served as subsidy or sewer commissioners, sheriffs, or deputy lieutenants did even more. Although, as we have seen, justices did much face-to-face work in administration and conciliation, they in turn depended on the parish officers to carry out many orders, serve warrants, escort suspects, collect taxes and so on. That is why the justices needed to approve the selection of high constables, and sometimes of parish constables too, as in Middlesex and Norfolk and probably elsewhere. These constables had a difficult role in carrying out the orders of the justices in both administration and law, while not angering their neighbours too much in pressing for obedience. In the end, compliance depended as much on consent as coercion, and early modern England provided powerful incentives for obedience.

7
Obedience

How were the English persuaded to obey the requirements of the state, the law, and their community values? Without regular policing or a standing army, the country could have been anarchic. But it was not. The early modern state used many means to encourage obedience and establish duties. First, people obeyed, because they were told they must. The campaign started early in life, with the children. Every child had to learn the Church's catechism off by heart. All those who were old enough were to be taught and examined by the minister in the church on Sundays; if they did not learn they were excluded from communion, and so from full parish participation – a strong sanction at a time of almost universal church attendance. The basic and simplest catechism was that of the new Book of Common Prayer prescribed for use in every parish church from 1559 onwards. Many longer and more complex catechisms were published in succeeding decades, and some ministers made the children learn them. The Prayer Book catechism began with duty to God, the first four of the Ten Commandments. God also enjoined duty to others, in the last six Commandments, to neighbours and parents. In learning the Prayer Book catechism, children had to say they should bear nobody malice and should refrain from stealing, and slander, lying and coveting other men's goods and wives.

In its treatment of the fifth Commandment, the exhortation to honour father and mother, the catechism extended the demand for obedience far beyond that due to parents. A child had to learn: 'to honour and obey the King, and all that are put in authority under him; to submit myself to all my governors, teachers, spiritual pastors and masters; to order myself lowly and reverently to all my betters'. So from early on, children were taught that God demanded that they obey all those in authority: parents, and also the monarch, schoolteachers, employers, clergymen, and magistrates.

Alexander Nowell prepared a more detailed catechism in Latin in the early 1560s for grammar schools, and published an English translation in 1570 for wider use. It was much longer and more difficult; yet even so, some bishops ordered young children to learn it. The bishops of the large diocese of Lincoln, and the populous diocese of London, required it. Nowell followed Luther and Calvin on obedience to all those in authority. As well as magistrates, ministers of the church and schoolmasters, there was a duty to obey 'all they that have any ornament, either of reverent age, or of wit, wisdom, or learning, worship, or wealthy state, or otherwise be our superiors'. All these have their power and authority, 'because by these it has pleased God to rule and govern the world'. So older, or cleverer, or more educated, or richer persons should be obeyed, as well as officials. The mind of man is loth to be 'under other's commandment' but it owed duty and obedience towards magistrates as to parents. 'They are given us of God, both for our own and public benefit'. Everybody owed someone obedience, and most of the people owed obedience to a great many around them who could be considered their superiors. Beside exhortation, there was threat: people who disobey parents or magistrates, misuse, or kill them, would suffer a vile life, or untimely death. God's displeasure would mean that not only in life, but in the world to come, such people shall 'for ever suffer the everlasting punishment of their ungodliness'. Children received powerful incentives to obey.[1]

William Perkins, in his best-selling catechism, *The Foundation of Christian Religion Gathered into Six Principles*, elaborated on the duty of obedience to just about everybody, and stressed it even more fiercely as deriving from God. Honour was due to superiors; 'in the Magistrate there is a certain image of the power and glory of God'. Images of God also applied to old men, and in a learned man is 'the likeness of the knowledge and wisdom of God'. So we must obey parents, and magistrates, ministers, our elders and 'those that excel us in any gifts whatsoever'![2] Perkins notes the promise in the fifth commandment of long life for the godly as a reward for their dutifulness. But if the Lord gave even obedient children a short life, all was still well, because he would reward them with eternal life in heaven. For Perkins, all were admonished to obedience because every higher power was the ordinance of God. Even if such higher powers acted cruelly, diligence and faithfulness to superiors was required; there could be no excuse on that account. But alongside strong support for hierarchy and the authority of the state, for preserving the public peace and order, Nowell, Perkins, and other catechists did also stress the reciprocal duties and obligations of superiors towards inferiors: they must govern wisely. Perkins wrote that superiors should conduct themselves as brothers, shine before their inferiors as examples of blameless life, display gravity and dignity, and provide everything that was good for their inferiors. So those who obeyed could at least expect good treatment from all above them. These catechisms pressed into the minds of children a very strong lesson of obedience.

Catechising in childhood was reinforced by Homilies and prayers. The Homilies printed in 1547 to be read in all churches, and ordered by Elizabeth to be used wherever the minister was not a licensed preacher, included *An Exhortation Concerning Good Order and Obedience to Rulers and Magistrates.* God had provided order, and it was necessary for the realm as for every household to accept it. Listeners were told that the powers of kings were directly ordained by God, who would ordain everlasting damnation for any who opposed them. 'Let no man think that he can escape unpunished that committeth treason, conspiracy, or rebellion . . . though he commit the same never so secretly'.[3] Magistrates likewise exercise God's will in judging and punishing on earth, so it was not lawful for inferiors and subjects ever to resist superior powers. Christ and the apostles are invoked as examples for patiently bearing injury from wicked men in authority without rebelling. Servants must be obedient to their masters whether good or evil. To resist authority was to resist God.

The 1570 Homily against disobedience and rebellion was long and much more vivid: it stressed obedience as the principal virtue of all virtues. Lucifer's rebellion against God, which led to his banishment to hell, was a warning against rebellion, which brings in 'all mischiefs and miseries'. God ordained obedience to kings and queens, and also to the heads of families, and to other governors and rulers. It was not for subjects to judge whether their monarchs or governors were evil, for that would lead haughty spirits to rebellion. The Homily included a prayer to God to defend Elizabeth, and one of thanks for the suppression of the 1569 rebellion. The third part dwelt on the dread punishments of God's wrath which awaited rebels, with terrifying scriptural examples, while good and obedient subjects would have peace, and the expectation of everlasting heaven.[4] Here were strong incentives to obey authority.

Regular prayers for the safety of monarchs gave a continual reminder to people of their duty, and how must they give thanks to God for the preservation of the royal life. The form of prayer to be used on the anniversary of Elizabeth's accession day stressed that the people had lived in safety under her rule, and hoped 'that we may in word, deed, and heart, show ourselves thankful and obedient'. Prayers such as that after rebellions and plots in 1569, in 1585 and during the dangerous times of the Spanish war also emphasised God's likely vengeance against enemies of the queen, with vivid similes referring to the 'jaws of cruel tigers' and the barbarous traitors who opposed her.[5]

Catechisms, Homilies and prayers provided early and continuing lessons in obedience. In addition, reciprocal obligations and duties interacted to encourage compliance. Partly it was self-imposed: duty to the community meant a surprisingly widespread participation in governing and the maintenance of order, despite the hierarchical emphasis of English society. Because enforcement of order was mostly done locally, there were people on the ground everywhere to monitor what was happening, and, crucially, with the power to take action if anything was amiss: little brother was watching you! Posts of various kinds carried responsibilities to make people comply, or see them punished if they would not. And that responsibility spread among a significant proportion of the settled male inhabitants, particularly as most communities were very small. Office in the parish as churchwarden, sidesman, or overseer of the poor; on petty or grand juries for quarter sessions or assizes; in small local manor or leet courts; as watchman or parish constable; and in town corporations, involved a huge number of men in administration and legal sanction. These officers were not imposed from above; most were chosen locally by their own neighbours.

Nearly all of those positions were temporary, so the share of power rotated among those eligible; plenty of people had a turn, but not a very long one. However, only men took part, except for the occasional female churchwarden before the Reformation. The churchwardens, usually two for each parish, held office for a year. They were selected according to the customs of the parish: in some parishes the office rotated around specific houses or hamlets; in many the inhabitants or householders made the choice; and in some the minister together with the parishioners decided. So the process of considering who was worthy was continuous. Churchwardens, assisted by sidesmen, had to be trusted as custodians of the goods of the church, which the parishioners themselves had paid for, and wanted kept in good condition. The churchwardens acted as spokesmen for the parish at visitations, and supervisors of the morals of the villagers; they presented to the church courts any transgressors who offended locals. As provision for helping the poor developed, the overseers of the poor had increasing responsibilities for handling money to help deserving cases. That money was provided reluctantly by the parish, and the overseer had to deploy it carefully, or suffer the anger of his neighbours.

Local responsibility circulated among many of the settled residents, even quite humble ones. Every person bound over by magistrates to appear at quarter sessions, or to keep the peace, or other conditions, had named two friends or neighbours to see the requirement of the recognizance performed, by standing as sureties and entering bonds, (as described in Chapter 6). In populous counties, such as Wiltshire or Essex, the numbers of people who thus appear in quarter sessions records, as guarantors not misdoers, are enormous: for instance, just one sessions in 1616 at Devizes, Wiltshire, listed nearly 300 names of sureties, for some 150 persons ordered to fulfil requirements, most of them for *bono gestu* [good behaviour]. There were four sessions a year, in nearly every county. Even if not every sessions counted on such a large number of sureties, the huge total of sureties involved every year made a substantial contribution to making their friends or relatives do as they had been ordered by the JPs, since otherwise their bonds were forfeit. The amounts sureties had to promise were often set high enough to mean the guarantors would suffer serious loss if conditions were not met; £10 for the principal and £5 for sureties was common, some were less, many were higher. For the quarrel between a butcher's wife and an innkeeper's wife at Calne, Wiltshire, in 1608, the sureties were for £20 pounds each. Relatives, often fathers, frequently stood surety, confirming the impression that much reported trouble involved young people. Tradesmen called on men in the same or other local trades, yeomen and husbandmen usually on other farmers. Even if some were angry that their friends were being pushed about, these sureties had been co-opted into keeping order.

General communal participation was a vital element in deciding which matters should be brought to a court for action, and in taking them forward. The possible matters included decayed highways and bridges, poor people building cottages on common ground, or without apparent means of support, and (especially) crimes. Informal processes were at least as important as the activity of any official. In cases of theft, the most common misdeed, the victim was usually responsible for investigating and finding a suspect, and depended on the help of relatives and neighbours. They could call on the constable, or headborough in some counties, who could assist the victim, neighbours, and any witnesses to search for the culprit.[6] But the constable was only a temporary part-time official and the involvement of interested parties usually lay behind an accusation and indictment: it was a self-help system of justice. The accusers had to go to a JP, along with the suspect, for interrogation, and had to give recognizances to appear, if the matter was to go to court. The victim and neighbours played the dominant role in the initial stages, and then witnesses had to help by turning up to give evidence at court. Although it was the propertied private persons who participated most often in these legal processes, they represented the wider community and its perceptions of morality. Presumably most of their neighbours agreed that they were helping to redress wrongs and enforce proper order.

Duty to the community and local responsibility for order could include service on a grand or petty jury, to present local problems to quarter sessions or assizes, and to decide whether alleged criminals should be indicted. Service on the grand juries for quarter sessions and assizes spread among quite a large circle of freeholders and each time, more were summoned than were actually chosen, giving the surplus, too, a sense of importance. (The landless poor were not called, however.)

Regions varied in their practice. In seventeenth century Cheshire, lesser landed citizens shared in enforcement through their membership of grand juries. In East Sussex, however, the jurors tended to be the more propertied men of the shire. The jurors called in Elizabethan Essex came from a wide spectrum of backgrounds. Just under a thousand men were called to be considered for jury panels in Cheshire between 1625 and 1659: 609 of them were chosen and sworn to at least one jury during that time.[7] From 1625 to 1642, sheriffs called between 24 and 40 freeholders for each quarter sessions, with 13 to 17 sworn in, and they called between 40 and 60 jurors for each assizes. The total number would have been higher, except that the majority served more than once, some many times: Philip Antrobus was the star grand jury man in Cheshire, serving an astonishing 49 times between

1625 and 1657; he was one of 28 who served more than 21 times. Of the 609 jurors, 165 were sworn only once, and nearly a hundred twice, so patterns of repeat service varied. No two panels involved precisely the same group of men and the presence of men who had previously taken part in deciding on presentments and indictments of misdeeds helped newcomers learn their duties and discharge their responsibilities in their county. Sir Richard Grosvenor in a charge to the Cheshire grand jury men stressed the importance of the position, and their duties to the community: 'You (Gentlemen) are the persons who are at this time trusted (as the eyes of your Country) to spy out and bring such to their deserved punishment'.[8] The eyes of the county were operating similarly all over England.

Cynthia Herrup's samples of East Sussex quarter sessions courts between 1594 and 1640, and some assizes, confirm John Morrill's Cheshire findings, although with certain differences.[9] In East Sussex, more than a hundred men served on a grand jury in any one year and few served repeatedly, so the total involved was greater. The Sussex assize grand jurors were men of gentry status, close to those who were JPs, while those for quarter sessions came from the modest yeomanry. By contrast, a Devon commentator in 1625 suggested that in that county most quarter sessions grand jurors were from below the richest yeomen. Despite these variations in the exact social position of men who served, responsibility for helping to maintain order relied in great part on local farmers or men of credit in the cloth or other trades. In their duty to the community, they briefly took on a legal mantle, when they presented violations or decided whether or not indictments should go forward. Afterwards, they reverted to their daily work, but perhaps with additional respect because they had been chosen as worthy to represent their community. For petty (or trial) jurors, large numbers of lesser landholders were empanelled for consideration – in East Sussex perhaps 400 annually. It was a less popular service than that of the grand jury, because jurors might be left waiting without ever being called, and the responsibilities were onerous without conferring as much status as grand jury service. Nevertheless, petty juries did mean yet more people taking part in enforcement of law and local administration.

Citizens assisted in social control even more locally in the lesser or 'leet' courts, in villages and small market towns. They aimed to stop trouble before it began. These courts took note of actions threatening good order and harmony among the inhabitants. The leet court or town jury made presentments, and also decided punishments, for matters of social misbehaviour or inconvenience which were in most cases not against the law, but against community expectations and might lead to conflict. These local courts presented 'scolds', both male and female, because scolding caused angry arguments and disrupted social relations. (Churchwardens presented scolds to ecclesiastical courts, too, as people 'out of charity' with their neighbours.) And even where they lacked formal authority they sought to control proprietors of disorderly alehouses and acted against sexual irregularity between unmarried people. Contrary to the view of historians who have argued for increasing prosecution of women due to a gender crisis – to men's fear of female sexuality – analysis of 265 smaller courts shows that a man and woman were usually named together for such conduct, and more so in the later sixteenth century than earlier.[10] These local courts also expressed worries about the divisive effects of poverty on their neighbours. Poor people who took wood from hedges for fuel, as well as kind inhabitants who took in destitute people or vagrant outsiders, were presented. Prosecution punished those presented, and aimed to discourage the rest from deviating. The bye-laws courts passed show the sorts of behaviour villagers and townsmen wished to prevent. The Manchester jurors in 1588 ordered that no single woman should keep house or room alone without a master; in 1589 they stated outright that single women 'at their own hands' following trades like bread baking were an economic threat, and also misbehaved with young men 'to the great dishonour of God and evil example to others', and should be made to serve under a master.[11]

Marjorie McIntosh in her analysis of these local courts found that not all of them reported these misbehaviours continuously. Even in the hard and worrying years of the 1580s and 1590s, 41 per cent of her sample reported none of them. Her study emphasises not how often people actually did scold, consort with people to whom they were not married, play unruly games in alehouses, or take wood from hedges – which we cannot know, but the significant occasions when neighbours decided to try to stop them. The local jury made its choice whether or not to report transgressors. They did so when stability was threatened, so there were regional variations as well as variations over time. In the 1580s and 1590s, when economic difficulties brought fears of misconduct by the poor and feckless, more leet courts took disciplinary action than had done in the 1520s and 1530s. This was in addition to the increasing activity of JPs, and church courts. Communities did actually want more control to make their neighbours obedient, and local juries helped to bring it about.

In London too, despite its great size, duty to the community involved many citizens. The court of aldermen was dominated by the city's elite merchants, but they did not operate alone. Joining in the work in the parishes, wards, and companies meant that a far wider range, and some of the lesser levels of society, helped to control the city. In any one year, about one in ten of London's householders held some kind of office in local government: although their families, servants, apprentices, and others too poor to be householders did not take part, it was a remarkably high proportion. London had a range of overlapping social and administrative connections, with artisans playing an important part in the middle ranks of the government of the livery companies. Even such a high level of participation still could not ensure total harmony, especially in so complex an environment with so many apprentices, crowds, and opportunities for disobedience. The Elizabethan aldermen could retain their authority without challenge, because they sufficiently fulfilled the expectations of their citizens and their duty to rule wisely. The city governors recognised that they sometimes needed to submit to demands for policy changes. They accepted prevailing ideals of responsible magistracy: they had to, because they could not secure compliance by coercion, any more than could the rural elites.[12]

The day-to-day local control in villages depended on the parish or petty constables, two in office at a time in every parish. They were part of the official surveillance system and dealt with disorder, but they also were part of their community and owed strong allegiance to it. They represented co-operation more than coercion. The JPs retained overall supervision of local administration and law-keeping; the parish constable was the man on the spot to take appropriate action – or not, if he so chose. The constable's vital role in dealing with administrative tasks, as well as preventing or dealing with trouble, goes far to explain the remarkable orderliness of English communities. It was only when government pressed too hard on the constables, for tax collecting or military provision, that their refusal demonstrated how far the state depended on them. Their communities also depended on them, continually. The office was rotating and unpaid, and it was very much a neighbourhood one, for which many men were eligible. The very long lists of candidates' names in the Middlesex, Wiltshire and other surviving records underline how wide the net could be. In the Middlesex administrative hundred of Osulstone, which included 58 parishes of the capital, High Holborn to Finchley, Clerkenwell to Ealing, 101 names were considered for new constables in September 1613: 34 were sworn, replacing men whose terms had finished. Lengthy lists in rural Wiltshire and Essex meant that an even larger proportion of each parish might take a turn as constable, since the parishes were less populated. No-one was constable for long – it was a burden briefly held, so each one was a real amateur at the job; their limited term of office may have helped to secure acceptance of their authority. The length of service for a constable varied; it was most commonly one or two years' service, although it was for longer in some counties. Although length of service was usually quite short, the same men could be chosen again later and bring their experience to the task. In Pattingham, Staffordshire between 1582 and 1640, 81 men were constables at some time: 18 of them served twice, six of them took three turns, one did it four times, and 56 of the 81 served only once. In the smaller village of Branston, Leicestershire, half of the 20 men who were constables at some time between 1611 and 1643 did it twice or more.[13] But in most places, it was rare for men to serve consecutive terms. In general, few seem to have served more than two or three terms altogether over a lifetime. There were roughly 9,000 parishes in England, making around 18,000 constables in office at any one time. By, say, two years later, a different 18,000 men were constables. So over any decade, somewhere between 80,000 and 100,000 men took on this responsibility. It was shared very widely.

A key point in the effectiveness of parish constables was their cohesion with their village or parish community. For the constables for each one were ordinary members of it, set apart only temporarily, and continuing their daily work at farm, bakery, last or loom. In some places eligibility rotated between specific houses; in most, local people selected their constables, who might be confirmed and sworn into office by leet court or quarter sessions. Selection was often made by the parish vestry, as in Essex, Norfolk, and London; or by the jury of the court leet; or simply by the inhabitants, as at Waltham, Leicestershire. So a constable belonged to his local community and he was also accountable to it. For some tasks, he could reclaim his expenses from the parish: constables' accounts show claims for travelling between villages or to the county town about assessing and returning taxes, or for escorting suspects to a gaol, or to the assizes or quarter sessions.

The neighbours had to pay the constable's costs, so they wanted the job done well, and themselves protected. Constables were not nobodies. In rural England it was chiefly the middling sort who served, yeomen and richer husbandmen, with some minor gentlemen and artisans. Some were quite substantial landholders from established families, with reasonable landholdings, men of credit and estimation. Their social solidity gave them respect from the villagers, without setting them too far above the rest. In towns the choice of men established in trade did the same. The illiteracy of some caused difficulties, since documents had to be read and written. Then community assistance meant that others, such as a clergyman, or a scrivenor, or a neighbour who could read, helped with written tasks. Illiterate constables did give scope for unscrupulous people to trick them, for instance into signing passports, which were a requirement for ordinary people to travel about England. As literacy increased this problem reduced.

As William Lambarde's handbook described, the constable's concern was to keep the peace. His tasks were to ensure that nothing was done to threaten breach of the peace, to pacify anyone he found actually breaking it, and to punish anyone who had broken it. A solemn charge to a new constable emphasised his serious duties: 'ye shall well and truly occupy . . . the office . . . and see the Queen's peace kept to the uttermost of your power'. Further he was exhorted not to be swayed by affection, and do all the duties well and truly 'as far as wit, power and cunning will extend unto'.[14] This attempt to turn ordinary men into earnest public officers gave them a consciousness of their role that could impress their neighbours into obedience. Of course, there were constables who failed to fulfil the thankless duties, or were discouraged when they met with bad temper and resistance – but many tried to do their duty, and frequently they succeeded.

The possibility of instantaneous public shaming (and personal discomfort) imposed by the constable helped people to opt for obedience. Constables could take immediate action, and had authority to punish minor offences on the spot: they put offenders in the stocks, to face the anger and ridicule of their neighbours, for an hour or a day. They could arrest suspects and demand assistance from others to do it, or raise the hue and cry after miscreants on the run. They could not stop all misdeeds, but constables could rapidly offer hope to victims of theft, by searching for missing items, and apprehending a presumed thief. They could be extraordinarily diligent: the constables and watchmen of Barling, Essex, caught a thief at 3a.m. with a stolen pig in his sack. Villagers and town-dwellers might be spared from theft or from the financial support of poor newcomers when constables rounded up and punished vagabonds. There were other, more mundane, duties which endeared the constables less to their neighbours: helping to assess and collect taxes of various kinds, delivering warrants and other legal documents, escorting evil-doers to JP or gaol, checking unlicensed alesellers, inspecting weights, organising gathering and transport of food for the royal table, and assisting with recruitment. These were unpopular but essential tasks, and at least the baton would soon be passed to another neighbour. Those who had already carried it co-operated because they remembered how much they had needed support during their term at the task.

The constables' presentments to the quarter sessions, or to petty or monthly sessions, listed the details of everything that was amiss – or were supposed to do that.[15] In Wiltshire, Norfolk and elsewhere they had lists of questions to answer. Sometimes they wrote out answers in detail, with the names of people who had built cottages without permission, or had blocked or damaged highways. An extreme example of damage which troubled others was the case of Roger Bridge of Aldham, Essex, who had made a pit in the highway, in which Benjamin Brice was drowned in January 1621; the pit was still not filled in April and was reported to the Easter quarter sessions as a great danger. Constables' presentments continually listed people who had not helped in repairs to highways or bridges: in Essex, Pissingford bridge remained decayed, in spite of repeated presentments in the early 1570s about who should mend it. Constables listed alehouse problems, lax provision for the poor, vagrants, and people absent from church. In Gissing, Norfolk, in 1607, constables reported on most of these issues, plus adherence to the statute of labourers, regulation of bread and ale, and drunkenness. Unlawful games, especially during the time of the church service and sometimes in the churchyard itself, proved more difficult for the constables to prevent, and appear on many lists. And as local or central government requirements altered, so the questions and answers varied.

Most of the people in a village or town, the conformers, would want offenders made to toe the line, and thus the constable's presentment acted as a communal complaint, not just that of an individual nark. Petitions to magistrates, complaining that an inhabitant misbehaved, sometimes carried the signatures (or marks) of villagers, as well as the constable's endorsement, reinforcing the fact that presentments reflected community opinion. In 1561, the two constables of Great Maplestead parish in Essex and two named parishioners made the presentment. On the previous Christmas Eve, 'we the said constables with divers others of the parish willing to see things well ordered in our said parish', having heard of 'matters much needful to be amended', searched suspect houses. The problem was a couple who may not have been really married, 'and how they live we cannot tell'.[16] The locals feared the couple might steal or become a burden, so they acted alongside the constables.

What should we make of the large number of presentments reporting all well, nothing amiss? Was everyone good, or were constables slack? Once, historians assumed that the constables were lazy, inefficient Dogberrys. More recently, especially with the opening up of local archives in county record offices, the evidence of a great deal of hard work by constables suggests that perhaps they told the truth – or rather, that nothing had happened that the community could not handle and wanted reported. Perhaps much of the time the people really were going to church, mending roads when required, going to the alehouse to drink and talk and not to brawl drunkenly. Or if they were not, nobody minded much. In 1571 a constable of High Ongar, Essex, said that all was well in his area because the leet and court met twice yearly, and problems 'are always reformed and brought into good order': a model community, obviously, or so it wished to be thought.[17] But the fact that they wanted to be thought capable of keeping order themselves, successfully, is as significant as if it were true.

Occasionally there are glimpses of constables' own view of their duty. Both high and petty constables accepted hard work as a duty and gave much effort. In 1572 Thomas Emery wrote a petition to the Essex JPs, pointing out that he had been one of the chief constables of the Chelmsford hundred for over ten years. He emphasised that it had been a long service, in which not only had he given 'great travail and pains' to carry out the duties, but had suffered great costs, and hindrance. Having done so much, now he requested to be discharged from the office. His claim was accepted; another man was appointed immediately to replace Emery. In the summer of 1617, Anthony Holloway and Richard Reason, constables of Amesbury, Wiltshire, walked all over the town at midnight to search all the inns and alehouses, to see what order was kept. But they would still have to attend their own work in the daytime.

The holders of public office gained obedience and co-operation because they were generally hard-working and seen to be useful. JPs made many orders to impose controls, but they also assisted people to settle problems and quarrels, either communal or personal. People expected JPs to fulfil that duty and provide assistance. On 6 July 1564 the inhabitants of Gyngrave, Essex, wrote to tell the JPs that John Patrick, yeoman, was a very troublesome person: he railed against the honest people of the parish, calling them thieves and villains, and sought to create strife and divisions with 'false lies and devices of his busy brain'.[18] So they requested a warrant of good behaviour for Patrick – and hoped that would bring him into line. It was not just Patrick's tongue which annoyed his neighbours. On 20 August he was indicted for obstructing a lane where inhabitants drove their cattle, and fined for it. Like many local conflicts, a whole range of issues mingled – but the community and the JPs were trying to solve them. In an unusually long report in 1620, the parishioners of Winterbourne, Wiltshire, sought a discharge from paying for the bastard child of Richard Maynard; he had apparently refused to pay himself, so they appealed to two JPs. The JPs made an order for payment: Maynard was to go to gaol till he found sureties for his performance of the order; and presumably the parish got what it wanted.

JPs helped individuals as well as whole parishes, and clearly tried hard to secure settlement of disputes by negotiation. In July 1566 Kenelm Throckmorton, an Essex JP, issued two recognizances and sent them to the clerk of the peace to show to the rest of the justices at the sessions. But he said that he was only doing this as a last resort: he had sought conciliation, but eventually sent the recognizances because 'I cannot otherwise end the matters betwixt the parties'. In a separate letter to the sessions, Throckmorton discussed a conflict over a verbal lease, which had boiled over at ploughing time.[19] He informed the justices that he had tried the best he could to sort out the matter and not trouble the quarter sessions with it, but could not bring the disputants to agree, and was forced to seek further action.

Individuals with very specific difficulties often approached JPs, who tried to assist them. A Wiltshire bone-setter gave information to the JPs on 9 April 1615, about a troublesome woman. She apparently alleged he had broken her neck bone when she was brought to him for treatment. But the bone-setter vigorously defended his expertise; he needed the JPs to trust him, to be certain that his practice was not ruined. Also in 1615, Anthony Fry, of Brinkworth, decided that a maid servant should be moved from her current employer (for unspecified reasons) and when one justice refused to make the order, Fry went to another JP and succeeded in persuading him to do as Fry wished. The organist of the parish church of Warminster had been appointed at a wage of 20 nobles yearly, agreed by all or most of the inhabitants. But in 1616 some refused to pay. The JPs did their best to come to the organist's rescue, by agreeing to call in the non-payers and endeavouring to make them pay. Thomas Doggett had the patent for his maimed soldier's pension stolen in 1622, so the overseers of the poor could not pay him; he asked the Wiltshire JPs to order a new warrant, and they did so, even though it had originally been issued in 1601.[20] Sixteen inhabitants signed a petition to Wiltshire Michaelmas sessions in 1628, that Edith Curtis, a poor widow with four children, be allowed to keep the cottage on waste and the garden with which she maintained the family. Two JPs negotiated with Sir Thomas Thynne, who opposed her, and persuaded him to let widow Curtis stay. Many people asked for assistance when their cottages were destroyed by fire, usually in the thatched roof, and injured soldiers requested help in times of war: the JPs attended to some of the petitions rather than leaving them to overseers.

The JP's power to impose a recognizance to keep the peace worked to help beleaguered people – although of course it displeased those bound over, and could be used maliciously. Unfortunately there is nearly always a tantalising silence in the records over the circumstances giving rise to such bonds, but very many people, both women and men, used the JPs' bond for the peace as a solution to local conflicts. Every sessions roll is stuffed full of such recognizances. Women too could get this remedy. At Michaelmas sessions in Essex in 1571 Mercy, wife of Thomas Strachie, secured a recognizance against Nicholas Smythe, gentleman, to keep the peace towards her. On 6 February 1608, Joan Brook, a butcher's wife in Calne, Wiltshire, obtained a recognizance against the wife of a local innkeeper to keep the peace towards her, and appear at the next quarter sessions: this rapidly settled the quarrel, and Joan Brook had the warrant cancelled a month later, before the sessions even met. Jane Hungerford, widow, got a JP's order for a recognizance on 2 December 1614 for Henry Long, innkeeper of Little Dean, Wiltshire, to appear at the next quarter sessions and meantime to keep the peace towards her.

Intervention by the justices could defuse tempers and resolve quarrels, even within a family. Thomas Norton, gentleman, and Alice his wife, had a serious dispute with Alice's son by a previous husband. It was over possession of lands and tenements, and in January 1622, one side of the family intended to indict the other for forcible entry into the property, which could only have exacerbated the dispute. But the family was persuaded to go to the Wiltshire JPs for arbitration instead of a criminal procedure, and the JPs in full sessions made an order, recorded in the minutes, to settle the matter with the consent of all parties – so saving everyone from trouble and increased bitterness. In these examples, and the many thousands of others like them which must have occurred in counties whose archives are lost, the JPs had given help to people with problems. To troublemakers the JPs may have appeared harsh. But to all the victims they provided retribution. No doubt the gratitude of those who needed such bonds helped to make them obedient, co-operative citizens.

Obedience was also encouraged by the developing arrangements for public welfare, especially the poor relief overseen by the JPs and urban authorities, who in this role appeared as supportive, and not simply punitive, figures. Charity alone could not cope with the rising numbers of destitute or partially employed people, and official action was needed if the poor were to be kept from desperate action. Cardinal Wolsey inaugurated a century of increasingly careful social provision for controlling disease, vagrancy, food prices and grain supplies, and assistance to the 'deserving poor', with compulsory work for the supposedly unwilling. Wolsey's innovations reacted to crises, but formed the pattern for further efforts. His 1527 commission for grain searches and market provision was followed in later decades by controls on corn badgers, in order to ensure supplies where they were most needed. A 1536 statute prescribed the duties of 'overseers of poverty and correctors of idleness', two to be appointed for each parish, and they were to be fundamental to the system of assistance. Hospitals were founded, as were institutions for 'setting the able-bodied poor to work' and 'houses of correction' to improve the morals or obedience of the disorderly and difficult, including recalcitrant single mothers.

It was in relief provided to the poor that Tudor policy did most to alleviate the disastrous effects of unemployment, of ill health or war injury leading to inability to work, of harvest crises threatening famine, of destruction of cottages by fire, and less often, the plight of single mothers and their babies. Statutes of 1536, 1572 and later additions culminated in the great Poor Laws of 1598 and 1601. They set up a regulated system for rating inhabitants of each parish and collecting money, deciding who in the parish needed help, and paying it out. For example, widows who could earn a little but not enough in, say, lace-making, received a supplement. Blind or infirm men and women who could no longer work on the land might get help. And destitute inhabitants received something towards basic food. All those who might at some time fall into difficulties, which meant probably half or more of the population, could feel slightly more hopeful that they would be helped, if need be. The poor laws were not totally inclusive: outsiders, vagrants, and single mothers without support still suffered, for parishioners naturally did not like having to raise taxes, and would not do so for these 'undeserving poor'. Vagrants and outsiders could be whipped or branded, and sent back to the parish from which they came; single mothers made to divulge the father's name so he could pay maintenance, and after the Jacobean statute of 1610, publicly whipped on market day. Money for poor relief could be hard for poor parishes to find, but it did provide a net to soften the worst blows: very few starved to death in Tudor and early Stuart England. Without poor relief, many would have died – and they owed such help to the laws made by the gentry in parliament, and the administration of the JPs, the treasurers appointed in quarter sessions, and the parish overseers. The poor laws demonstrated community concern and promoted social cohesion: support was available for the deserving, those who did their duty.

The citizen's duty included an obligation to inform on neighbours or on persons observed doing wrong: alehouse loose talkers, for instance, or people seen stealing, or suspected of it through flaunting fine new clothes or expensive objects. Presumably, people often avoided the duty to inform, but some spoke up and legal action followed. In April 1587, three men informed against Edward Tabor, innkeeper, of Fryerning Essex, for seditious words against the queen and the church service used in England. Most prosecutions for sedition came about from onlookers giving information, but this was worse because Tabor was a constable at the time and his neighbours expected more of him. In Lewes, East Sussex, at the summer fair in 1614, Richard Plawe, a visiting stranger, suggested to a fisherman's wife that she should check for her purse. When she found it missing, Plawe rushed after a man who was hurriedly leaving the fair, and grabbed him. The thief returned the purse, was examined and eventually convicted, all because of Plawe's sense of duty. Boasting at a Lindfield alehouse of his prowess as a thief by Edward Tab did not impress two fellow-drinkers. They reported him, and he was indicted for larceny.[21]

What was the balance between co-operation and coercion in seeking to make an obedient society in early modern England? Coercion obviously had a part to play, as in all societies, and it could be harsh; it is also easier to prove, since major contraventions of law leave records of prosecution, and often, of punishment. Fear of punishment certainly helped secure obedience. Serious crimes brought execution: prisons held criminals only briefly before trial, or as a short-term punishment, and they did not exist in sufficient number or size to provide long-term custody. Total opposition to the crown – treason – led to executions, around 300 of them in the 1530s under Henry VIII's treason laws, enacted to bolster his religious changes and his remarriage to Anne Boleyn. For crimes such as murder, burglary or theft of items valued at over twelve pence, and sometimes for witchcraft, the penalty was public hanging. Men and women might hang for theft of a bag of wheat, or a petticoat. This level of punishment aimed to impress with the majesty of the law, and to terrify the public and make them obey. In a state without a professional police force or army, it would not have been possible to hang those convicted without the acquiescence of the crowd, who could easily have rescued the convicts. Large crowds turned up to watch executions, especially at Tyburn in London – and they did not interfere. They learnt their lesson in obedience. Lesser crimes (mainly petty theft) or refusal of central or local government requirements such as tax-paying, could bring fines, short spells in the county gaol, whipping, branding, or a spell in the stocks. Faced with severe penalties, the instinct for self-preservation helped people to obey. But execution was a draconian measure which could not be applied to vast numbers of transgressors; far better to prevent the people from straying.

Propaganda, participation, surveillance, welfare programmes and punishments provided strong incentives towards order and obedience – but they did not always work. Of course. there was crime and disorder, and historians have tended to follow early modern commentators in judging that England was exceptionally unruly. William Lambarde, a JP in Kent and author of the definitive handbook for justices, bewailed in 1582 what he believed was a great increase in disorder, coupled with failure to punish it: 'sin of all sorts swarmeth and . . . evildoers go on with all licence and impunity'.[22] An Italian visitor also considered that England was full of robbers and thieves, and feared that disorder was increasing as never before, and was worse than elsewhere. At the beginning of the seventeenth century, Sir Thomas Challoner declared that economic depression 'brought more to the gallows in one year than a great part of Europe consumeth in many'.[23] That contradicts Lambarde in one sense, by suggesting at least that criminals were being caught and punished, although Challoner still thought England was particularly lawless. Some of the more notorious murders were described in lurid detail in pamphlets, contributing to the general sense of growing crime. But how realistic were the complaints and fears that increasing numbers of people were preying on society by committing crimes? Early modern England seems to have been lawless: however, concentration on crime exaggerates the frequency of trouble. Joel Samaha's study of crime and punishment in Elizabethan Essex suggested that there was a 400 per cent growth from the opening decade of Elizabeth's reign to the last, which seems to corroborate Lambarde's complaint. But there are problems here. Some assize files are missing for the 1560s so the earlier figures are too low. Samaha concentrates chiefly on felonies at assizes, the most serious prosecuted crimes rather than lesser misdemeanours, so that his results cover only a part even of prosecuted crime. Further, the tables which Samaha provides (on pages 19 and 21 of his study) reveal that 1596 and 1597 had by far the most reported felonies; both before and after this peak there were fewer. Samaha does admit that the rise may reflect greater determination by judges and grand juries to quell crime by more severe application of penalties, including hanging.[24]

The complaints of ever-increasing lawlessness need to be set within the context of a rapidly rising population, especially between 1550 and 1640, There were simply more people, so there were more potential victims as well as more possible malefactors. J.S. Cockburn endeavoured to overcome this bias by relating the numbers of serious crimes to population in three counties for varying periods between 1559 and 1625. He recognised the limitations of the assize indictments, and that the counties with comparable surviving sources are not necessarily typical. Essex, Hertfordshire and Sussex are all close to London, with many travellers passing through them, and not necessarily typical. Cockburn found that overall yearly averages of indicted serious crime in the three counties did not increase from 1559 to 1625; there were increases at certain times only, especially in the 1590s, rather than a steady rise. Cockburn compared wheat prices with indictments, and not surprisingly finds more property crime following the bad harvests of 1585–7 and the mid-1590s. His rough crime rates per head of population show low and fairly stable rates in two of his three counties, and a small rise in Essex.[25] If the crime rate remained generally steady, but the harsh years suffered higher rates of robbery, commentators in those years were correct in perceiving more lawlessness. But in easier times the English were not becoming a nation of thieves with no regard for society and order. The number of indictments at Wiltshire quarter sessions (there are no assize files until 1629) also suggest a steady but not enormous number of misdeeds. From a population of probably 100,000, Wiltshire justices indicted less than 90 people a year in six of the ten years 1615–24. The largest proportion was accused of larceny; assault or escape was the next largest category, with smaller numbers of trespass, illegal hunting and so on. The highest number indicted in the ten-year period was 129, including 78 larcenies, in 1623.[26] Although the assizes for Wiltshire probably handled about the same number of crimes, and of course dealt with more serious offences, it seems that contemporary fears of crime were exaggerated and most people were sufficiently obedient (or cunning) to avoid prosecution in the courts.

Jim Sharpe's detailed study of Essex crime from 1620 to 1680 emphasises that relative obedience. Sharpe shows a long-term decline in property crime, related probably to improved climate, harvests and economic conditions in the second half of the century. He too found high grain prices linked with rises in property offences, most notably in 1629–31. The 1620s had the highest level of serious crime up to 1680, coupled with harvest problems, depressions in the cloth trade, the plague of 1625, and the impact of troops for the war in Europe. Here too it seems that desperate need among the subsistence poor drove them to steal as a last resort, within a more general framework of orderliness. In all societies, some will thieve; when more did so, it was out of desperation.

The other side of the question is that of attitudes of the better-off, leading to fluctuations in prosecution, with more intensive efforts in tough times. In the years when everyone knew that prices were high and food and employment scarce, the local authorities might work harder to find and punish crime. In Essex they did so in the 1580s and 1620s, working with efficiency and diligence to enforce the law and punish miscreants. Sharpe wonders if historians should think in terms of 'enforcement waves' rather than 'crime waves': a useful insight for the early modern period.[27]

Persuasion reached everyone, and most people obeyed at least as far as necessary to stay out of trouble – though in tougher times more transgressed and more were caught. Friends tried to 'rescue' offenders from a constable escorting them to a JP, house of correction or gaol, yet, once recognizances were issued, a surprisingly high proportion of people appeared at quarter sessions, and most were discharged. In Elizabethan Essex 85 per cent of those bound over to appear did so; similarly, in January 1620 all but seven out of 65 turned up. Most of those ordered to come before Wiltshire quarter sessions appeared promptly, and defaulters were pursued further until they did. They probably complained among themselves, but eventually they obeyed. However, if most English men and women heeded the strictures of the Homilies on obedience, naturally there were also a few who criticised or insulted 'the higher powers', the magistrates, or the constables. We will look at these dissenters in the next chapter.

8

Dissent

Central and local controls achieved a remarkable level of obedience in early modern England. But many co-operated reluctantly, some grumbled, criticised or actively resisted authority. Enforcement of religious change upset some people and provoked animosity against officials throughout the period. Other complaints focused on the apparent failure of monarchs, nobles and officeholders to live up to the ideal notions of correct behaviour. And naturally, some men and women simply resisted doing as they were ordered. It is impossible to know how much private dissent remained hidden behind closed doors, leaving no record. Nonetheless, some was reported by neighbours, constables, or the victims of resistance themselves, and was prosecuted. The reaction of those present was crucial. If sedition or insult to authority figures occurred in alehouse, street, or private house, neighbours and onlookers were sometimes sufficiently convinced by exhortations to obedience, or fear of condoning treason, to report the incident. The very fact that criticisms came to light offers insight into the attitudes of the men and women who reported them, and who would not tolerate open denigration of rulers. The monarchs worked hard to promote images of majestic authority, royal virtue and care for the realm, but it is difficult to gauge how such notions were received across the realm. No monarch could please all their subjects, and some policies created vigorous opposition. Within the Privy Council and court, of course, there was always criticism and varying views. It was the voicing of opposition beyond that circle which worried governments. When regimes enforced change, felt insecure, or demanded extra burdens of tax or military service, then the voices of dissent grew louder. Even humble people expressed opinions about their leaders, and their complaints can tell us what was expected of rulers.

Apart from an outburst of popular opposition in 1525, Henry VIII achieved a fairly high degree of allegiance in the earlier part of his reign. But the tumultuous changes of the 1530s provoked bitter disagreement amongst ordinary men and women (as well as the rebellions of 1536–7). His efforts to divorce Queen Catherine, the break from Rome, and his marriage to Anne Boleyn excited dissent from people at all levels: it was not only Sir Thomas More and Bishop Fisher who objected to Henry's measures. Clergy hinted that the king was a heretic, when they were supposed to preach in support of the new supremacy law; some especially in the north, opposed Anne becoming queen. In 1533, James Harrison, a Lancashire clergyman was one: 'I will none for queen but Queen Catherine; who the devil made Nan Bullen, that whore, queen?' The notion that Anne was tarnished or unworthy as a wife for the king surfaced in many similar complaints. Worse, an Essex priest claimed later the same year that Henry was 'no king of right'.[1]

The king and Thomas Cromwell recognised the dangers of popular dissent, scurrility, and resistance to the novelties in church and state, and resolved to punish the worst ones severely – as shown by the penalties set down in the Succession Act and the Treasons Act of 1534, which made it treason to desire the death or deprivation of the king, to deny his supremacy over the Church, or to call him heretic or tyrant.

The nervous government investigated criticisms from all over the country, and although not all the perpetrators were punished, many were. Cromwell pressed for local justices to deal with the less dangerous critics, those who did not speak outright treason. Some were sentenced to the pillory, and even to have their ears nailed to it. But a Buckinghamshire tailor in 1535 went too far, when he asserted before witnesses that the king was a heretic, a traitor to God and his laws, and not the right king of England, and that furthermore, before midsummer day, he would play football with the king's head! He was tried and sentenced, though he may have escaped execution after all.

John Raven, of Over in Cambridgeshire, did not think much of Henry either. In 1536 he pointed out that Cardinal Wolsey and Sir Thomas More had both fallen from power, and he predicted that Thomas Cromwell who 'ruleth all' would soon follow them. Raven admitted that he had said the king was a fool, and self-willed, and Thomas Cromwell another; he considered that the king was failing to rule wisely as he ought. Raven's case offers a telling insight into the contrasting attitudes of those around him. The constable Robert Hornygold, surprisingly, warned him to deny the words he had spoken against the king, otherwise 'thou wilt sure to be hanged unless thy neighbours be good to thee'. The constable recognised that others in the village of Over might support the official line and be willing to see the critic hanged. And someone did denounce Raven, who then tried to transfer most of the alleged statements on to his accusers. There was an official investigation, but the outcome is not known. Many other villages must have experienced this kind of uncertainty about how to deal with critics of the king and of Cromwell: whether or not they came to be investigated or punished depended on how unanimous the neighbours and local officeholders were in their belief that such criticism was to be stopped.

Rumours and prophecies of all sorts abounded, especially that the king would soon die, or, in the mid-1530s, that Henry would be forced to flee the realm – wishful thinking by people to whom his changes in religion signified that he was failing in his duty to rule wisely, or, after the Boleyn marriage, that he failed to provide a moral example to his realm. Malicious or meddling neighbours accused people of such treasonable complaints against the king. An informer charged that John Lacy, bailiff of Halifax, composed a scurrilous rhyme which included the words 'That as for the king, an apple and a fair wench to dally withal would please him very well'. Local disputes involving Lacy had complicated the matter, and contrary statements about the rhyme meant that Lacy went free. Not all were so lucky, as continuing changes in church and state in the 1530s attracted much dissent. At least 394 people were denounced for treasonous words, and probably 63 of them executed between 1532 and 1540. Adding all treason trials, including those of the rebels from Lincolnshire and the Pilgrimage of Grace, there were 308 executions altogether in those years. At least another 400 suspects were investigated, but escaped death.

The young King Edward's death in 1553 was much mourned, but Mary was warmly welcomed, after overcoming Lady Jane Grey's short-lived attempt to become queen. Perhaps because of those events and her determination to impose Catholic policy, Mary and her Council were very concerned to punish critics who opposed her, in writing or speech. Apprentices were arrested in Norwich for singing anti-Catholic songs which they had learnt from a minstrel. A proclamation of August 1553 ordered people not to speak against the queen or her Council, and a stricter one followed in May 1554; written and spoken libels were to be punished. In 1555 the JPs were told to set a spy in every parish, and the Privy Council complained that the common people had become insolent, contrary to their duty of allegiance. The people may indeed have been more discontented – or the queen and her Council may have been less tolerant, especially when faced with bad harvests and war. Henry Machyn's diary notes a series of men and women put in the pillory in London for speaking against the queen, including three women in May 1554 for lies and sedition and for words 'touching the queen's proceedings and the Council'. In mid-1555, Richard Smith of Shoreditch, yeoman, was sentenced to the pillory, to have both ears cut off, £100 fine, and three months' prison for saying 'The queen is dead'.[2] One unfortunate woman was pilloried for reporting Mary's death on 12 November 1558 – only five days before Mary did, in fact, die.

There were reasons for hostile discussion of royal policies. The convinced Protestant minority opposed the return to Catholicism, while Mary's marriage to Philip II of Spain excited both political and popular opposition. Tavern talk was dangerous, as William Harris discovered after he claimed in a Deptford tavern in 1556 that the queen 'loves another realm better than this' (meaning Spain).[3] The Privy Council and the courts investigated such people, and many were tried for seditious words or treason. In only three and a half years from the beginning of 1554 at least 132 people were executed for treason: they included participants in Wyatt's rebellion, but even so this was a much higher rate than under Henry VIII. Such punishments did not convince everyone to cease their dissent: anonymous broadsheets or doggerel rhymes sung in the streets celebrated humble victims of Mary's policies, in contrast to those which had welcomed her arrival in 1553.

Queen Elizabeth attracted hostile comment during her long reign for failing to fulfil the aspirations of her subjects, but most of the criticism came at times of religious or economic stress. Critics came from a wide social and geographical range. At the beginning of her reign, the Privy Council ordered that Thomas Hall, of Huntingdonshire, who had spoken against her, should be punished, 'to the terror of others'. Despite this, dissent continued sporadically. Early in the reign, especially, priests spoke against her for not retaining the Catholic religion; later, the godly abused her for keeping too much of it. Mary Cleere must have agreed with the papal excommunication of the queen: in 1576 she declared that Elizabeth was not born to the crown, but that 'another Lady' was – meaning Mary, Queen of Scots. For that, Mary Cleere was sentenced to be hung, drawn, and quartered. In 1580 an Essex man claimed that 'the Mass was up in Lincolnshire . . . and some did say that we had no queen'; he was to be put in the pillory. Another man the next year called for a return to the Latin Mass, and condemned the queen for 'burning men's ears', and a tailor still believed that the pope was supreme head over all Christendom; yet neither were punished. Nicholas Haslewood, an Islington yeoman, wished the queen's death, and he hoped to see his enemies burnt in Smithfield; he received relatively lenient treatment, with a sentence to the pillory wearing a sign describing his contempt. Strong Protestants met trouble, too. Thomas Bedell of Writtle, Essex, found himself before the court of assizes for supposedly asking 'is the queen become a Papist now?' His defence was that 'those who are called puritans' said it. The jury decided that Bedell spoke scandalous rumours against the queen; after further legal proceedings the Privy Council considered the case, demanding Bedell's written submission and a fine. Godly men and women continued to complain that the queen was too popish, increasingly by the 1580s, when Protestantism was more firmly entrenched.[4]

Elizabeth promoted an image of herself as pure, goddess-like, careful of her people, but it did not always convince. Neighbours or fellow-drinkers in taverns reported people to quarter sessions for 'lewd', scandalous or insulting comments about the queen; some were investigated by the Privy Council. The Council recognised that people might not really mean what they said, and examined Robert Knight, to see whether he had spoken from malice, or from madness. In 1575, William Waller, gentleman was in the Fleet prison for 'very foul' speeches about Elizabeth, but he was eventually released on a £1,000 bond to appear before the Privy Council. Peter Moyses was sentenced to a penalty by Middlesex JPs for saying 'the queen is a rascall' in 1568, and others elsewhere used the term.[5] The queen's virginity seemed hard to accept. There were many rumours that she was pregnant, or had illegitimate children by the earl of Leicester, along with the tale of a newborn baby thrown onto the fire by the earl. (Such a lurid infanticide story was a stock allegation, directed against Sir William Darrell for instance in Wiltshire, and repeated in the seventeenth century too.) Women particularly were ready to believe that the queen had failed to live up to the model of purity – or perhaps with the uncertainty of the succession, it was actually hoped she had provided an son, even if illegitimate.

Elizabeth's care for her people seemed less effective after 1585, when war demanded soldiers and taxes, problems which worsened in the 'hungry 1590s'. Perhaps more were prosecuted, after a statute of 1581 increased penalties against seditious writing or words. In 1585 a weaver who had been pressed to serve as a soldier and felt a grudge, wailed that King Philip was a father to England and did better love an Englishman than the queen. A labourer in 1591 said 'let us pray for a father, for we have a mother already'. A bricklayer argued that warfare was not lawful and the queen no Christian. In 1602 a Clerkenwell yeoman wished 'a pox and a vengeance of all those whatsoever that made this statute for the poor . . . and a pox on all those that would follow her Majesty any more'. Many hoped for better times under a king.[6]

Yet James I also attracted dissent from ordinary people, particularly over his ecclesiastical powers. Middlesex quarter sessions in 1609 dealt with a man who claimed the king was but a temporal ruler, and in 1614 with an apparently more serious case against John Parish for persuading the king's subjects to deny royal authority in religion. General disrespect or blame of the king was punished from time to time. Neighbours in Staffordshire reported George Pannell, a trouble-prone alehousekeeper, in 1608 for making light of even the king's power to make him end a quarrel. When it was suggested he should 'leave higher powers alone', Pannell replied that 'rather than King James should make a wisp of him to dry his tail, he would cut his throat'.[7] A London man, presumably an office-holder, had to promise a £100 surety to appear before quarter sessions for asserting in 1611 'if the king's servants shall be thus used, and if the king take no order for it, he would have his crown pulled about his head'; others too thought the king should protect them better.[8]

The early years of James I's reign attracted less popular criticism of the monarch than had the last years of Elizabeth, probably because of peace and better harvests. The proclamations of James I's reign against licentious speech about matters of state might have increased caution. Perhaps justices were less anxious as the threat of Spanish invasion ended, and only prosecuted outright treason. Regional variations operated: from the 1580s, complaints seem to have been much more widespread in or near to London and in Essex than in Wiltshire, the only county with comparable records to those of Essex for the late sixteenth century. This may be because Wiltshire was an inland county with no fears that local dissidents might help invaders, and where there were fewer Catholics and zealous puritans to promote disaffection. Although some of these complaints by ordinary men and women stand out because they were vivid, even scurrilous, they were not really very numerous – or at least, not many perpetrators were prosecuted. On the home circuit assizes, covering Middlesex, Essex, Hertfordshire, Sussex and Kent, only 154 were accused under the sedition laws during the reigns of Elizabeth and James. Local courts dealt with others, as did the Privy Council. There was an undercurrent of provincial dissent, but it had been muted in insults to the monarchs themselves.

Later in James's reign and under Charles I, criticism became stronger, notably in the 1620s. James, and especially Charles, aroused grave doubts about the wisdom of their foreign policy, while Charles's repeated dissolutions of parliament and later imposition of Laudian church practices made for antipathy among the politically aware and the godly. Charles's forced loan was eventually paid by most, but at a huge cost in disaffection, even among the gentry. If the parliamentary gentry were at the forefront of opposition, they were not alone in their hostility. Entry into European war in 1624 meant recruiting soldiers and raising subsidies, leading to burdens for

Fig. 4: Some critics did suffer. A ballad on John Stevens, an apprentice tailor who was hung, drawn and quartered at Salisbury in 1632 for words against Charles I, was printed with this illustration. (*Roxborough Ballads*, III (1880), p. 155, Privy Council Register 1631–2, PRO, Pc 2/41, ff. 173, 175 for proceedings.)

the troops, their families, and vigorous resistance to the billeting of soldiers. Royal policy on the conduct of the war attracted widespread anger, after the disastrous losses of the Mansfeldt expedition and the extension to conflict with France as well as Spain, for which the duke of Buckingham received much blame.

The Suffolk minister John Rous worried in the mid-1620s that the king's proceedings had 'caused men's minds to be incensed', and he feared that a careless word would ignite reports of general insurrection. Rous's parishioners discussed their disapproval of the 1627 Ile de Rhe expedition and war with France, and their older discontents about parliament being 'crossed', about the expense, and the danger to English ships because of ill-advised royal policy. Rous noted much muttering, and strange rhymes and songs.[9]

Hugh Pyne, a Somerset JP, ridiculed the king to guests at Curry Malett, pronouncing Charles 'as unwise a king as ever was, for he is carried as man would carry a child with an apple'; Pyne believed he was not fit to be king. One of the guests must have blabbed, and the government wanted Pyne hung, drawn and quartered, but Chief Justice Richardson decided that although Pyne's words were wicked, they did not amount to treason – Pyne lived, although dismissed as a JP. In 1627 Pyne was committed for saying the king was governed by a company of upstarts: he resented the influence of the duke of Buckingham and others, believing that a king should actually wield power himself. Other Somerset men also denounced the king: John Williams was gaoled in 1629 for 'high and heinous words' against Charles; and many people elsewhere echoed these ideas. A Salisbury apprentice was hung, drawn and quartered in 1632 for treasonous words (see Fig. 4).

Such rhymes and songs, satirising monarchs or more frequently their ministers and courtiers, displayed severe disappointment with their performance of public duty. Several historians have recently investigated the eager appetite for news, and from the late sixteenth century the very rapid increase in provision of it, through newsletters, printed reports, and manuscript dissemination of political news, and anonymous critical or defamatory comment. Nobles and gentry in the provinces sought, and often paid for, regular newsletters from the court, which could retail gossip and opposition. Sir John Scudamore in Herefordshire, Sir Martin Stuteville in Suffolk, and the earl of Shrewsbury are just three examples among many. The most scurrilous and hostile comments mostly appeared in manuscript satires, epigrams and verse libels scattered in London streets or thrown into alehouses, and indeed composed in them, hiding the authorship. In 1576, one of the judges complained in Star Chamber that the spreading of slanderous libels, though odious in all well-governed commonwealths, had grown so common that he feared no officer 'should be free from the venom of such lewd spirits and pens'. Worse, the libel in question had been printed, to ensure a further spread. Some libels opposed royal plans, for instance Elizabeth's Anjou marriage project in 1579. Early in his reign James was castigated in libellous verses as indolent, enjoying court dances with his 'merry boys', and accused of using parliamentary subsidies to reward his Scots followers.[10]

Although some attacked the monarchs, many more attacked their ministers. Bishops provided a continuing target, including the invective printed in the Martin Marprelate tracts of the 1580s. Lewis Pickering, the author of a libel advocating 'not obeying government' which was pinned to the hearse of Archbishop Whitgift in 1604, was punished by Star Chamber in 1605. Most of the libels – epigrams, rhymes and verses – attacked prominent political figures. These men did not fulfil the ideal of authority: overweening ambition, corruption, sexual misbehaviour and disease, and selfish wickedness were alleged against them, often in scurrilous or even obscene terms. There were hopeful prophecies of the death or fall of Thomas Cromwell in the 1530s, and libellous ballads circulated. In Mary's short reign, critical papers were scattered in London streets. From the 1580s, there were written attacks on Lord Burghley, and then on his son Robert Cecil, later earl of Salisbury, accusing them of blighting the careers of opponents and hogging all power. 'Little Cecil trips up and down He rules both court and crown', lamented one caricature; many harped on his deformity as an outward symbol of the villainy of his nature. One libel addressed Cecil as 'Proud and ambitious wretch that feedest on naught but Faction'. The Cecils were commoners who had risen solely through their service to the state and they were accused of thwarting the old nobility:

> First did thy sire and now thy self by Machiavellian skill
> Prevail and curb the Peers as well befits your will.[11]

In a similar vein, some cast blame on Cecil and Walter Raleigh for provoking the abortive Essex revolt in 1601. Libels against Robert Cecil's financial policies, foreign diplomacy, even his enclosing of Hatfield Wood, shed light on a fund of bitter disapproval of the hunchback, who was compared with Richard III. (Yet the Council took no action on the spate of sarcastic libels at Cecil's death in 1612, because political tensions were not high.) James I's other Councillors and courtiers also rated low in the popularity poll of the libel-writers. Thomas Sackville, earl of Dorset, the Lord Treasurer, was castigated as 'Fill-Sack' for taking bribes, the earl of Northampton for being 'the Archpapist'. The king's favourite Robert Carr, earl of Somerset, attracted opprobrium for being grasping, as well as for the machinations surrounding his marriage to Frances Howard, and the associated Overbury murder scandal. An anagram went 'Francis Howard : Car finds a whore'. Authors and many copyists sent these opinions to gentlemen in the country, who often transcribed them into their commonplace books.[12]

Increasingly in the early seventeenth century hand-written 'separates' and printed information provided further fuel for criticism. 'Separates', accounts of notable events and of parliamentary proceedings, appeared in multiple copies and sold like pamphlets; interested squires like William Davenport in Cheshire borrowed and copied them. 'Corantos' discussed mostly foreign news. Additionally, verses and ballads sung and recited in alehouses or at fairs allowed even the non-literate to know more about their betters, and to form adverse opinions of them. Many songs and stories focused on the duke of Buckingham as the great grievance and source of folly in public affairs. His speedy rise, his amassing of money, office, and land, and his promotion of so many of his relatives provoked outpourings of mocking hatred. The poems and songs deriding him with their classical and current political allusions, were obviously written by educated people, but the scurrilous tone and jokes suggesting he had the pox probably influenced alehouse listeners too. Some substituted the first initial of his name, or sang 'The clean contrary way' to a popular tune. After Buckingham went with the expedition to France, it was hoped he would have a warm reception when he came home:

> London, prepare thy faggots
> Against the duke's return,
> And see thou hast them ready
> Laid for the duke to burn
> For he deserves them all.[13]

Most of the material appeared in London, anonymously; some was written by well-known satirists, or by Oxford and Cambridge dons and clerics. However, the hunger for news meant that eventually some could reach illiterate villagers. Word of mouth spread stories, as travellers, carriers and traders retailed the latest gossip in every inn they visited. London formed a continuous hub for the movement of people – and information – both to and from the countryside, and it was growing fast. More and more rural families had relatives in the capital to send them news. With higher levels of literacy, the capital remained the major source and target for libels and invective. But as entertaining comment the verses were readily transmitted to the provinces. It is impossible to estimate just how much reached the illiterate dwellers in villages and towns, but the gossip among humble Essex villagers, for instance, about Queen Elizabeth's supposed love-life with Leicester, suggests that some did. In 1628 a man imprisoned for repeating a tale about Buckingham claimed he had been 'drawn by the report of the common people . . . into the vulgar error of the time'.[14]

Derogatory words about a sovereign, chief minister or Privy Councillor attacked distant figures whom most people did not encounter. The nearer face of authority was that of JP, constable and other parish officers, such as the watchmen and overseers of the poor, the vicar and churchwardens, the manor and town officials. And despite widespread acceptance of order, there was more resistance the closer the contact. Many gentlemen as JPs helped victims secure redress, but occasionally they were criticised for failing the high standards of honour and fairness expected by their communities – or so it seemed to the discontented. Muttering in private left no record, but when the JPs heard of hostility or insult to themselves, they viewed it as a threat to their authority, since the maintenance of social harmony depended so much on willing deference. They considered it was vital to punish publicly those who showed disrespect, especially at times of national danger. Some gentlemen were particularly sensitive to derogatory remarks – and doubtless some did abuse their position, take bribes, show favour to friends and their followers, and punish those of enemies. Many such allegations were made by rival gentlemen in the course of factional disputes in Star Chamber, however, and were not necessarily true. Wiltshire faction leaders accused each other of abuse of office as JP, and especially as deputy lieutenant or subsidy commissioner. Such charges and counter-charges included taking bribes to free offenders or men summoned for military service, raising the subsidy assessments of enemies and lowering those of friends, neglect of duty as a JP, favouring cases against an enemy, keeping private sessions, and even bribing the gaol keeper to whip daily a woman imprisoned for having an illegitimate baby. The Star Chamber judges very rarely fined these men, suggesting that they were not convinced of any wrong-doing. In one case they fined both the rival accused. A few dismissals resulted from such claims, and serious abuse of office could be investigated by the court of King's Bench.

Occasionally those they attempted to rule spoke up against JPs, or complained of their decisions, while insults to a JP may have been due to his overbearing manner or unjust action. The records can be tantalisingly brief, and they rarely give the background to a dispute or describe personal attributes. Naturally, at times people simply resisted JP's orders and quarter sessions took action to remind them of the need to obey. One such man was Edward Glascock, gentleman, who was riding along an Essex highway in 1569 and had a fight with a husbandman travelling with his cart. Each went to a different JP for remedy. But Glascock made further assaults on his victim before witnesses, apparently flouting the JP's order: a petition to quarter sessions complained that either Glascock was not sufficiently bound to the peace, 'or else that he has small regard thereto'.[15] In 1587, another Glascock, Thomas, a labourer, was warned by a constable to appear before one of the Essex JPs for a misdemeanour, but contemptuously refused to obey the justice's warrant, insulting the constable, and threatening to shoot him for good measure. Even more contempt for the JPs was shown by John Powell during the same year, in Wiltshire, when he caused an affray in the court at quarter sessions. In 1591 William Alcock was reported to the Staffordshire JPs for continual disobedience, because he would not accept the commands of the deputy lieutenant nor of any justice of the peace. Walter Withers of Pilton, Somerset, was one of very many men and women who insisted on keeping alehouses without licence, but he annoyed the Somerset justices in 1610 because he was 'very malapert, saucy and obstinate' in his refusal to obey the order.[16] The drinkers who disturbed the sleep of the Somerset JPs at an inn during quarter sessions in January 1634 were probably simply drunk: when the revellers were told to go to bed, they replied with contemptuous and uncivil speech.[17] The justices were not prepared to tolerate such disrespect from their inferiors, however, and those who did not apologise next morning were to be reported to the Attorney General: perhaps the JPs were overreacting to a minor incident, or perhaps they really feared that insubordination would spread if not scotched.

People who were discontented with the behaviour of their JPs chose the obvious epithet – just ass – but many used excretory terms. Edward Dysmer allegedly declared that 'he cared not a fart for Sir Giles Wroughton', during a quarrel while fishing, and the Wiltshire JP determined to see him reproved. Dysmer was to appear before quarter sessions in July 1606, but Wroughton was ill and unable to attend. Wroughton wrote to inform the bench that the lewd stubborn fellow was still offering insults, despite having been bound over to submit to him. Wroughton emphasised the importance for all the JPs of maintaining respect for their authority, requesting them 'to deal with him in my absence . . . as you would I should do for any of you in like case'. Middlesex JPs, too, would not stand for insult to one of their number, and neither would the three men who informed on William Pettitt of Isleworth in 1615. Witnesses said Pettitt had called Sir Valentine Saunders a man of weak understanding not fit to be a JP, had said he 'would not care a louse for Saunder's warrant', and had rescued a man being taken into custody by that warrant. The JPs ordered Pettitt to be committed to prison till he put in good sureties for his conduct. John Noye, of Chiswick, gentleman, showed no deference when he was brought before Sir William Smith in July 1614, for severely beating a man at Hammersmith. When Smith demanded that Noye give sureties to keep the peace, or else be committed to prison, Noye brandished his sword and jibed 'Are you a Justice?'. Noye was ordered to put in sureties for good behaviour and to appear at next quarter sessions. In contrast, the Essex JPs in 1620 treated John Tabram leniently when he had to answer for slackness in office (probably as constable) and for abusing Richard Bennett esquire 'with lewd and bad speeches'. The bench considered Tabram's disrespect, but decided not to punish him, because they thought it insufficient in law to do so.[18]

Sometimes more specific accusations of misbehaviour are recorded. Anthony Fry complained bitterly in the presence of two Wiltshire JPs in March 1615 that when he had earlier gone to one of them, John Warneford, for justice, Warneford had refused. Fry claimed angrily that Warneford had spoken 'very rashly and perfunctorily' to him, whereas the JP whom he approached after Warneford's refusal had done as he asked: Fry implied that Warneford was a bad JP who had taken the wrong action. But Warneford and Sir Henry Poole saw the matter differently, and entered a memorandum in the quarter sessions file headed 'the abuses offered by Anthony Fry . . . to John Warneford esquire in the presence of Sir Henry Poole'. The bench also disapproved of Fry's outburst: he was required to give surety and appear at the next quarter sessions to answer for it. When he did so, he was given a warrant for good behaviour henceforth.[19] The Somerset quarter sessions in 1616 dealt with a more serious accusation of a JP's misbehaviour: a man declared that Mr Poulett was a crabbed knave who took bribes, half a crown for himself and the same again for his clerk.[20] In 1617, Wiltshire JPs punished Christopher Bigges, gentleman, of Stapleford harshly for 'divers insolent and contemptuous speeches, answers and behaviours' to the justices sitting in full sessions of the peace. Bigges had been convicted of a trespass, which he must have disputed, but he was also ordered to take the oaths of supremacy and of allegiance to the king; he was probably a Catholic recusant. The JPs considered his public outburst against them to be very serious: they entered an exceptionally detailed account of it, and kept him in prison for a week. He was bound to appear at next quarter sessions, with substantial men giving sureties for his appearance, and ordered to be of good behaviour in the meantime. For a gentleman such as Bigges, having to appear in front of the court was shameful, forming an important part of the punishment for disputing authority in public.[21]

In most of the incidents in which JPs were insulted or criticised, the real reason is unclear, but occasionally it is possible to uncover more background. The contemptuous accusation made by William Kidly against Sir Thomas Thynne, a Wiltshire JP, on 10 January 1629, that he would issue a warrant for a piece of bread and butter, was not a chance remark but part of a long and complex conflict. One part of it concerned a suspected horse thief supposedly named Dobbins from whom Thynne had taken a statement late in 1628. Thynne had requested Kidly, deputy bailiff to a neighbour, to take the statement and enquire in various places in Somerset and Devon where Dobbins claimed he was known; meanwhile the prisoner was to remain in the custody of the Warminster constables. Thynne's view afterwards was that Kidly had disregarded this plan, hoping to gain Dobbins's horses for himself should they turn out to have been stolen. Kidly instead took the prisoner with him up and down the country and finally to Salisbury where Dobbins somehow drowned and Kidly destroyed or lost the examination. Kidly later suggested that Thynne had been corrupted with gold, and soon after, was heard in a Warminster alehouse declaring that Thynne would grant a warrant against him for a piece of bread and butter. That is the sort of gratuitous insult which appears alone in some examples: here the context is clearer, with Kidly in the wrong, and possibly Thynne too. Three other men came forward on 27 January to accuse Kidly of taking bribes six months earlier to free them from jury service for a year; and a tailor went to Thynne to swear on oath that he feared Kidly would kill him or burn his house. The sudden surfacing of six-month old accusations suggests that Thynne was gathering evidence against Kidly after the Dobbins fiasco. Whatever the truth of Kidly's accusation, his railing against Thynne has a touch of self-defence. Perhaps, as in this example, accusations against JPs may frequently have arisen from tensions in local affairs, rather than implying general disrespect for their authority. In any case, such charges are rare in the records; it seems that JPs were respected, or at least feared.[22]

The JPs faced occasional insolence and disobedience, but it was their agents the constables who dealt most directly with the people, and who were at the cutting edge (literally sometimes) of enforcement. The parish constable was a temporary official, officiating only for a year or two, while maintaining his normal livelihood as farmer, butcher, baker or tradesman. Yet during his term he had a huge and difficult range of duties, many of which were likely to arouse conflict. He could call on neighbours for assistance, but generally it was the constable rather than his helpers who bore the blows if people resisted. Overseeing tax or military contributions, coping with unlicensed alehouses or rowdy drinkers, securing payment of child support by fathers, apprehending vagrants and suspected criminals and arranging their escort to a JP or to prison could all be risky tasks. Many constables achieved a high degree of obedience despite these hazards. Those who did not suffered often from unfortunate combinations of circumstances: the poverty of neighbours who had real difficulty in meeting demands, their angry temperaments when confronted, the determination of unlicensed alehouse keepers to continue their business, or support for minor malefactors by their friends.

The earliest detailed records suggest occasional problems. London with its concentrated and volatile population naturally experienced more frequent incidents. The Middlesex quarter sessions (which dealt with most of London except the City) saw far more frequent refusals to obey or pay, and abuse and assault on constables and their officers of the watch than a more distant county did: in one year for instance, 1615–16, there were 68 such incidents reported to the Middlesex JPs. London also experienced some of the most dramatic confrontations: in 1554 Robert Hill, then constable of Westminster, was watching out for disorderly rule at the house of Robert Most – an alehouse or brothel. But Alexander Darragh, a baker, resented Hill's surveillance, and hit him so hard that the constable died on the spot. London brothels and their customers created many conflicts: a Whitechapel baker was in trouble after he had been 'swaggering and drinking' all night in a notorious bawdy house in Turnmill Street in 1609, and next morning abused the constable. Grace Bull, the wife of James Bull, servant of the bishop of Ely, was in trouble in September 1615 for keeping a reputed bawdy house in London, and beating and abusing the officers of the watch in carrying out their duty.

Constables could face violence from all ranks of society. A tailor of St Clement Danes beat one of the parish constables in 1571 so violently that his life was in danger. In 1594, two servants of William Beecher, esquire, 'greatly abused the constable of Hoxdon as well by blows as by most opprobrious reviling speeches'.[23] Francis Higgins, gentleman, of Clerkenwell, and his wife Ann appeared before the quarter sessions for beating and locking up a constable who was trying to do his official work; they both acknowledged their fault, which cannot have been considered very severe, for they were fined only two shillings each. The 1590s saw more frequent attacks on constables, in some rural areas at least. The poor harvests made official demands harder to meet, and there was more distraint of goods and animals for non-payment. This often led to conflict, as people resisted the loss of a valuable animal, usually worth far more than the fine or amount owing. In Staffordshire in 1590 a group of Swinnerton inhabitants, including the miller, assaulted their constable. In Wolverhampton in December 1599 one of the constables, Robert Tunks, was assaulted by a cutler, and Tunks claimed that he was so intimidated by the threats of the local baker and his wife that he had not since dared to 'go openly about the business of his office'.[24]

Unlicensed alehouses formed a perennial problem and often led to abuse of constables who tried to close them. Nearly every constable was caught in a dilemma over any attempt to control alehouses. For poor people, including widows, to brew and sell ale was often the only way to support themselves and they were determined to continue: a constable trying to close an alehouse often met with fierce resistance. Yet there were constant calls to reduce the number and insist on licences from the JPs. Unlicensed alehouses appeared on practically every quarter sessions list of problems. In January 1620 an Essex brewer claimed 40 unlicensed ones were selling ale in Chelmsford and adjoining Moulsham alone. Local inhabitants on the other hand frequently did not want an alehouse retained. In the jury presentments and petitions to the JPs local inhabitants demanded action against unlicensed ones, and complained that the authorities were not fulfilling their duty. They objected to disorders which occurred, and to their servants spending time in them. So a constable sometimes faced strong pressure from his neighbours to implement any order against an alehouse. But drinkers disliked constables meddling with their pastimes, and often resisted them. In the summer of 1617 two constables of Amesbury, Wiltshire were checking on all the inns and alehouses at midnight, and reproved two local men, Coles and Skeane, for playing cards for ale – to which Coles responded with 'violent and undecent terms' and Skeane stabbed one of the accompanying watchmen in the thigh. The cardplayers admitted the attack, and Skeane was gaoled. In Calne, Wiltshire, unlicensed alehouse keepers Elizabeth Sherman, widow, and her two associates kept disorderly rule, but when they were forbidden to run the alehouse in 1608 insisted that they would do so nevertheless.

Thomas Chatfield, constable of Charterhouse Lane, London annoyed many of his neighbours in 1615–16, including vintners and their wives, one of whom lashed him with her tongue when he was carrying out his office. A gentlemen from Exeter was also accused of insulting Chatfield, and Henry Travis was sent to Newgate gaol for insulting and beating the constable, though he was soon freed and fined a mere two shillings. Those who were forced to answer for insulting Chatfield had good reasons though: in September 1616 Chatfield was brought before the quarter sessions himself for misdemeanors in his office as constable, was ordered to be dismissed immediately and to put in very good sureties for good behaviour and his appearance at the next sessions. However, he could not find sureties at first, and was gaoled, but was later bailed by a shoemaker and a merchant-tailor.

The complexities involved in a system of social control by amateur locals can be illustrated by two Cheshire cases from 1589. A curate, Robert Browne complained that when John Eyre had threatened to kill or maim him, he had requested a JP to take a bond from Eyre to keep the peace, and the JP duly directed a warrant to the constables of Tilston. But they had not done their duty, Browne insisted – for fear (because Eyre was unruly and would not obey them nor the queen's process, telling them he would 'have his way upon me'); or for affection (because Gregory, one of the constables, was Eyre's uncle); or for Gregory's fear of his father's displeasure, because Eyre was his landlord. Allegedly Eyre had also misbehaved in a nearby village, and when the constable there required him to keep the queen's peace he drew his dagger and wounded the constable's head 'most grievous to behold'. Here there was a hot-tempered man to control, but the constable's relationships to some raised a conflict of loyalties.[25] Another case of a constable's conflict between duty and friendship arose the same year. Margaret Clark of High Lea petitioned the Cheshire JPs because she had been beaten by Thomas Wilkinson, the son of her employer, and had a warrant issued to bind Thomas to keep the peace. But when she took it to the house of the only available constable, Richard Prince, he told her that in Thomas's position he would beat her every day, and declared that he would never serve the warrant. Thomas was at the time in Prince's house: he drew his sword, threatening to kill Margaret, then followed her and cut her with a dagger when she went to persuade a sheriff's bailiff to serve the warrant. The bailiff refused, declaring that it was not his job to do it. She requested the JPs to take a bond for good behaviour from Thomas, and pleaded with them to appoint a reliable officer 'to serve and do his duty accordingly'.[26]

People complained when the system failed them, or they thought those who exercised authority over them were mistaken or harsh. Yet respect for authority was often strong enough for people to report their neighbours for voicing dissent or insult. Drunken anger led to insults, especially if a constable tried to take action, but was not an excuse, and people were taken to court. Public talk, especially against the monarch or Councillors, brought retribution because of reporting by listeners. Isaac Felstead of Laindon, Essex, derided the Privy Council while was at market in April 1587, and found himself bound over on a recognizance for good behaviour. Three men informed on Edward Tabor, an innkeeper of Fryerning, Essex, in April 1588 for very lewd and seditious words against the queen and the divine service prescribed in England. Tabor was constable at the time: the JPs ordered his immediate dismissal, and his accusers were to be bound with good sureties to give evidence at the next assizes. Nicholas Haslewood must have worried some of 'the queen's faithful subjects' who heard his contemptuous talk in 1591, and probably thought his spell in the pillory was well deserved. John Brewer, a weaver of Witham, Essex, provided evidence against Henry Slinger of Ardleigh for disparaging talk about King James in 1621.

Informing meant trouble and expense, for those who did so in these cases had to travel to give their evidence to a court, yet they were prepared to do so.

All early modern regimes were nervous about hostile talk, and did their best to encourage the hearers to denounce any of their neighbours for it. Dalton's *Country Justice* noted that sureties for good behaviour should be granted against any who abused a justice of the peace (or a constable or other officer of the peace), and the owner of the Bodleian Library copy marked that section in the margin with two crosses, compared with the one cross he used for other categories. Popular derision of monarchs needed control: the Tudors and even James I knew that their rule rested on fragile foundations and feared that disloyal speech might encourage dangerous action. Many proclamations were issued to buttress royal authority and that of their officials. A 1538 proclamation against maiming the king's officials (mayors, sheriffs, bailiffs and others) ordered very severe punishment; in 1549 the Recorder of London requested a renewal – probably as a result of just one incident involving a sheriff, however. The anxieties of rule by a child and then by a woman led to a spate of proclamations limiting public discussion issued by Edward VI's government and by Mary Tudor. In May 1547 there was a proclamation against seditious rumours. The fears then felt seemed to be realised in the disturbances of 1549, and led to a series of new proclamations against sedition, which also ordered martial law against future rioters and against officers raising unlawful assemblies. In May 1550, one offered a reward for information on sedition and rebellion; further proclamations to suppress seditious rumours were distributed in July 1553, and in 1558, while another of 1558 placed possessors of heretical and seditious books under martial law.

Elizabeth issued fewer such proclamations than her two predecessors, but one appeared in the threatening international situation of 1587 just before the execution of Mary Queen of Scots. Elizabeth did use proclamations to control the use of guns, including that of 1579 against firing guns within two miles of a royal residence. James issued a proclamation after the Gunpowder Plots, and a special one in 1606 against a seditious rumour 'suddenly raised'. Charles I in contrast seemed more intent on issuing proclamations to control access to the court. Most of these proclamations appeared in response to a specific danger or fear, as a reminder of the need to maintain national cohesion. They did not entirely succeed, as we have seen. But there was not an extremely high level of recorded disparagement by the ordinary people of their monarchs, ministers in the central government and county justices, except when there seemed to be cogent reasons for discontent. Occasionally, however, more serious discontent over direct threats, such as to food supply or people's livelihood, spilled over from complaint to group protest and riot.

9
Riot

Complaint could turn from mere words to group action, and riot demonstrate serious discontent – but riots were scattered and rare. However, historians have suggested that riots *were* common, and were characteristic of a disordered and turbulent period. 'Riot' suggests unruly mobs running wild with no regard for authority at any level. But we need to look more closely at how riots started, who was involved, what they did, and what they were hoping to achieve. For riots in early modern England were not wild, undisciplined rampages. They did not intend to overthrow the monarchy, nor local authority, although they did seek attention. Nevertheless, governors local and central feared disorder among the people, and determined to prevent it if possible. Riots arose from dispute, and lawsuits sought to apportion blame afterwards. So we know about most riots because of the lawsuits which followed. That means that we do not receive a balanced account: the evidence comes from the conflicting allegations of interested parties in court. Gentry involved in disputes over politics or property rights frequently cited riotous behaviour by opponents in order to bring a lawsuit in the Star Chamber: serious threats to the peace formed one of the main concerns of that court, and nearly a quarter of cases in the Jacobean Star Chamber were allegations of riot. Riot could mean only three people meeting to attempt an unlawful act, or refusing to go home when ordered to by a magistrate. Those reporting riots exaggerated the numbers involved: they are often suspiciously large round numbers such as 100, or in more widespread disturbances 1,000 or 3,000.

Some events afterwards described as riots began at recreational events, others from hotheaded insult in alehouse or street. Brawling over grievances might become wider unrest if onlookers joined in; sometimes the troublemakers were prosecuted for brawls and assaults, other times for riot. In 1565, members of the Sampford family, of Essex, fought in public brawls, including one in the churchyard where Ellen Sampford, the wife of Richard Sampford, pulled out part of Thomas Sampford's beard and hit him over the head with a leg of mutton. After several violent disturbances involving the Sampford family and others, they were fined for assaults and brawls; elsewhere they could have been judged riots. Yet a rather odd event was prosecuted as a riot in Essex, in the summer of 1566. Peter Wentworth, esquire, Paul Wentworth, gentleman, and others, all from Lillingdale Lovell, Oxfordshire, were fined by Essex quarter sessions for riotously assembling in the marshes of Henry Baker, and making a 'silent affray' upon him (the reason is unclear; the two brothers later became famous for their outspokenness in parliament).[1] In Felsted, Essex, in July 1567, several men including three from the Cortman family were indicted for riotously assembling – to fish! Admittedly they also diverted a watercourse of Lord Rich to do so; still, fishing is not essentially a riotous activity. In an apparently riotous intervention in February 1589, 22 named men, including several yeomen, a carpenter, and a butcher, made an armed assault on the bailiff who was arresting John Wylde, yeoman, of Writtle, Essex, who had been outlawed for debt, and forcibly rescued him. Probably a large proportion of the village men took part, armed, but it was not called a riot. At festive times like Shrove Tuesday and Twelfth Night, young people indulged in inversion rituals and unseemly behaviour or worse. In the disorderly team sports between country communities, competition could become violent. Football and other games operated as combat between parishes, and involved all the young men. Contest was supposed to reinforce parochial loyalties, but drink and exuberance produced fights, if not outright riots, so that moral reformers wished to stop such disorder. In 1625, the men of Wilton in Wiltshire invaded the neighbouring village of Burbage, for a 'skimmington' a lively festive inter-village brawl, and ended up in the church court for it.[2] The definition of an event as riot lay partly with the person offended, partly with the constable or other officer who attended.

The parish constable could often do little when unruly crowds gathered, as shown in 1615 by the case of John Vizard, a Malmesbury man, described variously as 'labourer' or 'yeoman'. Clearly Vizard was a trouble-maker, and stirred up dissension locally by telling four men that their wives had sex with other men. He was also in trouble over his own sexual relations with six local women. Vizard took a strange action. He alleged he was to marry a London woman and led a procession through the town to the supposed wedding, in order, he claimed, to pre-empt action by any of his local 'conquests'. Perhaps it was an impudent charivari against himself, since he had met with disapproval for his lewdness from his neighbours and the JPs. From the viewpoint of the Malmesbury constable, Nicholas Mathewes, the event was a riot. Mathewes woke one morning hearing noise and drumming, and a crowd following the drum, saying they were off to Vizard's wedding, where none but cuckolds and cuckold-makers were invited. The constable complained later that a hundred people had been involved, and he dared not arrest anyone for riotous assembly. Afterwards, Vizard and five others were indicted for a riot, and sentenced to fine and imprisonment. If the constable could not stop the uproar at the time, he was vindicated after it with Vizard's conviction – even though the purpose differed from that of other riots, it had certainly disturbed the peace.[3]

Communal actions which local authority perceived as riotous disorder could be intended rather to sustain the moral order. The charivari or rough music did not comply with official notions of order; secular or church courts prosecuted villagers for such incidents. The drumming, commotion and noisy public play-acting ridiculed people who had contravened popular expectations of marital behaviour or sexual propriety. Married couples where the wife supposedly had sex with another man, either before or after marriage, attracted these punishments by their neighbours. Animal horns symbolized the cuckolded husband, and could be depicted, hung over a door, or paraded about. These incidents were often described as riotous, and involved public shaming, and noisy processions. In Beckington, Somerset, in 1609 William Swarfe's mare was allegedly paraded around the village wearing horns and a note summoning the owner to a 'court of cuckolds', while the villagers shouted derision about Swarfe during the procession. In Devizes, Wiltshire, and elsewhere, couples who had been convicted of extra-marital sex were sentenced to suffer being led around the town with clattering basins. A more elaborate procession occurred at Quemerford, near Calne, Wiltshire in 1618, where the masked figure leading the procession on a horse wore a white night cap, and horns. At the house of the victims, rough music (banging on saucepans etc) accompanied the display of rams' horns and bucks' horns waved high on forks. In this case there was violence: the door was forced as the crowd called for the husband to come out, and the allegedly unfaithful wife was thrown down and covered with mud. It was ritual shaming by a large group of men, some armed, with a drummer. But it was violent, and it was not accepted by the whole village. The couple took the matter to the quarter sessions for redress, and some neighbours gave evidence in support of them, rather than the rioters. Perhaps the Quemerford charivari was thought to have gone too far, and produced sympathy for its victims.[4]

Riotous behaviour could accompany the public 'carting' or 'riding' procession to ridicule husbands who failed to control their scolding wives. The next-door neighbours acted the events, with the actor-husband, or a straw dummy, sitting backwards on a horse in procession to the victim's house. Patriarchal values apparently influenced the attitudes of some early modern villages or towns enough for neighbours to enforce them. At Marden in Wiltshire in 1626, the procession followed two young fellows on a horse, one of them dressed in women's clothing to represent the wife, with drumming, and firing of guns when they reached the house of the offending couple. But the event was riotous, and the complaint about it went to quarter sessions. In a Suffolk procession of 1604, the target was a couple where the wife had beaten her drunken husband out of the house. But in court the participants denied illegality, insisting it was 'an old country ceremony used in merriment upon such accidents'. After a public mocking in Cameley, Somerset in 1616 caused trouble during village festivities, the participants likewise denied wrongdoing when they were taken to court for it. They told the JPs it was just a bit of innocent fun, 'without any hurt done or misdemeanours otherwise at all'.[5]

But hurt was done – to the victims, who sometimes took these matters to court, to their neighbours, who sometimes testified against the perpetrators, and to the local authorities who dealt with them because they were uncontrolled and riotous and might bring greater disorders. This was perhaps especially because participants often included men from the lower levels of local society, and some had been in trouble before. Nevertheless, such rituals had a controlling, not a destabilising purpose: they intended to make such an example of the offenders that others would fear to do the same, and thus to uphold the moral order. They aimed to punish people who flouted the norms of marital or sexual behaviour, to limit the disruption of relationships and avoid a burden on their poor rates of any bastard children. And local authority occasionally did not condemn, but actually condoned these performances. The constable of Burton on Trent led the procession against two people suspected of having illicit sex in 1618. The miscreants were paraded through the streets accompanied by rough music and shouts of 'a whore and a knave! A whore, a whore!', then set in the stocks.[6] The neighbours had requested action, the constable claimed it was an old custom in the town, and the justices apparently sanctioned it afterwards. However, very few charivari cases appear in surviving quarter sessions and ecclesiastical court records. That may have been because they were customary rituals serving a moral purpose, so the constables and churchwardens did not wish them punished. But probably charivari really were unusual; villagers normally dealt with offenders by the processes of law. The Wiltshire church courts dealt with very many cases of fornication and pre-marital sex, as did other ecclesiastical courts.

Many so-called rioters were not ordinary members of village or town communities acting on their initiative for their own local purposes, but followers or servants of gentry who incited them to 'riot' in the course of feuds. These participants were obedient: not to the ideal of order, but to their gentry and aristocratic superiors who persuaded them into disorder. They became one more weapon in faction-fighting among the elite. In such cases, it is hard to distinguish what really happened and what was at stake. Much of the supposed evidence comes from Star Chamber suits between feuding gentry, and allegations in the court exaggerated the riotous nature of events. In a typical case, the dispute in Northerden, Cheshire, between Edward Vawdrey and William Tatton in 1596 was part of a long-running feud between gentlemen, in which both claimed lordship of the manor. Each had enclosed common waste, built cottages on it and installed tenants, but denied the other's rights. Vawdrey claimed that when he legally tried to remove his rival's hedges from the common, twenty armed men of Tatton's stopped him; he also alleged assaults on his own tenants.[7] If there was a riot, it was deliberately provoked in defence of one gentleman against another.

The fierce gentry feuds of late Elizabethan Wiltshire also provoked allegations of riot. In a series of Star Chamber suits between John Thynne and Sir James Marvin, each accused the other of causing public riots at the Salisbury assizes, and at Warminster quarter sessions in 1589. This was doubly serious, because the affrays happened in front of JPs and judges assembled to impress upon the common people the need for order. Marvin denied causing any disturbance at the assizes, since he came with 15 or 16 servants 'weaponed only with their ordinary riding weapons'. He claimed that Thynne came out with a loaded pistol, with his 'rout of servants' who assaulted Marvin's followers and 'brake two of their heads'. This shameful affray was created by the very justices who were supposed to keep the peace. The related lengthy factional struggle between Sir John Danvers and Sir Walter Long led to violence and the murder of Long's brother, as well as riot. Sir Walter Long supported the claims of Danvers tenants to rights of common, and consequent hedge-breaking on Danvers enclosures. In 1596 the Star Chamber decided that Long was to blame, and he was fined £200 for 'a great riot' over the hedge-destroying incident. Twenty-eight people had been involved according to the judges: many Wiltshire yeomen were fined.[8]

In the 1590s Lord Dudley of Dudley Castle, Staffordshire instigated riotous actions against the Littletons with whom he disputed grazing rights. He allegedly gathered 600 tenants who seized hundreds of Littleton's cattle and drove them off into Worcestershire. In Star Chamber, one of the judges exclaimed that 'the riot was such as has not been heard of in the queen's time': Lord Dudley was heavily fined for two riots, 500 marks for one and £500 for the second, while lesser defendants were fined £20 for each riot.[9] Gentlemen used their tenants and servants to damage the interests of their rivals. In 1618 William Button and Edward Long of Lyneham, Wiltshire, started accusing each other of misuse of office. But Long also charged Button with organising violent intrusion into his deer park at midnight, killing deer, and assaulting his servants so that one lost the fingers of his right hand. Allegedly an encounter had been set up deliberately by Button, inveigling members of Long's family away to an alehouse beforehand. In these 'riots', the servants were simply tools of the gentry, and Star Chamber had to take the disorders seriously; as was the case with Sir Walter Long's fines, the punishments could be severe.

Feuding gentry provoked riots over enclosure, sometimes to discredit their rivals, for political advantage, and often to win support from their opponents' tenants. The tenants agreed because they wanted the enclosures removed. Other riots occurred because gentry landlords simply felt they had been disadvantaged by neighbouring enclosures, and they secured the co-operation of villagers to remove hedges and reopen fields. But the underlying problem was the trend towards enclosure. People tried to stop the change: one method was the enclosure 'riot'. The participants were not merely unruly peasants, but were reacting to disruptive changes in agricultural practice. These were due in part to a long-term and rapid increase in population, which doubled between 1540 and 1640, putting severe pressures on land and on food supplies. People sought new places to settle, moving into waste and woodlands. The 1586 statute against the building of cottages without four acres of land was bypassed continually, as JPs licensed poor people to build on former common land. There were more landless people, who had to subsist on wages for labour, or on textile and other artisan livelihoods. Grain supplies could not easily keep up with the population growth, especially with rising profits from raising sheep for the cloth trade. So landowners led the way in altering agricultural practice. They sought larger fields for pasture for sheep, in place of crops, and erected hedges to keep their animals from straying. Landlords also sought to exploit the land more, by raising rents and entry fines for manorial tenants, often ending in dispossession of small holders when times grew tough and they could not pay. Tenancies were consolidated into larger units to take advantage of rising prices, and farmers were reduced to wage labourers. Whether small holders lost land through eviction or indebtedness, whether gentry thought of capitalist exploitation or simply increasing production, the poorer people suffered.

Conflicts arose over land use rights, as landlords tried grazing more animals on the common pastures, depriving the rest of the villagers of feed for their own animals. Enclosure of forest for timber, or for hunting expeditions of the gentry and aristocracy, deprived tenants of their right to cut wood for themselves. In Kent, near Faversham, a London merchant bought woodland and started enclosing it. Husbandmen and yeomen living nearby claimed their right to pasture animals in the woods, and pulled down the fences – a violent riot, according to their opponent. Conflicts all over England involved differing specific local rights, but the same principles. For example, Thomas Box, lord of the manor of Nettlebed, Oxfordshire, angered the commoners by taking some of the common waste for his own orchard, and by enclosing the pond which they all needed to use for household water and cattle. He also put too many of his own animals on the remaining common, according to the tenants. This was typical of the grievances which arose. As landowners all over England increased their herds of sheep, claiming rights to enclose commons, removing the land from its customary uses by the whole community, protests followed. But riot was not always the first method of appeal.

Tenants tried legal methods to remove new enclosures on common lands. A common purse could be arranged, usually with the help of more prosperous farmers, in order to finance claims in the courts, even as far as Star Chamber. These lawsuits alleged illegal novel enclosures, often that they were created with force and intimidation by the encloser. In manorial courts discontented villagers claimed enclosures were contrary to the laws and ancient customs of the manor. These village courts, with juries drawn from the manorial estates, sometimes ordered enclosers to take down their new hedges. The manor court of Bakewell in Derbyshire in 1542 ordered the jurors themselves to level some enclosures made by John Sharp, gentleman, which had also obstructed the highway. Petitions for redress formed another way for tenants to reclaim their commons. In Middlesex, the tenants of four manors belonging to the Duchy of Lancaster protested to the officials, and in 1531 a duchy officer ordered restoration of common rights on one of the four. But when legal methods through manorial and other courts failed, when enclosers refused to obey court orders, and when petitions did not stop reduction of common rights, then a cross-section of people sometimes started to take down the enclosures. In the Nettlebed dispute, the commoners had complained to local gentry, who tried but failed to achieve a compromise. After that, one of the small farmers with some labourers and artisans decided 'to try by the course of common law their right to the said common of pasture' by clearing a way through the offending hedges – an action which was construed in Star Chamber as a riot.

These actions were normally taken by inhabitants of single communities; they were restricted local measures, in which relatively few people took part. In 43 cases alleging enclosure-riots in Star Chamber between 1509 and 1548, the number involved was generally under 30, and the action concerned very local agrarian grievances. Most of the Elizabethan cases before 1590 which Roger Manning studied specified less than 20 persons. Gentry-supported ones, such those between the feuding Wiltshire gentry alleged more: 30 or 100 rioters. But 100 seems improbable when the total population of a village might be only 45. When we have participants' names, there always turn out to be far fewer. For example, 27 armed rioters, supposedly in warlike manner, removed a fence around an enclosure in Enfield, Middlesex on 7 July 1589. They were said to be armed with swords, daggers, staves, knives and other weapons, and the rioters were named: they were the widows, servants, and wives of labourers, maltmen, a butcher, a shoemaker, a miller and a tailor. All were women! Some enclosure riots were larger, after the harvest failures and growing agrarian problems from the 1590s on. One big commotion at Ladbroke, Warwickshire, in 1607, allegedly involved several hundred rioters, and the Midlands and the Welsh borders saw the most frequent cases overall – with increased population and developing rural industry in cloth, coal, and iron in the Forest of Dean. Townspeople too suffered from enclosures of nearby common lands, and joined riots to reopen the land to traditional usage. In Lichfield in 1549 the bailiff encouraged the ringing of the bell to summon the people, to hear a proclamation to take their cattle and reclaim their common; a large number took spades and other tools and levelled the newly-made hedges and ditches. Since towns were small and most inhabitants expected to grow at least some of their own food, it was not surprising that they too protested angrily if enclosure threatened their rights.

Enclosure disputes were often very long-running; landlords tried a whole variety of tactics, as did tenants and freeholders, some of which led to violence. Armed response by landlords was alleged in many disputes over enclosure riots, where they were accused of starting the disorders. If this could be proved, then the villagers were not to blame. John Vicary in Somerset apparently countered his tenants' armed defence by firing at them with arrows, and later by hiring a band of Welsh ruffians to attack them. In Finedon, Northamptonshire the disputes continued for 30 years in the early sixteenth century. At first, the tenants complained to the King's Council, which ordered John Mulsho, esquire, to remove his enclosure on the common land. He did not. He was also accused of despoiling the village woods by cutting excessive timber; a complaint made frequently in these disputes. Lawsuits in the Star Chamber failed to resolve matters, and eventually, after some enclosures were removed by order of the sheriff, many of the villagers assembled to dig up the roots so that the hedges could not regrow. They worked at it for eight days, with the church bells knelling – it was seen as a riot, accompanied by shouting, but its purpose was methodically to return the land to the previous usage.[10] This was the pattern of enclosure riots. They followed traditional rituals, and the leaders sought to legitimise them. Thus the church bells were rung and proclamations were read by town bailiff or village constable ordering that the enclosures be cast down. As a further sign of legitimacy, these statements were often made in the king's name. The vicar of Hillingdon, Middlesex and 17 parishioners broke into a close of John Newdigate, esquire, on 12 May 1561, trampled the crop and dug up the soil. The rioters included gentlemen, yeomen, husbandmen, a baker, two blacksmiths and a tailor. Since the vicar had joined such a cross-section of the inhabitants, they must have felt they were in the right.[11]

Sometimes local governors themselves authorised anti-enclosure actions. In Chepping Wycombe, Buckinghamshire, the mayor and burgesses were accused of encouraging a midnight riot of hedge-cutting and burning, against a yeoman who had previously been ordered to remove the hedges which hindered common rights. This group action was implementing an order, not opposing authority. Though rioters were often described as armed, their weapons were bills and spades: tools for cutting down hedges and filling in ditches, rather than guns to kill. Of course, such tools could be deployed to wound, but more often the rioters sought to reclaim the land rather than to punish those who had enclosed it.

Sporadic local protests against land-use changes occurred throughout the period. They were much more widespread at times of severe hardship, especially when harvests failed. This may give an exaggerated impression of general disorder, because of the peaks in such protest. The mid-1530s, 1549, the late 1550s, 1590–1610 and the 1620s saw crises, accompanied by more frequent and more violent enclosure riots. In 1548, and especially in 1549, enclosure riots broke out in many parts of the country. The familiar grievances against enclosing landlords impelled these protests, encouraged by Protector Somerset's apparent disapproval of enclosure and the commissions of enquiry into it. In East Anglia, there was a major rising led by Robert Kett and discontented tenants and peasants elsewhere took their own action. Most local complaints were of landlords taking former common fields or meadowland to create enclosed pasture; some were against the deer parks of gentry and aristocracy. Colleges of the University of Cambridge had removed land from the common use, and suffered direct action in July 1549 when a large crowd marched to the sound of a beating drum to Barnwell priory just outside the town and pulled down the new fences.

Riots of this type occurred in many counties across the south, the Thames valley, and the midlands in the spring and summer of 1549. The gentry and aristocracy may have felt threatened by hedge-pulling crowds, but they did succeed in quieting most of the trouble fairly rapidly. In the midlands two leading aristocrats prevented the threatened rioting, partly by exemplary punishment of a few hotheads. The earl of Arundel headed off serious trouble in Sussex by holding a meeting with the people who complained of unfair treatment by gentry; Arundel told some of the gentry to take heed of the grievances, and his intervention defused the threat. Oxfordshire and Buckinghamshire were harder to pacify. A crowd of discontented commons killed deer at two properties near Thame belonging to Sir John Williams, then moved on to Woodstock, and next established a camp at Chipping Norton to publicise their grievances. Lord Grey had gathered an army to control the troubles, and he attacked the camp, taking 200 prisoners. Some executions followed. This movement had been on a different scale from the localised one-village anti-enclosure riots – a smaller version of the camps of Kett's rebellion, possibly involving Catholic opposition to the new Protestant government.

The Yorkshire disturbance of 1549 was much more violent, and potentially even more threatening to the gentry, with elements of full-scale rebellion. If enclosure underlay it, superstition, and religious opposition to the government's Protestant policy fired it. According to the Tudor martyrologist John Foxe, people in the North Riding believed a prophecy that the king, nobility and gentry would be destroyed, to be replaced by a government appointed by the commons, and this belief partly motivated the rising. The three leading conspirators planned to raise the people by lighting the beacons, and to murder some gentlemen so as to terrify the rest. They succeeded in gathering supporters, and in seizing four victims – men associated with the official suppression of the chantries. The rebel horde murdered the four, and then ranged around the county, thousands strong. But they did not attack the gentry in general, nor destroy enclosures, and it not clear what they really expected to achieve. Occupied with disorders elsewhere, the central government hoped to quieten the troubles by offering pardon to those who would disarm and return to their homes by 21 August. The leaders refused and continued trying to raise the common people, but they were captured and eight men were executed at York. Land-use changes had caused problems in Yorkshire as elsewhere, creating anger against the gentry; Catholicism and perhaps the prophecy added force to these malcontents. But this was quite different from simpler enclosure riots: from the beginning it aimed to murder gentry. The size and mobility of the rebellious band made it far harder to control, especially as there was no noble leader in that part of the North Riding to raise men quickly to fight it. In all, the troubles of 1548–9 were more severe and widespread than anything which followed, until perhaps the 1607 Midland rising.[12]

Between 1594 and 1597, successive harvests failed, causing distress and near-starvation for very many people. Pressure on resources intensified as population numbers had risen very rapidly in the two preceding decades. Shortages of pasture for grazing, and also of wood for fuel and building caused protests, with perhaps twice as many enclosure riots in 1590–1610 as in the preceding two decades. When James I, the new king, travelled through Huntingtonshire and Northamptonshire in 1603, crowds surrounded him, complaining that recent enclosures by Sir John Spence and other wolfish lords 'have eaten up poor husbandmen like sheep'.[13] If they hoped the king would take action to remedy the complaints, they were wrong. The grievance remained, and the revolt in 1607 in this region over enclosure and consequent depopulation (discussed in Chapter 10) stemmed from their distress.

The crown's own policy of forest enclosure led to simmering discontent and riots in the late 1620s. In the reign of James I the Lord Treasurer Lionel Cranfield commenced a policy of developing some royal forests in order to provide revenue. That meant overturning medieval law, so that the crown could end rights of common and lease out the forest lands at high rents. The crown's new tenants, rich outsiders, could then enclose and disafforest to put in their own private pasture or crops, replacing the woodland. There were commissions to press for the consent of the freeholders and copyhold tenants, with compensation, and the changes began. But the lesser inhabitants, many of them poor and without any compensation for their lost rights, considered the whole process unjust, since they had depended on the resources of the open forest, and their livelihoods were now threatened. In Gillingham forest, on the Dorset/Wiltshire border, from 1626, the inhabitants embarked on a long series of riots. In the first they threatened to destroy the new enclosures, for which they were prosecuted in the Star Chamber. Twenty-six inhabitants (14 men and the wives of 12 of them) were named, and seven were tried, with fines on four and not guilty decisions for the remaining three. Discontent worsened as the workmen started enclosing, and in 1628 some soldiers billeted in Shaftesbury helped the local people by destroying some enclosures, rather than preventing the destruction. The government took a serious view of the protests and four inhabitants were called before the Privy Council, but trouble escalated, with further destruction of hedges, killing of remaining deer, and threats to the workmen. Local authority seemed unwilling, or perhaps unable, to control these protests. Central government was more determined: 74 people suffered Star Chamber fines, 29 of them the very high sum of £200, considering that they were not wealthy. Many of those convicted were artisans connected with the Wiltshire cloth industry, or carpenters, shoemakers and so on; there were small farmers too.[14] The fines were severe, and the Gillingham people returned to obedience. But their protests were followed by the more extensive rioting in Wiltshire and Gloucestershire forests from 1630 to 1632 known as the Western Rising, considered in Chapter 10.

Harvest failures, with consequent high grain prices and hunger, led to another kind of rioting, the food riot. John Walter and Keith Wrightson identified around 40 outbreaks of grain rioting which worried the central government between 1585 and 1660. County and urban archives record some others. But the years of serious food difficulties (dearth) did not bring the widespread and violent rioting feared by governments. There was no great outbreak by the many-headed monster, the mobs of hungry and masterless men feared by the elite. Nevertheless, as Andrew Appleby has shown, the hard years of the mid-1590s created serious distress. A small number of poor people actually fell dead of starvation in the streets. Many more had to sell possessions in order to raise money for grain, as prices rose fast. They also resorted to the lower-grade grains and peas, rather than wheat. Malnourishment of those unable even by such means to find enough food led to a sudden increase of mortality; as people succumbed to disease, the number of burials rose to well above the average of normal times. Since even in normal harvest years a large proportion of the people had little beyond bare subsistence, we might expect that extra hardship created massive unrest. Those in authority certainly feared it in Elizabethan and early Stuart England, and occasionally they may have been right to fear. In 1586 in East Kent, where bad harvest coincided with severe unemployment, five men talked of a rising of eight or nine hundred men, who would not care for any justice of the peace nor nobleman. They talked of hanging the rich farmers who had corn. But the five were quickly arrested and punished. There was probably no real threat. In the west of England, unemployment in the cloth industry again worsened the impact of grain shortage and high prices. Walter Pate, a JP in Gloucester wrote to Lord Burghley describing the sufferings of the city's poor. In April 1586 a crowd of around 500 took the cargo of a ship held up by the tide on its way down the Severn to Wales, and soon after another shipload was taken. The JPs wrote to the Privy Council explaining the misery of the unemployed rioters, unable to buy food and forced to feed their children on grass, nettles and such things. Those in authority understood the reason for the direct action, even if they could not condone it.

More positive action occurred in Wye, Kent, in May 1595, when 20 women seized corn which was being taken to Ashford market. But they did not simply steal it. They claimed they would buy it, at a fair price, and this idea underlay many food riots. All the same, six of the women were indicted for riot. Other groups seized grain the following year. The assertion of fairness characterised grain riots. In hard times, the rioters aimed to prevent grain from being sent away from the areas where it was grown leaving insufficient for the local people and high prices to trouble the poor. They believed that was unjust. So transport or shipment of grain provoked the most active protest. Governments always took care to ensure food supplies for London, even during shortages. Hence the areas which in good years grew enough to supply the capital and the major towns were those liable to grain riots in bad. In the Home counties, Hampshire, the Thames valley and Norfolk, concern that scarce grain would be sent off to London provoked riots. Much grain was shipped out from the ports of Norfolk, creating high prices in Norfolk markets and agitation: in 1597 even the justices doubted there would be enough to feed the locals. What they feared did happen, with three or more food riots; a crowd boarded a ship and unloaded its cargo of corn to prevent it going. Bristol, one of the largest provincial cities, needed grain from Gloucestershire, Somerset and Wiltshire, which explains the clusters of grain riots there.

Around Canterbury too the bad harvests of 1594–7 created a crisis, which the justices recognised and described in a memorandum. They knew that by 1595 grain stored from previous years was gone, London offered higher prices to the farmers, grain went overseas, and towns did not regulate the markets. But the JPs' call for restrictions was overruled. By 1596 some desperate poor men thought of halting the corn for export. One of them proposed that they could stop the wagons, 'in her Majesty's behalf' but not touch the corn, and so they did. They refused to disperse, until the Dean of Canterbury ordered the wagons to return to Canterbury. Like so many other food riots, this one was not violent: the 15 or 20 people involved resisted authority only by stopping the wagons, and by refusing to go home when instructed by the high constable. The aim seemed to be to fix the grain price at a reasonable level, not to plunder. And the rioters displayed respect for order and a claim to act in the queen's name. At quarter sessions they received mild penalties from the justices, who understood why they had tried to solve an insoluble problem. Bigger disturbances near the Medway ports in 1605 sought to prevent grain going to ships for export. There were attacks on farmers, with one group of ten people seizing wheat, and a riot of allegedly 100 people, led by women.[15]

Women took a major role in food riots. In 1622 Margaret Baylie of Westbury, Wiltshire, tried with others to halt corn on the road when the owners were leaving the market; she beat the constable who stopped her. For her 'rebellious riot' and assault she was sentenced to sit in the stocks on the next market days in Devizes, Salisbury, and Warminster with the label 'notorious rioter', then go to gaol, and to the assizes for further trial. In Kent the same year, women attacked a corn merchant in Dover, presumably for trading grain to the continent. Bread prices were double the level of 1620, so there was a real problem. Worse was to come at the end of the decade, with the woeful harvest of 1630–31 and soaring food prices. The sheriff of Kent wrote to the Privy Council late in 1630 about his fears of general disorder: the poor were attacking corn carriers. He enclosed a rhyme which threatened a rising, but, more notably, expressed the need for higher authority to take action to help the poor, for fear that 'many will starve this year'. The verses continued:

> You that are set in place
> See that your profession you do not disgrace.[16]

However, by early 1631 food rioting had spread. Sir Walter Roberts was attacked at Cranbrook in Kent by a small crowd who seized the corn. They cried out that one half was for the king, and the other for them. Here again is the notion of justice, not theft. In five or six other disturbances the rioters, mostly women, complained of the low quality or inadequacy of corn provided. Women may have taken a major role because they looked after the feeding of their families, and in the hope of avoiding prosecution more easily than men, since theoretically they lacked legal identity. Or they may have acted with men accompanying them, sometimes dressed in female clothing, in order to show that they intended no violence or injury. The rioters tried to emphasise their desperate plight in the only way left to them if petitions had failed, and to encourage local authority to retain grain for them and to fix affordable prices.

Riots over land-use, over grain exports or prices sought justice and claimed legitimacy. They tried to find an immediate solution to their distress by destroying hedges, or commandeering grain wagons. Local authorities usually understood the reasons why the poor made commotions, and as well as prosecuting rioters, they also tried to negotiate. Both local and central governments increasingly developed policies to ease the burden of poverty for the most disadvantaged. Following the widespread distress of the 1590s, the Poor Laws of 1598 and 1601 codified methods of local taxing and distribution to assist poor families, exemplifying ideas of community responsibility and support. The Poor Laws embodied solutions which might decrease the incidence of disorder, even if they could not eliminate the impact of harvest failures. In this sense, the rioters slowly achieved a wider recognition of these problems, and action from those in authority.

Village riots were usually disciplined and well-focussed, but urban riots had less precise aims, and more violence. London's large, dense population contained hordes of recently arrived young apprentices and servants, far from their families and chafing under the control of their masters. The capital grew phenomenally, from perhaps 50,000 in the 1520s to 200,000 by the end of Elizabeth's reign, and visitors swelled the numbers during the law terms. Crowds milled everywhere, and the volatile mob could easily be swayed by rumours and stirred to action. The city had its own grievances, especially focussing on foreigners, who were accused of taking the work, food, and housing needed by Englishmen and women. The memory of the

Evil May Day riots of 1517, ostensibly against foreign artisans, lasted long in public and political consciousness. That riot had been suppressed by military force: 400 arrests followed it, with 14 executions. No doubt the lesson of those dangerous days helped to convince Henry VIII to back down in 1525 over the Amicable Grant, when London as well as the provinces resisted. During the widespread rural riots and two major rebellions of 1549, the City of London made extensive preparations to control unrest in the capital, expecting that news of the protests elsewhere would stir up Londoners. The preparations may have warned the citizens: they remained quiet. Despite conditions which often threatened turbulence, however, London experienced surprisingly few major riots before 1640. Ian Archer believes the relative stability owed much to various structures of authority in the capital which allowed communication of grievances. Aldermen, livery companies, parishes and wards maintained close contact between people, and a very high degree of participation. It has been estimated that one in ten Londoners held some office at some time in their lives. So grievances such as those against foreign artisans could be pursued by petition, and by pressure for action by the leaders of city, ward, or livery company.

Nevertheless, there were riots in London. In a brawl between apprentices and the serving men of Sir Thomas Stanhope in 1581, a brewer was accused of inciting 1,000 apprentices to make rebellion against the gentlemen and their servingmen. But the agitator was sentenced only to a whipping, so the authorities cannot have taken the threat seriously. Other brawls between apprentices and gentlemen degenerated into riots, including one in 1584; in 1590 riots against Lincoln's Inn probably also reflected tensions between apprentices and the young gentlemen studying law at the Inns of Court. Hostility to aliens surfaced too, with a riot of feltmakers in 1592 and circulation of anonymous libels attacking strangers. In 1595, a year of hardship everywhere, London experienced more serious rioting, although again with no casualties or damage. London swarmed with soldiers from the wars in Ireland and the Netherlands, apprentices were restive, and food expensive. In June there were riots over the high prices of butter and fish. An alleged 300 apprentices who invaded the market at Southwark insisted on the sale of butter at 3d. per pound, not the 5d. demanded by the sellers, and put out a proclamation that all butter be brought to the market, not sold privately. This is very much in the line of food riots elsewhere: an attempt to regulate food supply and the concept of a just price. In the fish riot, apprentices took fish from fishwives who had pre-empted the supply, but paid for it at the lord mayor's rates. Hostility to the lord mayor may have impelled more dangerous events of 29 June, when a larger crowd marched to Tower Hill, apparently to ransack gunmakers' shops, and stoned City officers. Their intentions are not clear: they were accused of plans to rob the wealthy, and take over authority, but these seem more like the exaggerations of alarmed officials. Punishment was accompanied by efforts to improve market regulation, so here too the rioters gained recognition of their problems.[17]

The riots on holidays and festivals, especially Twelfth Night and Shrove Tuesday, fall into a different category. Apprentices and artisans traditionally played in the streets; often they became boisterous. Some reported riots must have been due to high spirits; they occurred in London's open recreation areas, especially Moorfields, Lincoln's Inn Fields, and Finsbury Fields. On 26 December 1582 nine men from the Inns of Court caroused wildly, breaking windows of houses. A couple of days later, one of them interrupted the service in St Clement Dane's by repeatedly shouting 'falantido dilly'.[18] The evidence suggests that the window episode was more a drunken student prank than a riot for rejection of rule. Traditional rituals of misrule could also flow over into riot or even violence. Reported disorders often included the aim of reinforcing the moral order, or of being permitted to attack people that authority too disliked. Hence unruly groups attacked brothels, and theatres: places of entertainment that London's governors continually tried to eliminate. Groups of men, some described as yeomen, the rest of various crafts, repeatedly attacked Joan Leake's South Bank brothel on Shrove Tuesdays, from 1612 to 1614, and caused damage. A new theatre in Drury Lane attracted unwelcome attention on Shrove Tuesday, 1617, when a large mob destroyed the fittings and began to demolish the buildings, but were prevented, and prosecuted afterwards.

Shrove Tuesdays also provided occasions for young Londoners to express antipathy to foreigners, in actions which local officers considered riotous. Ambassadors passing along the streets occasionally suffered insults, increasingly so from 1616 as the crown's relationships with Spain and France aroused hostility. An additional, perhaps prime, reason for classing these activities as riots may have been that the ambassadors complained, and the authorities had to punish the perpetrators in order to maintain friendship with the country concerned. Gangs of youths publicly mocked ambassadors of Venice, Spain, and the Hapsburg Empire. In July 1618, a servant of the Spanish ambassador was thought to have killed a child: a large angry crowd pursued the servant to the ambassadors' house and smashed the windows, demanding the servant's surrender. Eventually the rioters were persuaded that the child lived, and they dispersed. The following year, a false rumour that the French ambassador's servant had murdered a local constable brought a mob to the embassy.[19] Disturbances on other traditional holiday festivals, such as May Day, Midsummer Eve, St Bartholomew Fair and Twelfth Night, were less frequent and less violent, although a riot erupted at Bartholomew Fair 1605. Generally, the holiday troubles were revels rather than riots, even though constables suffered assaults, or stones were thrown through windows. Drink rather than defiance of authority played the main part.

The problems of foreign war exacerbated tensions in the city in the late 1550s, 1590s, and 1620s. Returning soldiers had experienced the violence of war, they were discontented, and they had weapons. Soldiers in the city joined unruly youths in 1595. In the mid-1620s, unpaid soldiers and sailors returning from the fruitless campaigns rioted in London. They blamed the duke of Buckingham for failure to secure their pay, and his coach was smashed by a mob of 150 sailors in October 1626. The following month a larger crowd of sailors forced the gates of the house belonging to the treasurer of the navy; early in 1627, they smashed his windows, with threats to join the apprentices on Shrove Tuesday and make a memorable commotion. Disturbances by sailors or soldiers continued, in a period of more frequent, larger, and more threatening riots in the capital. On 10 July 1629 army officers objecting to an arrest by the sheriff started the Fleet Street riot. It surged through the streets around the Strand, as men from taverns joined in. Local officers could not quell the disturbance; the lord mayor and the sheriffs with some of the trained band faced barricades in the streets when they arrived. The violence caused serious injuries and two or three deaths: it was quite different from apprentices' pranks on Shrove Tuesday.[20]

We know more about riots in London than elsewhere because contemporary authority feared them more, more observers described them, and historians have devoted more attention to disturbances in the capital. York saw riots over civic elections, enclosure disturbances in 1524, 1534, and 1546, and religious disorders during the Pilgrimage of Grace in 1536. Shortage of grain was always a problem for urban areas when harvests were meagre, provoking riots to force the civic rulers to take remedial action – as happened in Norwich and Canterbury, York, Southampton, and Gloucester, and doubtless in other towns. Town rulers worried greatly about order, fearing that during harvest failures or widespread unemployment, more vagrants would enter the town and might riot if not carefully controlled. Shrove Tuesday, Twelfth Night, May Day and other festivals also provoked occasional disorders in the larger towns, although nowhere else had such a concentration of high-spirited students, apprentices and servants as London. Town riots had little impact outside the town concerned, and were usually quietened before the news could reach the government.

Historians of popular protest have found riots everywhere, but how prevalent and how dangerous were they really? As we have seen, London saw some lawless outbreaks, particularly in the 1620s – but the Middlesex quarter sessions prosecuted for very few riots, and in several of them only three or four rioters appeared. Rural riot, too, was quite rare. Essex quarter sessions records begin in 1556, and only occasional riots appear in them over the next 60 years. Wiltshire quarter sessions archives from 1572 to 1630 record very few riots, urban or rural: the indictments for a ten-year period from 1615–24 included a total of 27 riotous trespasses or arrests, compared with 424 indictments for the main category of misdeed, larceny. Any one village normally did not experience a riot even once in a lifetime. In those that did, it was likely to be controlled and in pursuit of a single goal which the rioters believed was justified. Perhaps enclosure riots were more serious. The offenders in these tended to come before the Star Chamber court, often because the riots had been instigated by competing gentry or nobles, who exaggerated the numbers and the violence. But enclosure riots organised by communities themselves aimed to right perceived injustice, not to create commotions. When farming practice and food supply were threatened, and complaint and petition failed, controlled rioting was the final resort. Enclosure rioters may have been fruitlessly seeking to reverse agricultural change, but they expressed ideas of communal good and the moral order – as did the food rioters, and even the makers of rough music. The people may have been hungry or angry in hard times, or disappointed that their governors were failing to solve the problems, but England was not continuously threatened by the 'many-headed monster' promising tumult, as some of their betters believed. Occasionally, rioters sought solutions through action, but they maintained the culture of obedience.

revenue, unless it was under £10 in which case they owed one-quarter. Better-off laymen should contribute one-sixth of their annual income or a proportion of their goods, poorer men less. These heavy demands came on top of the parliamentary subsidy granted in 1523, which people were still paying, and after trading difficulties had disrupted the cloth industry. Yet Wolsey and the king could not have foreseen the universal hostility the 'voluntary' grant was to provoke as soon the plan was presented to gentry commissioners and to the people, seeking agreement to pay. No-one agreed readily. Archbishop Warham, the bishops of Lincoln and Ely, and Thomas Benet in Salisbury diocese all reported that the clergy claimed that they could not find the amounts required and would not consent to pay, although some offered half. Laymen were even less forthcoming, and many refused outright.

Bishop West of Ely informed Wolsey of the lamentations of the people, and his fear of insurrection. Many had claimed it was impossible to raise cash: they would have to sell goods and cattle, but no-one could buy. The dukes of Norfolk and Suffolk met with more serious problems when they tried to secure obedience in the clothing areas of Suffolk and Essex. Although gentry were with difficulty persuaded that they should pay, the clothiers insisted that the Grant would leave them unable to employ their workers. The resulting fear that the cloth workers, especially, would starve without their weekly pay led to large gatherings of protesters at Stansted and elsewhere. Near Lavenham the two dukes met a crowd estimated at 4,000 or more, who hoped to halt the Grant, possibly with a petition to the king. The dukes saw this as a rebellion of the people, and they raised troops to put it down, although Suffolk's men warned him they would not fight their neighbours, with whom they sympathised. Soon, by careful handling, and a promise to inform the king of the grievances, the two dukes secured quiet: men came in their shirts and with halters around their necks to display loyal submission. In reply to Norfolk's question as to the name of their captain, a spokesman for the protesters declared, 'His name is Poverty'.[1] And Norfolk apparently recognised that real poverty indeed underlay the refusals; after reports of refusal and anger from elsewhere, Wolsey eventually did too. But no-one had opposed the king, they were all loyal. The cry from all was willingness to help, but simply inability to raise coin. So policy changed – the king purported to blame Wolsey for making the levy too harsh, the amount demanded was reduced by half, and by late May 1525 the plan was abandoned altogether. The Amicable Grant had failed completely; no money came in, making this the first successful Tudor revolt.

The people involved in the widespread troubles of the late 1540s in East Anglia and the Midlands claimed legitimacy as supporters of the government's social policy, against the misdeeds of greedy gentry landowners. The leaders of these revolts assumed they were on the same side as the government, and were reminding Councillors to bring the gentry into line. The enclosure of common land by landowners was often the main issue for the protesters, who saw themselves as representing the king against the men who should have being keeping the local world correct, but were failing. The statutes against enclosure needed to be enforced, yet the gentry not only failed in their duty to right problems, but themselves acted unjustly. When the landowners enclosed commons, the rest of the community might be deprived of traditional grazing rights. As Bindoff pointed out long ago, the rights of use of the common, and relations between landlords and farmers, involved a tangle of change and resistance which varied from village to village: local grievances had sparked lawsuits and riots before; now tenants were more insistent. Encouraged by the duke of Somerset's commissions against enclosures, villagers took action into their own hands to protect their necessary access to grazing. Pulling down hedges or new fences was the direct way to right a wrong, they reasoned, since the local JPs could not take action or would not. Rioters tore down hedges in Wiltshire and Somerset. By July 1549 there was widespread trouble of this kind.[2]

In Norfolk, the difficulties may have been more acute, or else the small farmers more determined to secure their old rights. A series of enclosure destructions united disparate groups and Robert Kett, who had his own grudges against local gentry, became the leader. Kett was a tradesman and small landowner, who had done some enclosing himself. Nevertheless he agreed to support the rights of the anti-enclosers, and in his leadership sought to establish their claim of legitimate action. The growing mobs destroyed hedges, and moved towards Norwich, where, in early July 1549, they set up a large camp on a common at Mousehold outside the city. Other groups of insurgents tried to seize towns such as Lynn and Yarmouth, and either joined Kett's forces, or established camps of their own. Other uprisings and camps began in Berkshire and Oxfordshire, the Home counties, Kent and Suffolk with similar aims. The men at Kett's camp aimed not at revolution, but results. They saw themselves as representing order, as shown by their petition and organisation. Every article of Kett's demands commenced 'We pray' in suitable deferential form. The list recommends solutions to specific problems, emphasising the need to enforce previous regulations or the king's rights. Many request a return to conditions as they were at the beginning of Henry VII's reign: an impossible hope in a time of rapid inflation which had itself contributed to the rebels' own problems. There was even a request for the king to take over courts leet; gentlemen had been using them to oppress tenants on their manors. And they requested a royal commission to consider the good laws, statutes and proclamations which had been hidden by JPs and other officials – that is, to force local government to act on those laws.[3]

The rapid organisation of a kind of 'mirror of government' in the camp, to replace the selfish and unsatisfactory local government by gentry provides further evidence of the legitimating principles Kett and his followers espoused. Many of the activists were the very men who ordinarily participated in governing: as constables and jurors, parish and manor officers.

Some were town-dwellers used to urban government, and they all wished to exert their pressure within a context of order. A government proclamation later in July complained indeed that bailiffs, constables and headboroughs used their authority not to suppress the risings, but to lead them. With Kett at the head, they created a 'county council' with two representatives for each from twenty-two of the thirty-two Norfolk hundreds, plus others for Suffolk and the city of Norwich (the hundred being a normal unit of administration). They observed forms and procedures, kidnapped a gentleman called Thomas Godsalve to write out their documents, the writs in the king's name by which Kett and his camp operated. Thus they sent out commissions signed by Kett to demand supplies of food, in terms similar to those for purveyance for the royal court. These legitimating statements appear throughout the East Anglian 1549 'campaign'. Camps in Suffolk, at the normal administrative centres of Ipswich and Bury St Edmunds also suggest the desire to mimic county government. In the Suffolk camps, too, the rebels acted as the local authority, to put matters right in ordinary quarrels – restoring a man to his copyhold, putting a man into possession of his step-children's property against a rival claim, and so on. Churchwardens and parish officers in two widely separated villages collected debts due, and took them to the camp at Mousehold to be used as if the camp had authority to do so.[4]

The camp also conformed readily enough to the newly established Protestant religious observance, thus demonstrating their loyalty and obedience. One of the Norwich ministers held services every day using the new Prayer Book, and other Protestant ministers also officiated at the camp, including Robert Watson who was one of Archbishop Cranmer's men. Seven of the articles of the rebels' demands express discontent with the current clergy, and press strongly Protestant solutions, such as ministers who preached, and taught the children the catechism. In religion too, then, the rebels, far from opposing the government, wanted faster progress to implement the reformation, and were confident they were not doing anything wrong there.

More surprising is that Norwich city leaders at first co-operated with Kett's multitude. The mayor, Thomas Codd, considered it would be unlawful to raise a force against them without the king's command. He and others, including the Protestant preacher Robert Watson, accepted Kett's demands for provisions from the city, and signed the commission to bring in cattle and other provisions. Codd, Watson, and Thomas Aldrich even signed the list of rebel demands to present to Protector Somerset. Perhaps they accepted Kett's own assumption of legality; perhaps they thought their endorsement might restrain the rebels; perhaps they hoped to protect Norwich from pillage – or perhaps they had no choice. Moreover there was a good deal of sympathy within the walls for the campers and their demands. Kett himself and his fellows had little expectation that force would be used against them, since they believed their aims reflected those of the government, of Somerset's enclosure commissions, and his desire to activate the statutes. Kett thought the government would listen. He was wrong. Despite all the effort to act as allies of the government, the campers were seen as outright rebels. The official reply to the petition was a sharp summons to disperse, and on refusal Kett was proclaimed a traitor. The violent suppression by the earl of Warwick's forces with many rebels killed, and the execution of Kett and other leaders, showed that their claims to be working within the framework of legitimacy had not convinced Somerset's nervous government. That lesson endured for over 50 years: there was not another mass protest of the common people on their own initiative until 1607.

The Midlands rising of 1607 also took place within a strongly loyal context. Economic difficulties provoked a campaign of direct action attempting to reverse enclosure, and to impress the government with the need for remedy. But the unlawful assemblies appeared very dangerous to central government officials. They also created problems of control for the local JPs, many of them enclosers themselves. The crisis stemmed from extensive and rapid enclosures in Northamptonshire, Warwickshire, and Leicestershire, where sheep grazing had replaced crops, and some villages had become completely depopulated as their old systems of farming were destroyed. A series of bad harvests, shortage of grain and high prices threatened hardship for the peasants by 1607. The high point of trouble occurred in the first week of June, with large numbers of people gathering in protest to remove the hedges and ditches around the enclosed fields. Protests must have been planned, since they broke out in at least eleven places at once; lesser risings followed sporadically. The people worked methodically to cut down the hedges, use them to fill the ditches, and level the ground again; arrangements were made to provide food over several days for the 'workers'. Although allegedly very large numbers joined in, they were organised, non-violent, and claimed justification. The supposed leader 'Captain Pouch' stood for unity, and claimed authority from the King to throw down enclosures to implement the anti-enclosure laws. Moreover, the leaders promised to stop, if the king would himself reform the recent enclosures which so hurt the poor. As in 1549, the protesters sought to enforce the king's own laws against disruptive landlords.[5]

The king took a different view. As news of the disturbances reached James and his Council, military suppression was ordered, but it was difficult to mount. Support for the destruction of enclosures was widespread, coming from the principal towns including Coventry, Leicester, and Northampton, as well as the rural population. Obedience had been stretched to the limit: trained bands refused to muster to fight the hedge-destroyers. In Leicestershire, the earl of Huntingdon managed to raise some forces; he frightened off most rioters, and threatened the rest. Near the Newton camp on 8 June, gentry armed their own servants and charged on horseback, killing 40 or 50 of the rebels, and capturing others, who were hung, drawn and quartered. The grisly example served to quieten the rising, and prosecutions against 900 or so participants followed. But there was some success, for royal commissions to enquire into offending enclosures commenced in July. This short revolt demonstrates that acute anxiety among the people could impel them to attempt to recreate previous rural conditions on their own initiative. It also illustrates the difficulties of control, if large groups determined on action without sanction.

The series of anti-enclosure riots between 1630 and 1632, sometimes called the Western rising, did not constitute one organised rebellion. Yet perhaps they can be considered as one, for they all opposed a single policy of Charles I, aimed to reverse it and reassert traditional practice. Unlike enclosure riots elsewhere, these actions occurred *within* the royal estates – the forests in Wiltshire and its Dorset border and the huge forest of Dean, no longer needed for royal hunting expeditions. Trouble resulted from the crown's determination to raise money by obliterating the medieval forest laws and rights of common so as to lease out the land at high rents. The lessees – courtiers, and relatives of the royal favourite, the duke of Buckingham – would kill the game, cut and sell the trees, and enclose areas to sublet for crops or grazing. But these changes signalled the end of a way of life for the humbler forest dwellers. They had depended on free access for firewood, building wood, and food – grazing their animals, and finding game, berries and nuts. The king, while compensating most of the gentry landowners for loss of their rights in the forest, would ruin the poorer inhabitants, including farmers and cloth workers, and the small village tradesmen such as bakers and blacksmiths. They reacted angrily.

When enclosing began in each of these western forests, the inhabitants tried to prevent the plans proceeding or to restore the forest. Groups stopped workmen making the enclosures, or destroyed the fences as they were made. In Gillingham forest Dorset, such protests had occurred intermittently over two years from 1626, in December 1628 forcing the sheriff to retreat when he arrived to apprehend around 100 people. Enclosure destroyers in Feckenham, Worcestershire, were confronted by the sheriff, a JP and a deputy lieutenant in 1631. These officers claimed that the rioters were in 'flat rebellion', slighting their authority and refusing to yield, so they arrested some of the people. Leases of 4,000 acres in and around Braydon forest provoked reaction, and large mobs estimated at 1,000 destroyed the lessees' enclosures in 1631; other disturbances occurred nearby in Chippenham forest. The destruction in the forest of Dean in March and April 1631 involved armed crowds alleged to be of 3,000, marching with drums and fife, tearing down the enclosures created for a member of Buckingham's family, and throwing an effigy of its local agent into the river.[6]

Clearly these were substantial anti-enclosure disturbances, yet no-one was killed, almost no-one hurt, and little property was damaged other than enclosures. But Charles I and his government took a tougher stance than had been the case in earlier reigns, perhaps partly because the destruction was in crown forests, but also from an official ideology of closer control. The lessees had paid much, and now pushed for harsh punishment. Charles and the Privy Council saw the disturbances as serious insurrections against the crown, and wanted to use armed force to suppress them; the Council complained bitterly to the sheriffs and JPs for not acting more robustly. Since the estimates of the large numbers involved were made by those local authorities eager to prove the difficult task they had faced in attempting to quell them, we may assume they are inflated. The rioters had expressed no overall rebellious ideology: they were mostly humble men and women, and apparently simply reacted to the local forest closures with direct force. Artisans and husbandmen, with a few yeomen, comprised the majority of the 74 convicted for the Gillingham riots, and the 34 fined for Braydon riots. Few of the Dean forest participants are known.[7] Yet they were prosecuted by commissions of rebellion issued from the Star Chamber. Charles and his Privy Council thought they were seeing a rebellion, in these spontaneous, dogged efforts to oppose one small part of his policy. Eleven years later, the king faced a real rebellion.

In the third category of greater disobedience, three sixteenth century rebellions sought major changes in official policy, with the reversal of Protestant religion, and alteration in the personnel of government. All found extensive common support, with leadership from gentry and nobility. By far the biggest and most determined was the first of these: the Pilgrimage of Grace in 1536, in the north. It did not seek to overthrow Henry VIII; here too the leaders claimed legitimacy – that they were pressing the king for a return to the old, correct ways, from which he had been led by evil advisers. The Pilgrimage and the Lincolnshire rising preceding it involved a potent mixture of grievances, and of supporters; religious, economic and political demands and fears mingled. A leading theme was to show the king the errors and misdeeds of authority. In religion, he had been misadvised in breaking from Rome, in the divorce, and in allowing 'heretic' bishops into the church in England. Bishop Longland of Lincoln received special criticism from the Lincolnshire rebel group, because he had assisted the king's divorce, and his officers were enforcing the new religious policies. For the northern rebels, the Ten Articles, Cromwell's injunctions, and the reduction of saints' day holidays had broken down traditional religious life. Dissolution of the abbeys ranked very high among the government's mistakes. The rebel leader, Robert Aske, declared that the lords had failed in their duty, and not told the king about the poverty of the north, and the importance the abbeys had in helping the poor people, so that the dissolution caused distress. He argued that because the incomes from abbey lands now went elsewhere, there was a severe lack of currency in the north. Aske thought official policy ill-judged; Sir Thomas Tempest thought it was illegitimate. Tempest argued that the parliament which passed the dissolution statutes lacked the proper authority; that it was a body of yes-men under the control of Thomas Cromwell.[8]

Cromwell's misgovernment formed a prominent grievance which the Pilgrims wanted redressed; article 8 of the Pontefract articles asserted that Cromwell, with the Lord Chancellor [Thomas Audley] and Sir Richard Riche subverted the good laws of the realm and required punishment.[9] Rumour claimed the government planned further threats to traditional parish worship, and, it was also feared, to the chalices, plate, and even to the buildings of local churches. Cromwell's role in forwarding religious change was bad enough. But his evil government was seen as high-handed as well as wrong-headed and self-serving. He was accused of allowing even his servants to command sheriffs, JPs and other men, who had to obey or be threatened with punishment for treason. His low birth meant he was seen as aiming too high, even rumours suggested at the crown itself. Aske explained that the rebels' greatest grudge was 'against the Lord Cromwell, being reputed the destroyer of the commonwealth'.[10]

For the threat to 'the commonwealth' was a major reproach against the government, and a rallying cry for the Pilgrimage. One aspect was economic distress, with high food prices following a bad harvest in 1535 and a mediocre one in 1536. Yet the government seemed to have overlooked these problems: a subsidy was collected in 1535 and 1536, even though it was peacetime. The government apparently had embraced novel principles of peacetime, perhaps even regular taxation, without the justification of wartime defence needs. The subsidy was unfair, and perhaps impossible to collect, wrote Archbishop Lee in December 1536. But further unjust taxes were rumoured: on baptisms, marriages and burials; on eating white bread or white meat; on ploughs – all of which would affect the poor. The First Fruits and Tenths were innovative higher taxes on the clergy. For the nobility and gentry, the new Statute of Uses constituted an attack on traditional inheritance arrangements and a threat to their property. And the king took counsel from men of low birth, rather than high, men who profited from their positions, particularly Cromwell and Riche. The 'things amiss' provided a long list of matters which the Pilgrims intended to petition the king to remedy.

So the protesters considered they were acting legitimately to gather, to demonstrate, to draw the attention of the king and persuade him to make changes in government policy and personnel. The massive participation – nobles, gentry, clergy and commons, both peasants and townsmen – underlines their belief that the risings were legitimate, necessary, and would bring results. Since they considered they were gathering for proper purposes, the commons turned to the usual local authority figures, and persuaded nobles and gentry to lead. Later the gentry insisted they had agreed through force, or the threat of force, or because it was safer to take charge and keep order if the people threatened to become unruly. The sheriff of Lincolnshire, Sir Edward Dymock, 'induced' perhaps to participate, wrote letters under his official authority in the name of the king to command attendance and bring in men from other villages – and the men responded. Loyalty to Henry VIII was stressed by all, throughout. The Lincolnshire gentry wrote to the king on behalf of the common people, their intention to serve God, the king and the commonwealth.

The rebels' methods of gathering the people together emphasised the supposed legality of doing so. They followed traditional procedures, organising musters by the usual methods in divisions, as if for military service. The lesser local leaders of village and township, the yeomen and tradesmen accustomed to minor authority as constables, and churchwardens, played a vital role in co-ordinating the risings. Without them, mustering would not have raised so many men. However, once armed and gathered, the crowd could be violent, and the murder of the Bishop of Lincoln's chancellor expressed defiance. But they marched ten thousand strong to Lincoln without serious trouble, and there drew up articles to petition the king. The gentry later claimed that it had not been a military advance, but rather a move to petition the king. The Lincolnshire marchers thought they had not offended the king; all expected some redress of grievances. And when the king's negative reply and command to go home arrived, reluctantly they obeyed.[11]

The same loyal intention animated the much more extensive rising further north, starting in Yorkshire under the leadership of Robert Aske. Aske asked every man to swear to be true to God, the king and the commonwealth. The oath he wrote emphasised the preservation of the king, the purification of the nobility, and the removal of low and evil Councillors. The pilgrims were to take the cross before them, for the restitution of the Church and suppression of heretics and the oath was to be sworn on a holy book.[12] Though many took the oath under pressure, they felt it to be binding. Even gentry who had opposed the Pilgrims joined them after being made to swear – Sir William Fairfax, Sir Francis Bigod, Sir James Layburn and others. But prominent as legitimating sanction was the name – a Pilgrimage of Grace for the Commonwealth – and the religious aim and imagery. Their banners and badges proclaimed the Pilgrims' righteousness. The badges of the Five Wounds of Christ showed Christ's sufferings, and now his Church suffering. Other groups carried their traditional religious symbols, such as the banner of St Cuthbert under which the Durham men marched. Monks marched with the Pilgrim army, and parish priests led their flocks, carrying the church cross before them. The Pilgrim songs expressed spiritual concern for the Church and its danger, the loss of abbeys, and, crucially, the commons' duty to help the Church. So the protest appeared as a holy enterprise: it was a justified holy crusade to right wrongs.

The Pilgrimage further justified itself by formal organisation and structure: it was *not* just a mob on the rampage. Captains, including Aske, settled the men into companies for regular musters. After they marched to York, probably ten thousand strong, and took possession of the city, the Pilgrims asserted the peaceful intention to petition the king – and Aske determined to keep order meanwhile. Goods were to be paid for, men kept quiet. The captains agreed to plans for restoring local abbeys, and posted them up in public. As the movement spread rapidly across the north, it remained disciplined, although there was some damage, for instance to Bishop Tunstall's palace. And more gentlemen joined as leaders, such as Robert Bowes and Sir Christopher Danby. Nobles fell in with the rebels by sympathy, compulsion or some combination of the two, as Lords Lumley and Latimer, Scrope, Conyers did. Lord Darcy at the royal castle of Pontefract crucially gave in and joined them. The earl of Westmorland's heir, and two Percy brothers of the earl of Northumberland added their prestige to the undertaking.[13]

The rebels' council became an unofficial government of the north, with Aske as 'grand captain'.[14] Members of the king's Council in the North either joined the rising or fled. Money and supplies were levied, garrisons manned and watches kept. And order did prevail: only one person was killed, by accident, a remarkable achievement. When royal forces moved north they feared to confront the force of some 30,000 pilgrims, and they arranged a truce. Two gentlemen took the rebel petition to the king. To hear the royal reply, a Great Council assembled at York. It was an ad hoc northern parliament, with 800 members: gentry and commons, to sit as representatives of parishes and wapentakes. There was also a 'convocation' of clergy to debate religious issues. A delegation was appointed to meet the duke of Norfolk at Doncaster: ten knights, ten esquires and twenty commoners, representing an ordered and orderly society. The Pilgrimage adhered to many of the methods of regular authority, in a hierarchy of control, with nobles and gentry taking leading parts (although Aske's anomalous commanding role exceeded his lawyer/gentleman's traditional place). The Pilgrimage justified itself as legitimate, and was controlled with an astonishing sense of order.

Order mattered, because the Pilgrims believed they were in the right. Theirs was not merely a selfish uprising: their oath declared 'Ye shall not enter in this our Pilgrimage of Grace but only for the love that ye do bear unto Almighty God his faith, his Holy Church militant': it was to preserve the king, purify the nobility and expel evil Councillors.[15] And they were seeking to enforce the law of God, by restoring abbeys for His service. Nobles, gentry, and commoners shared the conviction, which explains why a very high proportion of all the able-bodied men joined the Pilgrimage. The estimated 30,000 in the main army appeared to Norfolk at Doncaster to be 'the flower of the north',[16] another 5,000 mustered in the Lake counties and marched to Lancaster. They intended not to disobey the king but to present such force to him that he would appoint better advisors, reverse the recent incorrect or unfair laws, and reinstate the abbeys, so that they could then obey. When the king's representative Norfolk promised concessions and consideration of their demands, they agreed to disband and go home. And they went, tearing off their rebel badges.

Thirteen years later, in Devon and Cornwall, the government of Edward VI faced serious efforts to reverse religious change. The dissolution of chantries, and the new English prayer book ordered for use from Whitsunday 1549, provoked opposition which claimed to be a legitimate call for a return to the old religion. But the opponents seem to have been more obdurate and rebellious than those of the Pilgrimage, or Kett's revolt. In the previous year resistance had become violent in Cornwall with the murder of William Body, a commissioner enforcing the new religious scheme. Moreover, the mob had made a novel claim, and one which was taken up by the rebel leaders in 1549. For they denied outright the regime's authority to make the new religious laws, since Edward VI was still too young. They insisted that until Edward reached the age of 24, religion rightfully should be retained as it was at the end of Henry VIII's reign, and so they should keep the Latin mass, the chantries and images which were now prohibited.[17] These claims tried to halt religious change for over a decade to come. In early June 1549 the decision of the town government of Bodmin to protest against the new prayer book provided an official element in the opposition. Groups of local people assembled in a camp nearby, encouraged by priests, and found two prominent gentleman, Humphrey Arundell and John Winslade to be the leaders. So far the rising looked orderly – encouraged by the mayor, endorsed by priests, and led by gentlemen. But violence toward gentlemen, the subsequent siege of Plymouth and an advance towards Exeter suggest militant intentions from the start. A rebel statement made a call to kill the gentry, for then there would be the Act of Six Articles and ceremonies as in Henry's time.

At Sampford Courtenay in Devon, the first use of the new English service on 10 June provoked outright disobedience: crowds demanded a Latin mass next day, said by the willing priest. Clearly, the people were resolute, and set about further action. Gentry – JPs – who might have halted protest did not, either too scared of the commons, or in sympathy with their conservative religious aims. The mob would not readily accept gentry orders, for they murdered a gentleman who called on them to obey. The protest was developing into a dangerous rebellion, as more armed supporters gathered and marched towards Exeter. Their camp outside the city and defensive works on the approach roads, and taking hostage some Exeter gentry and merchants, all proclaimed their stern determination to make authority respond. The rebel demands would overturn government policy and bring a return to old ritual with Latin mass, wafers at communion, baptism only on holy days, reimposition of the Act of Six Articles, and Henry VIII's statutes kept, until Edward came of age. Protector Somerset had printed for distribution his long reasoned reply in the king's name, in which he damned the 'assemblies' as against all order and of a kind never attempted against a sovereign. The king's youth was no deterrent to his laws, because he has the crown by God's ordinance and descent from Henry VIII, not depending on being adult. It sought obedience by persuasion.[18]

But the Cornwall and Devon rebels maintained a lengthy siege of Exeter, and widened their demands – adding complaints about the failings of parish clergy, about taxes on sheep and cloth which hit the Devon farmers, and about lack of government action to assist the suffering poor. The final set of articles returned to more strictly ecclesiastical and theological conservatism, refusing to accept the new service because it was like 'a Christmas play'. Demands included the restoration of abbey lands, the re-establishment of institutions of traditional devotion. Also, oddly, they wanted restrictions on the number of servants employed by gentlemen, perhaps to weaken the power of Protestant gentry. These articles were uncompromising in tone. Where Kett's men had said 'we pray', the Exeter articles each began 'We will have'.[19] Moreover, the rebels wanted to take no chances, and demanded hostages until the king granted the demands by parliamentary statute; the hostages to be 4 lords, 8 knights, 12 esquires and 10 yeomen.

Historians have varied in their interpretations of the reason for the size and vehemence of this revolt. Robert Whiting emphasised the economic grievances, against gentry, against taxes on sheep, further rumoured taxes and lack of help in food shortage. Joyce Youings believed politics had a crucial role, the old Courtenay interest seeking to reassert its local power: one of the leaders had been a Courtenay man.[20] Though economic and class conflict may have influenced the revolt, religious conservatism was clearly vital. Clergy influenced the revolt and the articles, but the common people willingly acted. They defended the mass as the only legitimate form for regular church services. While the rebels justified their action by the law of God, representatives of the law of the land joined in, or failed to act against it. Town governors were among the leaders, notably in Bodmin, with the mayor Henry Bray, the ex-mayor and five burgesses involved in the protest; and in Torrington the mayor's participation again gave the protest an official tone. Some gentry also led, rather than opposed, the uprising. Humphrey Arundell was the most prominent gentleman involved, with land holdings in Cornwall, and he, with the mayor of Bodmin, was chosen to present the last set of rebel articles to the king. John Winslade and his brother, Robert Paget, and Sir Thomas Pomeroy joined. And gentry in local government decided not to prevent the protest. For some such as the JPs in Cornwall, their expressed fear may have been genuine. Others probably sympathised enough with the widespread antipathy to the new religious prescripts to allow the rebels to continue. Sir Hugh Pollard was cautious, and Sir John Arundell allowed masses to be said in Dorset. If local government could not or would not halt the rising, royal forces had to be sent, but even Lord Russell's army took some time to quell it. Russell succeeded after skirmishes and an outright battle, and several thousand of the king's subjects died for their disobedience.

The common people did not rebel again in favour of the Catholic religion until the Northern Rebellion of 1569, and that began as an aristocratic conspiracy with wider purposes. Some of the aims were political, and its leaders were the earls of Northumberland and Westmorland, initially plotting with the duke of Norfolk. While the Pilgrims, the Western rebels and Kett's protesters had proclaimed, and believed, they were totally loyal to the monarchy, the Northern earls intended to determine the succession to the throne, and perhaps to overthrow the monarch. While earlier revolts believed that their demands were legitimate and that the government would co-operate once it understood them, the northern leaders knew theirs would be considered treasonous. The initial plans involved a range of aims and the participants had differing priorities, but all plans centred on the deposed and now captive Mary Queen of Scots, who claimed to be the rightful occupant of the English throne, as a Catholic who rejected Elizabeth's legitimacy. The duke of Norfolk hoped to marry Mary, restore her to her Scottish throne, and assure her succession to the English crown. His nerve broke when faced with Elizabeth's disapproval: he fled from the court, and disobeyed the queen's summons to return. If he could not continue the plan with her agreement, he must abandon it or fight. He chose the first option, submitted to Elizabeth and was sent to the Tower.

The ideas for a joint attempt with the earls of Northumberland and Westmorland in the north, and Norfolk in East Anglia, to free Mary Queen of Scots from captivity in England had developed piecemeal. The northern earls' priorities differed from Norfolk's concentration on the marriage, and they probably also had separate plans to liberate Mary. For them, two other issues mattered vitally: the restoration of Catholicism, and their own power in the north. Other northern nobility and gentry shared the hope that releasing Mary and gaining possession of her person might force concessions on religion from Elizabeth. The earls had suffered erosion of their power as the crown shifted authority away from old northern aristocracy to reliable nominees, making the earl of Sussex President of the Council of the North, the queen's cousin Lord Hunsdon Governor of Berwick, and the disreputable Sir John Forster Warden of the East March. Thus a desire to recover their traditional leadership reinforced the earls' determination.

A wide range of the leaders of northern society apparently took some part in the early intrigues, so the earls and their allies might expect strong support for action to free Mary. Northumberland claimed later that many gentlemen had been prepared to act, 'if the quarrel should be for reformation of religion, or for nominating of the heir apparent': these had been accepted as legitimate causes for action.[21] After Norfolk's retreat to his East Anglian base in late September 1569, the spread of rumours of an imminent rising in the north contributed to a general atmosphere of unrest. No clear plan existed however, and Norfolk's arrest disrupted even the previous vague projects. Without Norfolk's support, the risks of failure were apparent, and the earls and Dacre decided not to rebel, until better plans and foreign help could ensure success.

But renewed pressure for a rising from the influential Norton clan and Thomas Markenfeld made the nobles reconsider. With Norfolk now in the Tower, any action could be treason. Discussions by the chief plotters, with some Catholic priests, about the legality of rebellion against their anointed prince demonstrate their concern. They sent a message to Rome seeking a declaration of support for a revolt – but the papal bill excommunicating Elizabeth came too late to ease their consciences. Continuing rumours of insurrection during October culminated in the queen summoning the two earls to court. Now their obedience was put to the test. They stalled, fearing arrest, but then with the pressure of their gentry associates, and their wives, eventually agreed to resist: the countess of Northumberland declared they would be weak cowards if they gave up now. Still they asserted they were loyal and obedient subjects, even while Westmorland, the Nortons and Markenfield started training and calling in armed horsemen, collecting armour and weapons. On 14 November with the reluctant company of Northumberland, they rode into Durham with a force of perhaps 60, in an ill-planned rebellion, and with doubts about whether or not their Catholic morality condoned it. Yet they still hoped to remove the queen's evil advisers, especially William Cecil, and change her policies. In Durham cathedral they pulled down the Protestant communion table and had priests celebrate mass. Then, insisting on their loyalty to the queen, they called on her subjects of the Catholic faith to restore the old, correct ways.[22]

By claiming to act in the queen's name in the true interest of the realm, and in duty to God and Catholic religion, the rebel leaders sought to justify their actions, and to raise forces who would accept this claim. To buttress it, their proclamations to the people to muster the men were also in the queen's name. As they marched southward they rallied support along their path: it was no longer simply a conspiracy of nobles and some ardent Catholic gentry – the cause had gained popular backing and an army of around 5500 men by 21 November, although the armour was deficient. The government responded by ordering the earl of Sussex, Lord President of the Council of the North to start raising an army to oppose the rebel force. That took some time, especially as the rebels sometimes persuaded the men who had been mustered by Sussex to change sides. Even some of the men in Barnard Castle, defended for the queen, joined the rebels instead.[23]

The difficulties Sussex had in gathering his army point up the relative success of the rising in gaining support for the expressed intention of the leaders: to restore Catholicism, and ensure its continuation by making Mary successor to the throne. Sussex commented on the popularity of their cause in the north, and complained that many gentry came to serve in his royal force when called, while they sent others of their family to the rebel side. And as the rising continued, the convinced Catholics could see results. Catholic worship was revived where the rebels gained. In Durham cathedral the altar was raised and masses said. In many churches (including about 70 in Yorkshire), the rebels destroyed the Protestant service books, and in some churches, set up altars and held masses. Prominent Protestants, including the dean and bishop of Durham, had property destroyed or plundered.

The apparent progress towards restoring Catholic worship partly explains the patterns of recruitment. Despite the assertions of many historians, the rebel force did *not* depend on the tenants of the leaders following them. The earl of Westmorland and his family gathered some Neville tenants, the Nortons and Markenfield some of theirs (if only by threats in Norton's case). But very few of the rebel horde were tenants of the earls; over 80 per cent were not.[24] The earls gathered their following chiefly in the places they passed through, and by their methods. Their proclamations of the cause, and their use of the ordinary methods of mustering men for military service brought in the majority of their force; Northumberland used his royal offices as steward of Richmond, for instance, to gather men, so some followers were actually the queen's tenants, not the Percies'. The proclamations and calls to musters were issued in the queen's name (claiming to be required to save her from evil counsel, and restore Catholicism). So, despite raising an army, taking Barnard Castle from the queen's commander there, and seizing the port town of Hartlepool, even this rising claimed legitimacy.

Some doubts persisted, however. The earls needed Mary Queen of Scots to legitimate their undertaking; but the Council was determined they should not capture her and she was moved further away from Tutbury to near Coventry. The earls did not continue their march south, but retreated after they reached Branham Moor near Leeds. Sussex succeeded in recruiting an army to confront the insurgent force, and marched north. As the queen's army approached, the leaders of the rising abandoned their enterprise, preferring flight into Scotland. Surprisingly, almost no-one died during the six weeks of the crisis – most of the injuries happened to the men who jumped from the walls of Barnard Castle to join the rebels! And a relatively small proportion of the people of the north took part, perhaps 6,000, with neutrality or support from more. It was much more a conspiracy of the elite than a rising of the people, with no ordinary economic grievances of the ordinary people mentioned. The queen determined that such insurrection should not happen again, and around 400 of the poorer rebels were executed. About 80 of the leading gentry who had taken part, including many of the Norton family, and the two earls and the countess of Northumberland, were indicted and condemned but many had fled the country.[25] With likely leaders gone, perhaps the punishments provided sufficient warning. Whatever the reasons, the crown did not face another large-scale rising for 70 years.

Two rebellions shared certain characteristics with the revolt of the earls. The leaders were aristocratic or gentry conspirators, they wanted to force their monarch to change policy or advisors. Both risings more directly challenged the monarch; and both tried to involve London, and leaders of both were men who had lost power at court. Neither rebellion had enthusiastic commons participation. In contrast with other risings, Sir Thomas Wyatt's rebellion against Mary Tudor in 1554 hoped not for Catholic but for Protestant revival. The plans of the conspirators of 1553–4 derived from Queen Mary's decision to marry Philip of Spain: Protestants who had held office under Edward VI feared the permanent Catholicism and Spanish influence which would follow such a match, and they faced permanent exclusion from influence at court, if Philip arrived as royal consort with his entourage. The plot envisaged a marriage between Elizabeth Tudor and Edward Courtenay, a man with some royal blood, and putting Elizabeth on the throne in place of Mary. The initial plan proposed risings across England just before Easter 1554, led by Sir Peter Carew in Devon, Sir James Croft in Herefordshire, Thomas Grey duke of Suffolk in Leicestershire, and Sir Thomas Wyatt in Kent, with French help at sea to block Spanish ships. But, as with the northern earls, rumours of plotting reached the government and a summons to court precipitated action. Carew attempted to raise Devon against an alleged Spanish invasion, but could achieve neither gentry nor commons support in a county which had suffered after the 1549 rebellion five years before. In Leicestershire Suffolk's proclamation against the marriage raised only a hundred or so of his tenants. In Herefordshire, Croft did not even try.

But it was different in Kent. Wyatt managed to recruit a small force, of around 2,000, mainly from the Medway valley, and began a march towards London. Sir Henry Isley raised a smaller force, but was defeated by the sheriff. The Council sent 500 Whitecoats from London against Wyatt, but, led by the Protestant Brett, most of them defected to Wyatt, crying 'we are all Englishmen'. The march on London proceeded, the rebels assuming that Londoners would support them and their cause. They reached Southwark on 3 February, but found London Bridge closed and defended. However, the rebels crossed the Thames at Kingston and on 7 February they entered London marching along Holborn to Ludgate and scattering defenders as they went. But although presumably some Londoners sympathised, the expected hordes did not turn out to help. The queen had made a personal appeal for loyalty, and Wyatt had been proclaimed a traitor. Trapped by the earl of Pembroke and Lord Clinton and their forces, and finding Ludgate closed against them, Wyatt and his followers surrendered.

Wyatt had raised forces in the name of the queen, allegedly for her preservation and for her protection against foreigners and evil advisers. But while other rebel leaders before and after believed their own propaganda, and claimed they were acting legitimately, Wyatt and Carew had to mount their rebellion by deceit. Carew tried announcing in Devon that Spaniards had landed. According to John Proctor's account, Wyatt's proclamations told various stories: that the sheriff Sir Robert Southwell and Lord Abergavenny supported their cause; later, that they were traitors against the queen. Wyatt declared that the Spanish had landed in arms at Dover. When his followers began to desert he announced that the queen's officers were hanging any who had been with the rebels; he concealed the royal pardon with which Mary had tried to forestall rebel action. Wyatt and his allies did not mention their hopes for Protestantism, and above all, said not a word about deposing Mary and installing Elizabeth on the throne. They really were rebels against the monarch, but they did not dare admit it, even to their followers. Nevertheless, they could not persuade more than a tiny number to rise, and their attempt was over in two weeks. The most treasonous revolt had little support, and no mass of the common people to fight for it.

The earl of Essex, to his surprise, gained even less support in London when he tried to raise revolt in 1601. His rising involved no principle of religion or grievance of the people, as others had done. Essex, as one of Elizabeth's closest advisors and her favourite, had been right at the centre of power: he stood proud in his insignia as earl marshall of England, and had been hailed as commander of the naval action at Cadiz against Spain in 1596. He had suitors fawning on him, and public acclaim, with a following especially in Wales. But after military failure in Ireland, he lost the queen's favour, and she refused to renew the farm of the customs duties on sweet wine which had provided his chief income. Without the influence with the queen needed to reward followers with his patronage, nor the wine duty, Essex by late 1599 seemed an outsider with no way back to power.

Yet he thought there was a way. With his circle of friends, the young earl of Southampton, Sir Charles Danvers, Lord Cromwell, Lord Mounteagle, Henry Neville and others, he plotted to confront the queen and force her to recognise his strength, and to reinstate him. He planned a triumphal progress through London to the queen at Whitehall, with his followers and the huge crowd of supporters who would rush to his call. On 8 February 1601 Essex and his inner circle went to seek support from the Lord Mayor of London, but without success. When Essex tried to raise London himself, that too failed. The refusal of the Londoners to declare for him might have showed Essex that his was not a cause for which the people would risk their lives, but he marched with a small force through Ludgate towards Whitehall. After some confusion, Essex and his friends were confronted by loyal noblemen and confined in one of the great houses along the Strand. Essex only gathered about 200 men on the day. In the event this was not a dangerous uprising which threatened the monarch's person, but a petulant demonstration by a disappointed aristocratic politician. The queen, her principal advisor, Robert Cecil, and the Lord Chancellor saw it as outright treason, and Essex and some of his advisors were soon executed, although Essex insisted at the end that he had meant no harm to the queen.

Between 1525 and 1640 six rebellions had failed to achieve their objects and instead had destroyed their leaders. By far the largest was the Pilgrimage of Grace, with support from all levels of northern society and many clergy, and 35,000 or more men taking part. It had never intended to threaten the monarch, and Aske persuaded the nobles not to march on London. But it was so extensive that Henry could not put it down by force, and deceitfully offered concessions to persuade the rebels they would be heard. The Western rebellion produced a smaller but still significant armed force, with specific and coherent aims; it too would not consider the overthrow of Edward or his Protector Somerset, though it did demand that Cardinal Pole be admitted to the Council. Kett's rising had much popular adherence, though it was not a rebellion at all but a demonstration for the implementation of government policy. Wyatt certainly opposed the monarch and intended to replace her with another. The revolt of the northern earls was not the rising they had planned, and may have hoped to succeed by rescuing the Queen of Scots and using her as a figurehead: it raised a substantial army which was active for six weeks until the leaders fled. Essex in contrast had personal ambition, and tried to take his complaint to the monarch in person: his rising lasted only a few hours. But, as we saw, the resistance in 1525 to the Amicable Grant had succeeded in making the monarch change a policy.

And there was at least one other successful rebellion. On the death of Edward VI in July 1553, government was in the hands of the duke of Northumberland, who had his daughter-in-law, Lady Jane Grey, proclaimed queen. Northumberland controlled the Council, the Exchequer, the Tower, and was well defended by military men. It appeared that the next heir by Henry's will, his elder daughter Mary, would not gain the throne, and observers were convinced that the duke's plan would succeed. But Mary, by holding firm and insisting she was the rightful queen, gathered enough gentry and popular support around her in East Anglia to overturn the government and take the throne. The English people were always reluctant to support causes they felt to lack legitimacy, and they were easily persuaded that Mary Tudor should be their monarch. The rebellions which had raised the most support were those in favour of restoring a previous status quo. And over the 115 years, out of a total of many million, perhaps 15 million, who reached adulthood, fewer than 50,000 ever actively rebelled: most of them in the Pilgrimage. Hardly any actually fought. The English were not a people prone to violent rebellion.

Conclusion

When William Lambarde and other magistrates delivered their charges to juries they harped on fear – fear of social chaos and the wreck of the state – and exhorted their listeners to be vigilant. Circuit judges warned JPs as well as assize juries that 'if you fail of your duty this must be as a place where every man's person and estate are subject to rapine and spoil'.[1] They overstated the dangers, but they were well aware of the limits of authority, and of how far order depended on the willing co-operation of people throughout English society. The gathering of tax for the state, or even to help the local poor, pointed up those limits. Henry VIII had to abandon his 'Amicable Grant' in 1525, and yields from each subsidy fell steadily later in the sixteenth century, as both gentlemen assessors and borough leaders levied smaller sums. They recognised that higher demands might lead to resistance, and the crown could not control the subsidy commissioners. Even Lord Burghley assessed himself at the rate applicable before he received his title. No wonder Francis Bacon commented that the English 'were the least bitten in the purse of any nation in Europe'.[2]

Authorities at every level in early modern England confronted a dilemma: how to achieve conformity to the requirements of state or locality without putting so much pressure on people that they refused to co-operate. Difficult decisions had constantly to be made about the level of threat, and the punishment to impose for failure to conform, while avoiding over-leniency. John Spencer, vicar of Aveley in Essex, was reported to the quarter sessions in 1592 for claiming in the hearing of many parishioners, 'I will be lord and king of Aveley and I will make the best of you all inhabitants of Aveley to stoop', supposedly in derogation of royal authority. But the JPs did not think that he offered a real threat to Queen Elizabeth, and he was treated simply as a disturber of the peace. In 1614, John Parrish of Stepney apparently tried to persuade people that James I had no supremacy over the Church. The justices tried to make him change his view and swear accordingly. But although he refused, they allowed his case to drift on, without decisive action. Again, they must have concluded that he was relatively harmless. Magistrates needed to be careful: unpunished sedition might lead to trouble, but they could not treat local loudmouths too harshly without risking wider insubordination. At least until the 1630s, the Privy Council recognised that the people must accept direction from above, but not oppression, and Star Chamber punished lesser authorities for being overbearing. Bailiffs and other minor officials who used too much force in carrying out their duties could suffer the shame of standing in public, wearing papers in their hats detailing their misuse of authority; often they were fined or imprisoned, and sometimes they had to ask forgiveness of those they had maltreated.[3]

After the risings of 1607, ambiguous responses reflected the dilemma. Robert Wilkinson preached before royal commissioners at Northampton, showing much sympathy for the poor who had been expelled from their holdings because of the extreme covetousness of some enclosing landlords. He thought that a stranger, 'finding here so many thousands and thousands of sheep' and no people, might wonder if sorcery had transformed men into beasts – or 'what sheep were these, to throw down homes, towns and churches'! Wilkinson did not consider it surprising that those suffering hardship as a result of enclosure should run mad and riot. He called on judges, magistrates and others to meet the just complaints of the poor, for the disorders had been a lesson not to grind their faces. But he also spoke of the danger which came when men took up their spades to reclaim land for tillage, and then used them as weapons; rioters must be punished severely, or else they would eventually 'level states'. King James too was aware of the delicate balance needed to preserve social stability, declaring in his proclamation after the disturbances that such insurrections 'do seldom shake or endanger a crown'. Although a few were executed, the king offered pardon to all who would submit, and at least 143 did so. And the government set up a commission to enquire into the depopulation, hoping to prevent further troubles.[4]

While governments recognised the need to conciliate their people because the whole system of authority depended on consent, they feared that too much leniency or laxity would allow the unruly to go too far. No doubt much negligence was not confronted or punished. But there were efforts to discipline sheriffs, bailiffs, jurymen, JPs and others who failed to fulfil their duty. A leet juror who in 1562 put in a blank paper instead of a verdict was ordered to stand at every leet session for the next seven years, wearing a paper on his head advertising his contempt. Occasionally, whole juries were sentenced to fines or brief imprisonment. In 1580 and 1581, Gloucestershire and Herefordshire juries which had failed to find men guilty were fined and imprisoned, and sentenced to wear papers detailing their fault, both at Westminster and in Herefordshire, and to attend sermons to teach them their duty. Their appearance at Westminster was specifically to provide a spectacle of shame which would be widely observed and reported, to encourage others to do their duty towards God, the queen and the realm.[5]

JPs who blatantly failed to do as government required needed careful handling. Many suffered temporary or permanent dismissal, as we saw in Chapter 3. And a few were hauled before Star Chamber to be disciplined. In 1552 Sir Francis Leek suffered a spell in the Fleet for insolence to an assize justice. A Suffolk JP in 1555 was reprimanded for absence from sessions and assizes; Sir Thomas Packington was sent to the Fleet and fined £10 in 1570 for not doing his duty. In 1577 Simon Harcourt was imprisoned and dismissed as a JP for using the office for revenge, violently putting in the stocks one Buttle, 'a mean man' who could easily be oppressed: he had jeered at his victim, calling the stocks 'Buttle's buskins'. Probably these were a small minority of the JPs who used the office unfairly – but a government which understood its limits could not risk alienating too many of the office-holders whose voluntary work made it function.[6]

These limits, and the need for widespread consent, underlay the concern about criticism and the anxiety of authorities to control it. As well as investigating complaints about constables or justices, central government tried to buttress their authority, and punished wild words. In Mary's reign, Roger Whitfield was sentenced by Star Chamber to a whipping and the pillory for speaking against the magistrates sitting at sessions, while Gabriel Pleydell went to the Tower for discrediting the actions of the assize justices. Vilifying other officeholders attracted similar penalties, sometimes with the requirement to ask forgiveness. But Lord Chancellor Ellesmere trod carefully in 1609 when dealing with Thomas Coo, who had a complex of grievances against Ellesmere, and alleged he would be able to bring the complaints of 5,000 others. When Coo moaned to Lord Treasurer Salisbury, Ellesmere commiserated with his colleague for the trouble from 'so idle and turbulent a broken-brained fellow'. Salisbury treated Coo's insults ironically, noting that when Coo had done with railing at Ellesmere, he himself would be the butt 'and then I shall be a raven and no swan'.[7]

Verbal complaints in public, and slanders and libels spread in manuscript or print worried governments – concerned for the system of authority to work harmoniously in appearance as in fact. In 1576 the bishop of Chichester brought a Star Chamber suit against Thomas Hills, a city official, for distributing a printed libel deriding him, his chancellor and the archdeacon, scattering copies in the cathedral. Hills was sentenced to a spell in the Fleet prison, to the pillory with one ear nailed to it, to wear a paper at Westminster Palace, at Chichester market, and at the next assize in Sussex, and to pay £50 fine. The Privy Council and judges hoped that such widely advertised exemplary punishment would halt criticism. One of the judges noted that such slanders had been well punished there lately, but complained that they had nevertheless grown so common that 'no estate neither high nor low shall be free from the venom of such lewd spirits and pens'. He believed that defamation even of a private person was a great offence, but a worse one to 'touch in that sort the meanest officer, though he were but a constable'. If unpunished, they would 'breed in arrogant and malicious minds such boldness, as they would presume to march by degrees even to the highest magistrates under the queen, in contempt of her authority'.[8]

Every monarch and government in our period demanded acceptance of policies which tested the obedience of some, or of many, of their subjects. The religious changes under Henry and each of his three Tudor successors, the financial and military requirements of wars, the misgovernment by favourites at the early Stuart Court – all brought those who objected to them into conflict with authority. Yet only a few were punished harshly, many lightly or not at all. After Henry VIII had imposed major changes in 1532–6, he was lucky, or cunning, to quell the resulting protest, the largest of the sixteenth century, the Pilgrimage of Grace. His successors also managed to weather protest by a mixture of persuasion and pressure. But under Charles I official attitudes hardened. His policies provoked strong opposition, and expressions of disaffection were sometimes more harshly punished than in the preceding reigns. Most of those who criticised Elizabeth got off with a small fine or the pillory. But when Hugh Pyne derided Charles I's capability in 1629, Chief Justice Richardson wanted Pyne hung drawn and quartered – though the punishment was not carried out. Reaction was also harsh to slanders against Lord Keeper Coventry in 1630, when he was accused of taking a bribe and making Chancery a hell where no subject could retain his own lands. Richardson proposed to order Bonham Norton, the main proponent of the slander, to pay a fine of £2,000, and £3,000 damages (equal to £2,000,000 and £3,000,000 now) plus putting him in prison for life. Although the others present, the Privy Councillors, demanded less, they all wanted severe fines.[9] Charles I's government failed to perceive the dilemma of early modern rule, and misjudged what his subjects would accept. An indication of hostility was the strong public reaction to the pillorying and ear-lopping of the puritan pamphlet-writers Prynne, Burton and Bastwick in 1637: sympathetic Londoners dipped their handkerchiefs in the blood of the three martyrs.

Although they were sometimes strained – by Henry VIII in the 1530s, by Elizabeth in the 1590s, and by Charles I in the 1630s – long-established habits of obedience remained. Such habits were so strongly ingrained that when the leading villagers of Swallowfield, Wiltshire, devised a set of rules in 1596 to govern themselves, they followed the traditional precepts of jury charges and constables's articles for petty sessions. Their own requirements were exactly those their social superiors would have wanted, with exhortations to local harmony and 'the better serving of her Majesty'. Even during the momentous political turmoil after 1640, such conventions of obedience survived. When the middling sort and labouring poor acted violently against gentry and clergy in the 'Stour Valley Riots' of August 1642, they attacked targets identified as enemies by parliament – Catholics (who were believed to be amassing weapons to support the king) and Laudian clergymen. Parliament even sent messages of support after the initial outburst, reinforcing the plundering crowd's belief that it acted in accordance with parliaments' wishes.[10] These riots were against the state's apparent enemies, not the state; the rioters meant to uphold social order, not challenge it. The English were remarkably obedient to authority, national and local. Only when a significant section of the governing order itself had become so alienated as to launch armed resistance to Charles I were people ready to be led, or coerced, into deliberate rebellion against their king. Then, but not before, William Lambarde's fears of the wreck of the ship of state were realised.

Notes

Place of publication is London unless otherwise stated.

Introduction

1 Buchanan Sharp, *In Contempt of All Authority: Rural Artisans and Riot in the West of England 1586–1660* (Berkeley, CA, 1980); B.L. Beer, *Rebellion and Riot: Popular Disorder in England during the Reign of Edward VI* (Kent, OH, 1982); A. Fletcher, *Tudor Rebellions*, (1968; 4th edn, revised by D. MacCulloch, 1997); R.B. Manning, *Village Revolts: Social Protest and Popular Disturbances in England 1509–1640* (Oxford, 1988); P. Slack (ed.), *Rebellion, Popular Protest and the Social Order in Early Modern England* (Cambridge, 1984); D. Underdown, *Revel, Riot, and Rebellion: Popular Politics and Culture in England 1603–1660* (Oxford, 1985); J. Brewer and J. Styles (eds), *An Ungovernable People: the English and their Law in the Seventeenth and Eighteenth Centuries* (1980); E.B. Fryde, *The Great Revolt of 1381* (Historical Association, 1981); L. Stone, 'Interpersonal Violence in English Society', *P&P*, CI (1983), 22–33; Joel Samaha, 'Gleanings from Local Criminal Court Records: Sedition Amongst the Inarticulate in Elizabethan England', *Journal of Social History*, VIII, 4 (1975), 61–79.

2 *William Lambarde and Local Government: His Ephemeris and Twenty-nine Charges to Juries and Commissions*, ed. Conyers Read (Ithaca, NY, 1962) pp. 74, 84–87; J. Hawarde, *Les Reportes del Cases in Camera Stellata 1593 to 1609*, ed. W.P. Baildon (1894), pp. 186–7.

3 N. Phillipson and Q. Skinner (eds), *Political Discourse in Early Modern Britain* (Cambridge, 1993); J.P. Sommerville, *Royalists and Patriots: Politics and Ideology in England 1603–1640* (1999); Glenn Burgess, *Absolute Monarchy and the Stuart Constitution* (London and New Haven, CN, 1996).

4 Joan Kent, *The English Village Constable 1580–1642* (Oxford, 1986).
5 L. Gowing, *Domestic Dangers: Women, Words and Sex in Early Modern London* (Oxford, 1996); Tim Stretton, *Women Waging Law in Elizabethan England* (Cambridge, 1998); R. Houlbrooke, 'Women's Social Life and Common Action from the Fifteenth Century to the Eve of the Civil War', *Continuity and Change*, 1 (1986), 176–83.
6 K. Wrightson, 'Two Concepts of Order', in Brewer and Styles (eds), *Ungovernable People.*
7 G.R. Elton, *Policy and Police: the Enforcement of the Reformation in the Age of Thomas Cromwell* (Cambridge, 1972); Richard Cust, 'News and Politics in Early Seventeenth-Century England', *P&P*, CXII (1986), 60–90; A. Bellany, '"Raylinge Rymes and Vaunting Verse": Libellous Politics in Early Stuart England, 1603–1628', in K. Sharpe and P. Lake, (eds), *Culture and Politics in Early Stuart England* (1994), pp. 285–310; P. Croft, 'The Reputation of Robert Cecil: Libels, Political Opinion and Popular Awareness in the Early Seventeenth Century', *TRHS*, 6th series i (1991), 43–69; M.J. Braddick, *Parliamentary Taxation in Seventeenth Century England: Local Administration and Response* (Woodbridge, 1994).
8 *L&P*, XI, 705.
9 *Poems and Songs Relating to George Villiers, Duke of Buckingham*, ed. F.W. Fairholt (1850).
10 *The Winter's Tale*, Act 3, scene 3; Paul Griffiths, *Youth and Authority: Formative Experiences in England, 1560–1640* (Oxford, 1996).
11 J.E. Martin, *From Feudalism to Capitalism: Peasant and Landlord in English Agrarian Development* (1983), chs 9 and 10; Hawarde, *Reportes*, pp. 367–8.

Part I

1 Monarchy

1 *Quarter Sessions Records for Somerset*, II, 1625–39, Somerset Record Society, XXIV, pp. xxiv–xxv.
2 G.B. Harrison, *The Elizabethan Journals, being a Record of Those Things Most Talked of during the Years 1591–1603* (1938, reprinted 1955), p. 326.
3 R.W. Heinze, *Proclamations of the Tudor Kings* (Cambridge, 1976); F.A. Young, *Proclamations of the Tudor Queens* (Cambridge, 1976); P. Hughes and J.F. Larkin, *Tudor Royal Proclamations* (3 vols, New Haven, 1964–9); J.F. Larkin, *Stuart Royal Proclamations*, I (Oxford, 1973); II (Oxford, 1983).
4 For reproductions of the images: Roy Strong's many books, esp. *The Tudor and Stuart Monarchy*, 3 vols (Woodbridge, 1995); *The English Iconography: Elizabethan and Jacobean Portraiture* (1969); *Holbein*

and Henry VIII (1967); *Artists of the Tudor Court* (1983); *Gloriana: Portraits of Queen Elizabeth* I (1987); also S. Anglo, *Images of Tudor Kingship* (1992); and original royal portraits in the National Portrait Gallery, London.

5 C. Lloyd and S. Thurley, *Henry VIII: Images of a Tudor King* (Phaidon, 1990, reprinted 1995).
6 Strong, *Tudor and Stuart Monarchy*, I, plate 64.
7 Lloyd and Thurley, *Henry VIII*, p. 32.
8 Strong, *Tudor and Stuart Monarchy*, I, plates 15, 39, 80.
9 *Ibid.*, esp. plates 107 (Mary I by Eworth, 1554) and 108.
10 Strong, *Gloriana*; Strong, *The Cult of Elizabeth* (1977).
11 National Portrait Gallery, widely reproduced; Strong, *Tudor and Stuart Monarchy*.
12 G.C. Brooke, *English Coins* (1932, 3rd edn 1950) has photographs of coins of each monarch; C.E. Challis, *The Tudor Coinage* (Manchester, 1978); *Tables of English Silver and Gold* (1763); Ashmolean Museum, Oxford, Heberden Coin Collection. (I am grateful to the Keeper for permission to examine the Tudor and Stuart coins.)
13 Challis, *Coinage*, Appendix 11.
14 S. Thurley, *The Royal Palaces of Tudor England: Architecture and Court Life 1460–1547* (1993), with illustrations and plans.
15 J. Loach, 'The Function of Ceremonial in the Reign of Henry VIII', *P&P*, CXL11 (1994), 43–64; S. Anglo, *Spectacle, Pageantry, and Early Tudor Policy* (Oxford, 1969).
16 Anglo, *Images*, pp. 36–7, 58–9, 104–5; J.S.Morrill (ed.), *Oxford Illustrated History of Tudor and Stuart Britain* (Oxford and New York, 1996) facing p. 225.
17 J. Richards, 'Mary Tudor as "Sole Queene": Gendering Tudor Monarchy', *HJ*, XL, 4 (1997), 895–924; Anglo, *Images*; Anglo, *Spectacle*, pp. 319–22; *The Diary of Henry Machyn*, ed. J.G. Nichols, Camden Society, XL11 (1847), p. 42.
18 *Machyn*, p. 180.
19 *Letters of John Chamberlain*, ed. N. E. McClure (2 vols, Philadelphia, 1939), II, pp. 606–9, 616.
20 C. Haigh, *Elizabeth I* (London and New York, 1988; 2nd edn 1998), p. 157.
21 J. Richards, '"His Nowe Majestie" and the English Monarchy: the Kingship of Charles I before 1640', *P&P*, CXIII (1986), 87–9.

2 Nobility

1 L. Stone, *The Crisis of the Aristocracy 1558–1641* (Oxford, 1965, reprinted with corrections 1979), esp. section V. See also G. Bernard (ed.), *The Tudor Nobility* (Manchester, 1992), ch. 6.
2 S. J. Gunn, *Early Tudor Government 1485–1558* (1995), esp. pp. 33,

39, 43, 45, 54, 71; S.J. Gunn, *Charles Brandon, Duke of Suffolk, c. 1484–1545* (Oxford, 1988), pp. 35–8.

3 Gunn, *Early Tudor Government*, pp. 33, 71; D. Starkey, *The English Court* (1987), chs 1 and 3.

4 G.R. Elton, *Reform and Reformation: England, 1509–1558* (1977) and other works, differs from D. Starkey, *The Reign of Henry VIII: Personalities and Politics* (1985) on the role of faction in the rises and falls of Henry VIII's ministers.

5 D. Hoak, *The King's Council in the Reign of Edward VI* (Cambridge, 1976); J. Loach and R. Tittler, *The Mid-Tudor Polity* (1980).

6 Henry Brandon's line died out in July 1551, and the title transferred to Grey through the female line.

7 Stone, *Crisis*, esp. pp. 212, 250–61.

8 S.J. and S. Watts, *From Border to Middle Shire: Northumberland 1586–1625* (Leicester, 1975).

9 Stone, *Crisis*, part III.

10 Roger Lockyer, *Buckingham: The Life and Political Career of George Villiers, First Duke of Buckingham* (1984).

11 M. L. Bush, *The Pilgrimage of Grace: A Study of the Rebel Armies of October 1536* (Manchester, 1996).

12 S.J. Gunn, 'Henry Bourchier, Earl of Essex (1472–1640), and R.W. Hoyle, 'Henry Percy, Sixth Earl of Northumberland and the Fall of the House of Percy' both in Bernard (ed.), *Tudor Nobility*.

13 J.R. Dias, 'Politics and Administration in Nottinghamshire and Derbyshire, 1590–1640' (unpublished D. Phil. thesis, Oxford, 1973); B Coward, *The Stanleys, Lords Stanley and Earls of Derby 1385–1672* (Chetham Society, 3rd series, XXX, 1983).

14 A. Wall, 'Patterns of Politics in England 1558–1625', *HJ*, XXXI, 4 (1988), 947–63; Bernard, *Tudor Nobility*, ch. 6.

15 P. Williams, 'County Government', *Glamorgan County History*, IV (Cardiff, 1974), 143–201, esp. 186.

16 Coward, *The Stanleys*, p. 119.

17 Wall, 'Patterns of Politics'.

18 C. Holmes, *Seventeenth Century Lincolnshire* (Lincoln, 1980), pp. 79–104.

19 C. Cross, *The Puritan Earl: The Life of Henry Hastings, Third Earl of Huntingdon* (1966); T. Cogswell, *Home Divisions: Aristocracy, the State and Provincial Conflict* (Manchester, 1998); T.G. Barnes, *Somerset 1625–1640: A County's Government during the 'Personal Rule'* (Cambridge, Mass., 1961).

20 G. Scott Thomson, *Lord Lieutenants in the Sixteenth Century* (1923); J.C. Sainty, 'Lieutenants of the Counties 1585–1642', *BIHR*, Special Supplement no. 8 (1970); V. Stater, *Noble Government: The Stuart Lieutenancy and the Transformation of English Politics* (Athens, Georgia, 1994).

21 Stone, *Crisis*, esp. pp. 199–223; P. Williams, *The Tudor Regime* (Oxford, 1979), pp. 109–35; Bush *Pilgrimage*, esp. pp. 152, 231; G. Bernard, *The Power of the Early Tudor Nobility* (Brighton, 1985), ch. 2.
22 L. Boynton, *The Elizabethan Militia* (1967); J.P. Cooper, *Land, Men and Beliefs: Studies in Early-Modern History*, ed. G.E. Aylmer and J.S. Morrill (Hambledon, 1983), ch. 4 'Retainers in Tudor England'.
23 Stone, *Crisis*, pp. 214–17, 288.

3 Gentry

1 William Lambarde, *Eirenarcha, or Of the Office of the Justices of Peace*, (1581, numerous editions thereafter).
2 Due partly to reliance on J.H. Gleason, *The Justices of the Peace in England 1558–1640* (Oxford, 1969): he sampled only six counties in five individual years between 1562 and 1636, which obscures the extent of change; moreover, he used composite lists of men who had been JPs at some stage of a year, but not necessarily all of it. See T.G. Barnes and A. Hassell Smith, 'Justices of the Peace from 1558 to 1688 – a Revised List of Sources', *BIHR*, XXII, (1959); and evidence in this chapter.
3 *L&P* prints precisely dated commissions issued during the 1530s, with the names. In 1534 a remembrance for Cromwell recommended dismissal of 10 named prominent JPs in Yorkshire, *L&P*, VII, no. 1669.
4 PRO, C231/1 and C/231/4: big ledgers listing documents produced by the Crown Office. I have examined both in detail. A new commission was issued for every addition or removal of a justice, but not simply for a death.
5 Cecil made many lists, often annotated.
6 J. Guy, 'Thomas Wolsey, Thomas Cromwell and the Reform of Henrician Government', in D. MacCulloch (ed.), *The Reign of Henry VIII* (1995) pp. 53–7.
7 A. Hassell Smith, 'The Personnel of the Commissions of the Peace, 1554–1564: A Reconsideration', *Huntingdon Library Quarterly*, XX, (1958–9), 301–12.
8 M. Bateson (ed.), 'A Collection of Original Letters from the Bishops to the Privy Council, 1564', *Camden Miscellany*, IX (1895).
9 *Ibid.*, pp. 63–4, vi.
10 BL, Landsdowne MSS 121/10 and 53: long lists of dismissals, the latter with comments; Barnes and Smith, 'Revised List'; *CSPD*, 1603–10, p. 368; *Diary of Walter Yonge, esqire*, Camden Society, XL1 (1847), p. 50. Lord Keeper Thomas Egerton's papers mention JPs ordered to be dismissed, see Conclusion.
11 J. Hawarde, *Reportes*, p. 106, and pp. 159–60, 186, 368.
12 A. Hassell Smith, *County and Court: Government and Politics in*

Norfolk 1558–1603 (Oxford, 1974), ch. 4 for Norfolk dismissals discussed below. R. Cust, 'Wentworth's "Change of Sides" in the 1620s', in *The Political World of Thomas Wentworth Earl of Strafford 1621–1641*, ed. J.F. Merritt (Cambridge, 1996), p. 67, 74.

13 Hassell Smith, *County and Court*, p. 84.

14 Wall, 'Patterns of Politics' for following paragraphs.

15 *Ibid.*, p. 947.; A. Wall, 'Faction in Local Politics 1580–1620', *WAM*, 72/3 (1980), 119–33.

16 J.T. Cliffe, *The Yorkshire Gentry from the Reformation to the Civil War* (1969) p. 282.

17 Peter Clark, *English Provincial Society from the Reformation to the Revolution* (Hassocks, 1977), p. 264.

18 Longleat MSS, Thynne Papers IV, f. 266; BL, Harleian MSS, 6995/35.

19 A. Wall, ' "Points of Contact": Court Favourites and County Faction in Elizabethan England', *Parergon*, Bull. of the Australian and N.Z. Assoc. for Medieval and Renaissance Studies, new series VI (1988), esp. 216–20; Thynne Papers, V, ff. 136–8, 173.

20 Hassell Smith, *County and Court*, pp. 64–8.

21 BL Harl. MSS, 6994/41; 6996/48, 6996/64; Wall, '"Points of Contact"', 221.

22 HMC, *Hastings*, II, p. 62

23 D. MacCulloch, *Suffolk and the Tudors: Politics and Religion in an English County 1500–1600* (Oxford 1986), pp. 100–04, 184, 197–206.

24 S.L. Hollings, 'Web of Power: The Function and Connections of Courtiers and Great Ministers in the Patronage Network During the Reign of James I' (unpublished Ph.D. thesis, University of Sydney, 1983), pp. 192–8. Barnes, *Somerset*, Appendix notes omissions and reinstatements.

25 HMC, *Salisbury*, XII, p. 562–3.

26 J. Hawarde, *Reportes*, pp. 159–60, 368.

4 Towns

1 P. Slack, *Poverty and Policy in Tudor and Stuart England* (1988), esp. pp. 48–9; A. Appleby, *Famine in Tudor and Stuart England* (Stanford, CA, 1978).

2 P. Slack, 'Poverty and Politics in Salisbury 1597–1666', in P. Clark and P. Slack (eds), *Crisis and Order in English Towns* (1972), p. 169.

3 J.F. Pound (ed.), 'The Norwich Census of the Poor in 1570', *Norfolk Record Society*, XL, (1971).

4 N. Goose, 'English Pre-industrial Economies' in J. Barry (ed.), *The Tudor and Stuart Town* (1990), pp. 77, 87.

5 J.S. Cockburn, 'The Nature and Incidence of Crime in England 1559–1625', in J.S. Cockburn (ed.),*Crime in England 1550–1800*

(1977); J.A. Sharpe, *Crime in Early Modern England 1550–1750* (1984), esp. pp. 101–2.

6 P. Slack, *The Impact of Plague in Tudor and Stuart England* (1985); Slack, *Crisis and Order*, pp. 169–70; D. Palliser, *Tudor York* (Oxford, 1979), p. 227.

7 D. Palliser, 'Civic Mentality and the Environment in Tudor York', in Barry (ed.), *The Tudor and Stuart Town*, pp. 222, 226; D. Underdown, *Fire from Heaven* (1993).

8 Palliser, 'Tudor York'.

9 Underdown, *Fire from Heaven*; Slack, 'Poverty and Politics in Salisbury 1597–1666', pp. 182–94; P. Clark, '"The Ramoth-Gilead of the Good": Urban Change and Political Radicalism at Gloucester 1540–1640', in Barry (ed.), *The Tudor and Stuart Town*, pp. 244–73; P. Clark (ed.), *The Transformation of English Provincial Towns 1600–1800* (1984), ch.10.

10 E.M. Shepherd, 'The Reformation and the Citizens of Norwich', *Norfolk Archeology*, XXXVIII (1981), 44–58.

11 HMC, *Salisbury*, V, pp. 537, 454–5, VI, pp. 88, 133, 153; XI, pp 234–5; F.O. White, *Lives of the Elizabethan Bishops* (1898); BL Harl. 6997/93, f. 180; BL Lansdowne 87/54–5, ff. 156–8; R.C. Hoare, *Modern Wiltshire* (6 vols, 1830), VI, pp. 298–9, 312–13; PRO STAC8/39/13.

12 Barry, *The Tudor and Stuart Town*, pp. 25–9, Palliser, 'Tudor York', ch. 4.

13 C.J. Hammer, 'Anatomy of an Oligarchy: the Oxford Town Council in the Fifteenth and Sixteenth Centuries', *JBS*, XVIII (1978), 1–27.

14 J. Goring, 'The Fellowship of the Twelve in Elizabethan Lewes', *Sussex Archeological Collections*, CIX (1981), 157–72.

15 R. Tittler, *The Reformation and the Towns in England: Politics and Political Culture, c. 1540–1640* (Oxford, 1998), chs 7–9, and Table I; C.F. Patterson, *Urban Patronage in Early Modern England: Corporate Boroughs, the Landed Elite, and the Crown, 1580–1640* (Stanford, CA,1999), esp. chs 4 and 5.

16 J.T. Evans, *Seventeenth-Century Norwich: Politics, Religion and Government 1620–1690* (Oxford, 1979), ch.3.

17 D.M. Palliser, *Chester 1066–1971: Contemporary Descriptions by Residents and Visitors* (Chester, 1972), p. 11.

18 *Records of Maidstone* (Maidstone, 1926), esp. pp. 211–12, 72, 97.

19 R. Tittler, *Architecture and Power: The Town Hall and the English Urban Community c. 1500–1640* (Oxford, 1991).

20 I. Archer, *The Pursuit of Stability: Social Relations in Elizabethan London* (Cambridge, 1991); J. Boulton, *Neighbourhood and Society: A London Suburb in the Seventeenth Century* (Cambridge, 1987).

Part II

5 The family

1 [Heinrich Bullinger] *The Christen State of Matrimony* (1541 trans. Coverdale, many later editions); Edmund Tilney, *A Briefe and Pleasant Discourse of Duties in Mariage, called the Flower of Friendship* (1571 edition), sig.Cj.
2 A. Kingsmill, *A Viewe of Man's Estate . . . Wherunto is Annexed a Godly Advice Given by the Author Touching Mariage* (1574, but written *c.* 1560, he died 1569); [D. Fenner], *The Artes of Logike and Rhethorike . . . The Governement of the Familie* (Middleburg, 1584); R.C. [Robert Cleaver], *A Godlie Forme of Household Government* (1598; 1600 edn used here, revised by John Dod and republished several more times); Henry Smith, *A Preparative to Marriage* (1591, also included in *The Sermons of Mr Henry Smith* (1676); T. Salter, *A Mirrhor Mete for all Mothers, Matrones, and Maidens* (1579); W. Perkins, *Works*, III (Cambridge 1609; he died 1602); T. Bentley, *The Monument of Matrones Conteining Seven Several Lamps of Virginitie...* (1582); P. Stubbes, *A Christal Glasse for Christian Women: Contayning an Excellent Discourse of the Godly Life and Christian Death of Katherine Stubbes* (1591, under slightly different title; 1592 and later edns as given here); William Harrison, *Death's Advantage Little Regarded . . . Two Funerall Sermons at the Burial of K. Brettergh* (1602); J Mayer, *A Patterne for Women* (1619).
3 C.F. Tucker-Brooke, 'The Life and Times of William Gager, *Proceedings of the American Philosophical Society*, XCV, 4 (1951), 404–29; W. Heale, *An Apologie for Women* (Oxford, 1609); *DNB*; W. Whately, *A Bride-bush, or a Wedding Sermon* (1617, preface says preached in Banbury in August 1608; 2nd, enlarged edn 1619 as *A Bride-bush or, a Direction for Married Persons*), pp. 99, 107 (1619 edn).
4 M. Ingram, '"Scolding Women Cucked or Washed": A Crisis in Gender Relations in Early Modern England?' in J. Kermode and G. Walker (eds), *Women, Crime and the Courts in Early Modern England* (1994), pp. 48–80.
5 *DNB* for all except Cleaver; prefaces to their books.
6 Tilney, *Briefe and Pleasant Discourse*, sig. C iiij; Heale, *Apologie*, p. 15.
7 William Gouge, *Of Domesticall Duties* (1622, 3rd revised ed. 1634 used here), pp. 355, 4, 269–74.
8 P. Seaver, *Wallington's World: A Puritan Artisan in Seventeenth Century London* (1985), pp. 79, 23.
9 'An Homelie of the State of Matrimonie', *The Second Tome of Homilies* (1587; this Homily first printed 1563).
10 Sir Thomas Smith, *The Commonwealth of England* (1621, earlier editions 1581, 1583), p. 120.

11 M. St Clare Byrne (ed.), *The Lisle Letters* (Penguin one volume edition 1983, abridged from 6 volumes Chicago, 1981). Examples include letters on pp. 277, 280–1, 133–4, 139–41, 298.
12 A. Wall, 'Elizabethan Precept and Feminine Practice: the Thynne Family of Longleat', *History*, LXXV, 243 (1990), 23–38; A. Wall (ed.), *Two Elizabethan Women: Correspondence of Joan and Maria Thynne 1575–1611*, Wiltshire Record Society, XXXVIII (Devizes, 1983).
13 HMC, *De Lisle and Dudley*, II, pp. vii, 100, 153–4.
14 As n. 10.
15 J Raine (ed.), '*Wills and Inventories from Registrar of the Archdeaconry of Richmond*', Surtees Society, XXVI (1853), pp. 13–14, 12, 70–71; *North Country Wills 1553–1558 in Lambeth and Somerset House*, Surtees Society, CXVI (1908), pp. 172–3; *Merchants and Merchandising in Seventeenth-Century Bristol*, ed. P. McGrath (Bristol Record Society, IXX (1955), App. III: Wills, p. 52.
16 *North Country Wills*, p. 195; PRO, Prob. 11/101/quire 23; PRO, Prob 11/133/quire 34.
17 *Wills from . . . Richmond*, Surtees Society, XXVI (1853), pp.73–5; *Ecclesiastical Proceedings of Bishop Barnes, Bishop of Durham 1575–1587*, Surtees Society, XXII (1850), Appendix, pp. cviii–cix, pp. cxxv–cxxvii; p. cxxxi; *Lancashire and Cheshire Wills*, Chetham Society, V (1860), pp. 57–9.
18 F. Heal and C. Holmes, *The Gentry in England and Wales, 1500–1700* (1994) pp. 48–9; *DNB*; D. Durant, *Bess of Hardwick* (1977).
19 K. Acheson, *The Diary of Anne Clifford 1616–1619* (New York and London, 1995), p. 10; K. Hodgkin, 'The Diary of Lady Anne Clifford: a Study of Class and Gender in the Seventeenth Century', *History Workshop Journal*, Spring (1985), 158.
20 A. Friedman, 'Portrait of a Marriage: the Willoughby Letters of 1585–6', *Signs*, II, 3 (1986), 542–55, esp. 550, 552.
21 Gouge, *Domesticall Duties*, p. 289.
22 N. Bashar, 'Women and Crime in Seventeenth Century England' (unpublished PhD thesis, University of Sydney, 1986), pp. 55–6. Bashar's essay, 'Rape in England between 1550 and 1700', *The Sexual Dynamics of History*, ed. London Feminist History Group (1983), pp. 28–42, deals with a variety of contexts.
23 J. Sharpe, *Crime in Early Modern England*, p. 55; Bashar, 'Women and Crime', pp. 65–6.
24 R. Houlbrooke, *The English Family 1450–1700* (1984), pp. 71–2, 69–70; Heal and Holmes, *Gentry*, pp. 60–68; A. Wall, 'For Love, Money, or Politics? A Clandestine Marriage and the Elizabethan Court of Arches', *HJ*, XXXVIII, 3 (1995), 511–33; PRO, Prob 11/137/ quire 38. Conversely, parents sometimes refused to allow a marriage even after their negotiations had commenced and the couple longed to marry, as in the case of Elizabeth Isham and John Dryden in 1630–31: J.R.

Priestley, 'Marriage and Family Life in the Seventeenth Century' (PhD thesis, University of Sydney, 1988; to be published by Manchester University Press), pp. 51–5.

25 Heal and Holmes, *Gentry*, p. 63, A. MacFarlane (ed.), *The Diary of Ralph Josselin, 1616–83* (1976).

26 Heal and Holmes *Gentry*, p. 82; Longleat MSS, Thynne Papers, I, ff. 154–6.

27 *The Life of Adam Martindale*, ed. R. Parkinson, Chetham Society, old series, IV (1845), pp. 5–8.

28 A. Wall, 'Deference and Defiance in Women's Letters of the Thynne Family: the Rhetoric of Relationships', forthcoming in J. Daybell (ed.), *Women's Letters and Letter-writing in England 1400–1700*; D. Cressy, *Birth Marriage and Death: Ritual, Religion, and the Life Cycle in Tudor and Stuart England* (Oxford, 1997); D. O'Hara, '"Ruled By My Friends": Aspects of Marriage in the Diocese of Canterbury c. 1540–1570', *Continuity and Change*, VI, 1 (1991), 9–41; R. Houlbrooke, *English Family Life, 1576–1716, An Anthology from Diaries* (Oxford, 1988), p. 55.

Part III

Much of this part is based on long runs of court records of several counties. Quotations are noted. Unless otherwise indicated, Essex examples are from ERO, quarter sessions bundles Q/SR/1 [1556] onwards. Wiltshire examples: WCRO quarter sessions Great Rolls [GR], four sessions per year from 1603, and Minute Books, 1574 onward, with two short gaps. The earliest Minute Book has been translated into English: *Minutes of Proceedings in Sessions, 1563 and 1574–1592*, ed. H.C. Johnson, Wiltshire Archeological Society, Records Branch, IV (1949). London examples: *Middlesex County Records*, old series I and II, ed. J.C. Jeaffreson [hereafter *Midd. CR*] and *Calendar to the Sessions Records*, new series, I, II and III [hereafter *Midd. SR*], ed. W. le Hardy. Staffordshire examples: *Staffordshire Quarter Sessions Rolls*, vols I to VI [1581 to 1609], ed. S.A.H. Burne, William Salt Archeological Society (1929, 1930, 1932, 1935, 1940, 1948–9).

6 The practice of authority

1 *WAM*, XIV (1874), 194–5.

2 *L&P*, XIII, App. 5; *L&P* through the 1530s for this paragraph.

3 *Ibid.*, XVI, 645.

4 *WAM*, XIV, 196; *Sir Henry Whithed's Letter Book*, vol. I 1601–1614, Hampshire Record Series I (1976), pp. 10, 13, 67.

5 *WAM*, XIV, 208–16.

6 *Lambarde and Local Government*, esp. pp. 74, 58–9.
7 *Ibid.*, pp. 86–7, 130, 95.
8 M. Dalton, *The Country Justice* (1619), sig. A3, pp. 22, 27. This manual contains 372 pages of instruction!
9 *Ibid.*, sig. A3.
10 M. Bateson (ed.), *A Collection of Original Letters from the Bishops to the Privy Council, 1564*, Camden Miscellany, IX, n.s. LIII (1895); *The Official Papers of Nathaniel Bacon of Stiffkey, Norfolk, as Justice of the Peace, 1580–1620*, Camden Soc., 3rd series, XXVI (1915), pp. 24–7.
11 Assize judges were told to lecture local JPs on their circuits; sometimes all JPs currently in or near London were also called to the Star Chamber, *L&P*, XIII, App. 5, Hawarde, *Reportes*, 20, 106, 159–60, 186, 368.
12 *L&P*, XIII, 34; XIV, part 2, App. 6.
13 *Lambarde and Local Government*, pp. 67–8, 73; Dalton *Country Justice*, sig. A3.
14 V.M. Larminie, 'The Godly Magistrate: the Private Philosophy and Public Life of Sir John Newdigate', *Dugdale Society*, Occasional Papers, no. 28 (1982), esp. pp. 15–17; Bacon, see n. 10; R. Cust and P. Lake, 'Sir Richard Grosvenor and the Rhetoric of Magistracy', *BIHR*, LIV, 129 (1981), 40–52.
15 *The Papers of Sir Richard Grosvenor, 1st Bart (1585–1645)*, ed. R. Cust, Record Society of Lancashire and Cheshire, CXXXIV (1996), esp. p. 169; PRO, Prob 11/162/quire 110.
16 A. Hassell Smith, 'Justices at Work in Elizabethan Norfolk', *Norfolk Archeology*, XXXIV (1967), 93–110.
17 *Official Papers of Sir Nathaniel Bacon*, and *Supplementary Stiffkey Papers*, ed. F.W. Brooks, Camden Miscellany, XVI, 3rd series (1936) [Bacon's notebook].
18 *Quarter Sessions Record for Somerset*, I. Most did not attend every session. The total number who might have attended varied, perhaps around 35 to 40; notably fewer JPs attended in Charles I's reign.
19 *Minutes of Proceedings*; *WAM*, XIV (1874), 200–8, 237.
20 Longleat MSS, Thynne Papers, VI, f. 152.
21 *Notebook of a Surrey Justice*, ed. G. Leveson-Gower, Surrey Archeological Society, IX (1885), esp. pp. 175–9, 188.
22 *The Casebook of Sir Francis Ashley, JP, Recorder of Dorchester 1614–35*, Dorset Record Society, VII (1981), esp. pp. 10, 29, 31, 34, 41.
23 J. Samaha, 'The recognizance in Elizabethan Law Enforcement', *American Journal of Legal History*, CCLI, 3 (1981), 189–204, explains how recognizances were used.
24 H. Langeluddecke, '"Patchy and Spasmodic": the Response of Justices of the Peace to Charles I's Book of Orders', *EHR*, CXIII (1998), 1231–47.
25 ERO, Q/SR/112/8.
26 Larminie, 'Newdigate'. p. 10; Heal and Holmes, *The Gentry*, p. 181.
27 WCRO, GR Hil. 1617, 186, 92.

7 Obedience

1 *Nowell's Catechism* (1570); Parker Society edition, pp. 130–33; I. Green, *The Christian's ABC* (Oxford, 1996), esp. pp. 451–8.
2 W. Perkins, *Works*, I (1612), pp. 49–53:'The Foundation of Christian Religion Gathered into Six Principles'.
3 *Certain Sermons or Homilies* (1547) and *A Homily Against Disobedience and Wilful Rebellion* (1570), critical edition edited by Ronald B. Bond (Toronto, Buffalo and London, 1987), pp. 161–70 (other editions available).
4 *Ibid.*, pp. 209–48.
5 *Liturgies and Occasional Forms of Prayer Set Forth in the Reign of Queen Elizabeth*, Parker Society (1847), esp. pp. 580–1, 585.
6 J. Kent, *The English Village Constable 1580–1642* (Oxford, 1986); C. Herrup, *The Common Peace: Participation and the Criminal Law in Seventeenth Century England* (Cambridge, 1987); J. Sharpe, *Crime in Early Modern England*, ch. 4.
7 J.S. Morrill, *The Cheshire Grand Jury 1625–1659*, Leicester Department of English Local History Occasional Papers, 3rd series, 1 (1976).
8 *Ibid.*, p. 23.
9 Herrup, *Common Peace*, ch. 5.
10 M. K. McIntosh, *Controlling Misbehaviour in England 1370–1600* (Cambridge, 1998) pp. 73–6; and *JBS*, XXXVII, 3 (1998): special issue about the book and issues raised.
11 McIntosh, *Controlling Misbehaviour*, p. 111.
12 I.W. Archer, *The Pursuit of Stability: Social Relations in Elizabethan London* (Cambridge, 1991), esp. pp. 14–18.
13 Kent, *Village Constable*, ch. 3.
14 W. Lambarde, *The Duties of Constables, Borsholders, Tithingmen and Suche Other Lowe Ministers of the Peace* (1591); ERO, D/DBy. Z.1 [A Precedent book], pp. 37–9.
15 Kent, *Village Constable*, chs. 5 and 6 for tasks.
16 ERO, Q/SR/4 (undated).
17 ERO, Q/SR/36/36.
18 ERO, Q/SR/11/27, and Q/SR/12/6. At Easter 1566 the constables listed articles for enquiry at the petty sessions, including vagrancy, breaches of the peace, rumours of sedition, etc; there are very many examples of constables' concern to keep all in order.
19 ERO, Q/SR/19/20, 21 and 22. Samaha, 'The recognizance in Elizabethan Law Enforcement', and recent work by Steve Hindle and others confirm the importance of conciliation.
20 WCRO, GR Easter 1615, nos 107, 120, 39; Orders in Quarter Session Minute Book 1616–1621, Warminster Session [1616]), Minute Book 1621–26, Midsummer [1622].

21 Herrup, *Common Peace*, pp. 81, 82.
22 *William Lambarde and Local Government*, pp.67–8.
23 Cockburn, 'Nature and Incidence of Crime' in *Crime in England*, p. 49
24 J. Samaha, *Law and Order in Historical Perspective: the Case of Elizabethan Essex* (London and New York, 1974).
25 As n. 23.
26 Tables in M.J. Ingram, 'Communities and Courts: Law and Disorder in Early Seventeenth Century Wiltshire' in Cockburn, *Crime in England*, p. 112; Sharpe, *Crime in Early Modern England*, p. 55 for assizes comparisons over seven or more decades.
27 J. A. Sharpe, *Crime in Seventeenth-Century England: a County Study* (Cambridge, 1983), p. 210.

8 Dissent

1 G.R. Elton, *Policy and Police: The Enforcement of the Reformation in the Age of Thomas Cromwell* (Cambridge, 1972), a full study of opposition in the 1530s; quotes in this and next three paragraphs: pp. 9, 100, 278, 304.
2 *Diary of Henry Machyn*, esp. pp. 42–3, 62–5; *Midd. CR* I, p. 23.
3 D. Loades, *The Oxford Martyrs* (1970), pp. 237–8.
4 *Acts of the Privy Council (APC)* 1558–70, p. 58; F.G. Emmison, *Elizabethan Life: Disorder* (ERO Publications no 56, 1970), p. 40–3, 44–5, 49; *Midd. CR*, I, p. 195; *APC* 1571–74, p. 283; Samaha, 'Gleanings . . . Sedition amongst the Inarticulate', p. 71.
5 *APC* 1571–5, pp. 365; 354–5; *Midd. CR*, I, p. 147. Rascal meant low-born, or common.
6 Emmison, *Elizabethan Life: Disorder*, pp. 49–50, 55, 59; *Midd. CR*, I, 283–4
7 *Staffs QSR*, VI, pp. 76–7.
8 *Midd. CR*, II, p. 76, and see n. 10.
9 *The Diary of John Rous*, ed. Mary E Green, Camden Society, 1st series, LXVI (1856), pp.12, 19; *Quarter Session Records for Somerset*, II, pp. xxiv–xxv.
10 P. Croft, 'Libels, Popular Literacy and Public Opinion in Early Modern England', *Historical Research*, LXVIII no.167 (1995), pp. 266–85, p. 276.
11 P. Croft 'The Reputation of Robert Cecil', pp. 43–69.
12 *Ibid.*; Cust, 'News and Politics'. A. Bellany, 'Railing Rymes' and 'Mistress Turner's Deadly Sins: Sartorial Transgression, Court Scandal and Politics in Early Stuart England', *Huntington Library Quarterly*, LVIII, 2 (1995), pp. 179–210 considers the scandal over the Somersets and Overbury as a turning point towards more scurrilous criticism of courtiers.

13 *Poems and Songs Relating to Buckingham*. This song is on p. 18.
14 A. Fox, 'Rumour, News and Popular Political Opinion in Elizabethan and Early Stuart England', *HJ*, LX, 3 (1997), 597–620.
15 ERO, Q/SR/30/1; Thomas Glascock /102/36.
16 *Quarter Sessions Records for Somerset*, I, pp. 36–7, 46–7.
17 *Ibid*., vol. II, p. xxv.
18 WCRO, GR M 1605, 247; T 1606, 122; *Midd. CR*, II, pp. 117, 99; ERO Q/SR/230/7, 67.
19 WCRO, GR E 1615, 39, 120; Minute Book, 1610–1616, Warminster, July [1615].
20 *Quarter Sessions Records for Somerset*, II, p.xxv.
21 WCRO, GR H 1617, 50, 51, 199v.
22 Longleat MSS, Thynne Papers, Box 59, ff. 156–69, 188.
23 *Middx. CR*, I, pp. 217–8.
24 *Staffs QSR*, IV, p. 194.
25 Cheshire Record Office, QJF 19/2, f. 27, QJF/19/3, f. 30.
26 Cheshire Record office, QJF 19/2, f. 28.

9 Riot

1 ERO, Q/SR/19/14. (Lillingdale Lovell then was a detached Oxfordshire enclave in Buckinghamshire.)
2 Underdown, *Revel, Riot and Rebellion*, p. 110.
3 WCRO, GR M 1615, 107; Minute Book 1610–16, Michaelmas 1615: the court ordered fines and prison; he was still under surveillance the following year when the minutes for the Devizes session noted his recognizance in the high sum of £40, with his father and a blacksmith as sureties.
4 M. Ingram, 'Ridings, Rough Music and the "Reform of Popular Culture" in Early Modern England', *P&P*, CV (1984), 79–113, discusses these two and other cases.
5 D. Underdown, 'The Taming of the Scold' in A. Fletcher and J. Stevenson (eds.), *Order and Disorder in Early Modern England* (Cambridge, 1985), ch. 4, pp. 130–33.
6 Ingram, 'Ridings, Rough Music', 105.
7 Manning, *Village Revolts*, p. 65.
8 Wall, 'Faction in Local Politics', 120–5 [132–3 for Long–Button conflict below]; Hawarde, *Reportes*, pp. 391, App. iii; PRO, Estreats of Fines in Star Chamber.
9 Manning, *Village Revolts*, p. 67.
10 Examples for this and previous four paragraphs, Manning, *Village Revolts*, pp. 88, 41–5, 68–9, 71, 82–3. The comment is mine.
11 *Midd. CR*, I, p. 40.
12 Beer, *Rebellion and Riot*, ch. 6.

13 J. Nichols (ed.), *The Progresses of James I* (4 vols, 1828), I, p. 104, from a pamphlet printed in 1603, slightly misquoting Thomas More's *Utopia.*
14 Sharp, *In Contempt of All Authority*, pp. 85–9, 127–8.
15 J. Walter and K. Wrightson, 'Dearth and the Social Order in Early Modern England', *P&P*, LXXI (1974), 22–42; and P. Clark, 'Popular Protest and Disturbance in Kent, 1558–1640', *Economic History Review*, 2nd series, XXIX, 3 (1976), 365–381; Sharp, *In Contempt of All Authority*, pp. 15–16.
16 WCRO, GR E 1622, 257, and T 1622, 165; Clark, 'Popular Protest', 369–70.
17 Archer, *Pursuit of Stability*, esp. pp. 1–7
18 *Midd. CR*, I, pp. 134–5.
19 K. Lindley, 'Riot Prevention and Control in Early Stuart London', *RHS*, 5th ser. XXXIII (1983), 109–26.
20 *Ibid*,. pp. 113–15.

10 Rebellion

1 G. Bernard, *War, Taxation and Rebellion in Early Tudor England: Henry VIII, Wolsey and the Amicable Grant of 1525* (Brighton, 1986), p. 111.
2 S.T. Bindoff, *Kett's Rebellion 1549* (Historical Association, 1949).
3 Fletcher and MacCulloch, *Tudor Rebellions*, 4th edn (1997), Document pp. 144–6; ch. 6; D. MacCulloch, 'Kett's Rebellion in Context', *P&P*, LXXXIV (1979), reprinted in Slack (ed.), *Rebellion, Popular Protest*, ch. 2.
4 Bindoff, *Kett's Rebellion*, p. 16; MacCulloch in Slack (ed.), *Rebellion, Popular Protest*, p. 48.
5 J. Martin, *Feudalism to Capitalism: Peasant and Landlord in English Agricultural Development*, Part III, Case Study: the Midlands Revolt of 1607.
6 B. Sharp, *In Contempt*, ch. 4; E. Kerridge, 'The Revolts in Wiltshire against Charles I', *WAM*, LVII (1958–60), 64–75.
7 Sharp, *In Contempt*, pp. 127–30.
8 C.S.L. Davies, 'The Pilgrimage of Grace Reconsidered', *P&P*, XLI (1968) reprinted in Slack (ed.), *Rebellion, Popular Protest*; C. Haigh, *English Reformations* (Oxford, 1993), pp. 143–50; M.L. Bush, *The Pilgrimage*. Aske's statement is printed in Fletcher and MacCulloch, *Tudor Rebellions*, pp. 132–3.
9 *Tudor Rebellions*, p.136.
10 C.S.L. Davies, 'Popular Religion and the Pilgrimage of Grace', in Fletcher and Stevenson *Order and Disorder*, ch. 2; p. 72.
11 S. Gunn, 'Peers, Commons and Gentry in the Lincolnshire Revolt of 1536', *P&P*, CXXIII (1989), 52–79.

12 The oath is printed in Fletcher and MacCulloch, *Tudor Rebellions*, p. 132.
13 Bush, *Pilgrimage*, for detailed discussion of leadership; R. Hoyle, 'Thomas Masters' Narrative of the Pilgrimage of Grace', *Northern History*, XXI (1985), 53–79.
14 Davies, 'Popular Religion and the Pilgrimage', p. 62.
15 See n. 12.
16 Davies, 'Popular Religion and the Pilgimage', p. 61, n.8.
17 Haigh, *English Reformations*, pp. 170–76; F. Rose-Troup, *The Western Rebellion of 1549* (1913), a full coverage, with documents reproduced in Appendix. Demands also printed *Tudor Rebellions*, pp. 139–41.
18 Somerset's reply sought to refute each rebel demand: J. Foxe, *Acts and Monuments of the English Martyrs*, ed. G. Cattley and S. Townsend, V (1838), pp. 732–6.
19 See n. 17 for references for Western rebel demands, n. 3 for Kett's. Somerset prepared a further set of answers against the rebel claims.
20 R. Whiting, *The Blind Devotion of the People* (Cambridge, 1989), pp. 34–8; J. Youings, 'The South-Western Rebellion of 1549', *Southern History*, I (1979), 99–122.
21 Northumberland's examination reproduced in Fletcher and MacCulloch, pp. 151–2.
22 S. E. Taylor, 'The Crown and the North of England, 1559–70: A Study of the Rebellion of the Northern Earls, 1569–70, and its causes' (unpublished PhD. thesis, Manchester, 1981) is the fullest account of the revolt. This discussion follows her interpretation, which differs from others.
23 *Ibid.*, pp. 192–214.
24 *Ibid.*, pp. 216–19, 251–9. Ch. 7, 'Participants', examines more extensive lists than those in the *Calendar of State Papers, Domestic.*
25 *Ibid.*, pp. 334–40.

Conclusion

1 Lambarde, see Introduction; BL Add. Ms 32,518, f. 129.
2 R. Schofield, 'Taxation and the Political Limits of the Tudor State', in *Law and Government Under the Tudors*, ed. C. Cross, D. Loades and J. Scarisbrick (Cambridge, 1988); M. Braddick, *Parliamentary Taxation*, p. 271. Braddick shows big increases in the tax burden in the seventeenth century, mainly after 1640.
3 ERO Q/SR/120/25, /121/50; *Midd. SR*, I, pp. 291, 333.
4 R. Wilkinson, *A Sermon Preached at North-Hampton the 21 of June Last Past, Before the Lord Lieutenant of the County and the rest of the Commissioners there assembled upon the occasion of the late Rebellion and Riots in those Parts Committed* (1607).
5 HEH, EL 2768, ff. 21v, 25v, 46–9; EL 2652, ff. 10–12.

6 HEH, EL 2652 f. 15v; EL 2768 f. 68v.
7 HEH, EL 2768, ff. 25, 25v, 68; EL 2652, ff. 8v, 12v, 14, 17v; EL 5745–76; R.B. Manning, *Religion and Society in Elizabethan Sussex* (Leicester, 1969), pp. 104–7.
8 HEH, EL 2768, f. 67–67v.
9 HEH, EL 7950, ff. 1–24.
10 S. Hindle, 'Hierarchy and Community in the Elizabethan Parish: The Swallowfield Articles of 1596', *HJ*, XLII, 3 (1999), 835–51; ERO, Q/SR/18/61 and other examples in Essex; J. Walter, *Understanding Popular Violence in the English Revolution* (Cambridge, 1999), esp. ch. 2, and pp.329–30.

Select bibliography

For background or further reading. Place of publication is London unless stated.

Introduction

P. Slack (ed.), *Rebellion, Popular Protest and the Social Order in Early Modern England* (Cambridge, 1984); Keith Wrightson, 'Two Concepts of Order: Justices, Constables and Jurymen in Seventeenth-century England', in J. Brewer and J. Styles (eds.), *An Ungovernable People: The English and Their Law in the Seventeenth and Eighteenth Centuries* (1980).

1 Monarchy

For monarchs and government, and background to following chapters: G. Elton, *Reform and Reformation: England 1509–1558* (1977); S. Gunn, *Early Tudor Government, 1485–1558* (1995); D. Starkey, *The English Court from the Wars of the Roses to the Civil War* (1987).

More detailed studies of monarchs: D. Starkey, *The Reign of Henry VIII: Personalities and Politics* (1985); J. Loach, *Edward VI* (London and New Haven, CN, 1999); D. Loades, *The Reign of Mary Tudor* (1979); C. Haigh, *Elizabeth I* (1988, 2nd edn, 1998); R. Lockyer, *The Early Stuarts: A Political History of England 1603–1642* (London and New Haven, CN, 1989); K. Sharpe, *The Personal Rule of Charles I* (Yale, N.H. 1992)

On imagery: Roy Strong's many books, e.g *The Tudor and Stuart Monarchy*, I & II (1995), or *The English Iconography: Elizabethan and Jacobean Portraiture* (1969); S. Anglo, *Images of Tudor Kingship* (1992); C.E. Challis, *The Tudor Coinage* (Manchester, 1978); S. Thurley, *The Royal Palaces of Tudor England: Architecture and Court Life 1460–1547* (1993) includes illustrations and plans).

On ceremony: J. Loach, 'The Function of Ceremonial in the Reign of Henry VIII', *P&P*, CXLII (1994), 43–64; J.M. Richards, 'Mary Tudor as 'Sole Queene': Gendering Tudor Monarchy', *HJ*, XL, 4 (1997), 895–924.

2 Nobility

L. Stone, *The Crisis of the Aristocracy 1558–1641* (Oxford, 1965, reprinted with corrections 1979) remains the key reference. G. Bernard (ed.), *The Tudor Nobility* (Manchester, 1992) for the early Tudor nobility with studies of individual nobles; S. Adams, 'Eliza Enthroned? The Court and its Politics', in C. Haigh (ed.), *The Reign of Elizabeth I* (1984), pp. 55–78.

Books on individuals or families: The *Dictionary of National Biography* (currently being revised) has brief histories. See also B. Coward, *The Stanleys, Lords Stanley and Earls of Derby 1385–1672* (Chetham Society, 3rd series, XXX, 1983); for the exercise of outstanding regional influence, N. Williams, *Thomas Howard Fourth Duke of Norfolk* (1964); C. Cross, *The Puritan Earl: the Life of Henry Hastings, Third Earl of Huntingdon* (1966); T. Cogswell, *Home Divisions: Aristocracy, the State and Provincial Conflict* (Manchester, 1998) for the problems of the fifth earl of Huntingdon.

3 Gentry

P. Williams, 'The Crown and the Counties', in Haigh (ed.), *Reign of Elizabeth*, pp. 125–46.

County studies include: A. Hassell Smith, *County and Court: Government and Politics in Norfolk 1558–1603* (Oxford, 1974), an excellent start, with material relevant to gentry officeholding in general. T.G. Barnes, *Somerset 1625–1640: A County's Government during the Personal Rule* (1961) is still good. P. Clark, *English Provincial Society from the Reformation to the Revolution* (Hassocks, 1977) is long and detailed on Kent; C. Holmes, *Seventeenth-Century Lincolnshire* (Lincoln, 1980) and D. MacCulloch, *Suffolk and the Tudors: Politics and Religion in an English County 1500–1600* (Oxford 1986) both have material on gentry politics and competition.

Instability in office: T.G. Barnes and A. Hassell Smith, 'Justices of the Peace from 1558 to 1688: A Revised List of Sources', *BIHR*, XXII (1959); J. Guy, Thomas Wolsey, 'Thomas Cromwell and the Reform of Henrician Government', in *The Reign of Henry VIII: Politics, Policy and Piety*, ed. D. MacCulloch (1995), pp. 48–57; A. Wall, 'Patterns of Politics in England 1558–1625', *HJ*, XXXI, 4 (1988), 947–63.

4 Towns

General studies and collections of essays: J. Barry (ed.), *The Tudor and Stuart Town* (1990); P. Clark and P. Slack (eds), *Crisis and Order in English Towns* (1972); P. Clark (ed.), *The Transformation of English Provincial Towns* 1600–1800 (1984).

Charters and politics: R. Tittler *The Reformation and the Towns in England: Politics and Political Culture, c. 1540–1640* (Oxford, 1998), chs 7–9, and Table I; C.F. Patterson, *Urban Patronage in Early Modern England: Corporate Boroughs, the Landed Elite, and the Crown, 1580–1640* (Stanford, 1999), esp. chs 4 and 5.

Presentation: R. Tittler, *Architecture and Power: the Town Hall and the English Urban Community c. 1500–1640* (Oxford, 1991).

Individual towns: I. Archer, *The Pursuit of Stability: Social Relations in Elizabethan London* (Cambridge, 1991); W. MacCaffrey, *Exeter 1540–1640: The Growth of an English County Town* (Harvard, 1958); D. Palliser, *Tudor York* (Oxford, 1979); D. Underdown, *Fire From Heaven: Life in an English Town in the Seventeenth Century* (1993) (about Dorchester); P. Slack, 'Poverty and Politics in Salisbury' in his *Crisis and Order*.

5 The family

General introduction: R. Houlbrooke, *The English Family 1450–1700* (1984).

On household order: S. Amussen, *An Ordered Society: Gender and Class in Early Modern England* (Oxford, 1988); K. Davies, 'Continuity and Change in Literary Advice on Marriage', in R. Outhwaite (ed.), *Marriage and Society: Studies in the Social History of Marriage* (1981), pp. 55–80 remains a good approach to the conduct books; A. Wall, 'Elizabethan Precept and Feminine Practice: the Thynne Family of Longleat', *History*, LXXV, 243 (1990), 23–38 for the godly books and some reaction in practice.

Particular aspects: A. Erickson, *Women and Property in Early Modern England* (1993); D. Cressy, *Birth, Marriage and Death: Ritual, Religion, and the Life Cycle in Tudor and Stuart England* (Oxford, 1997); D. O'Hara, '"Ruled by My Friends": Aspects of Marriage in the Diocese of Canterbury c. 1540–1570', *Continuity and Change*, VI, 1 (1991), 9–41; F. Heal and C. Holmes, *The Gentry in England and Wales 1500–1700* (1994), ch. 2; M.Ingram, '"Scolding Women Cucked or Washed": A Crisis in Gender Relations in Early Modern England?', in J. Kermode and G. Walker (eds.), *Women, Crime and the Courts in Early Modern England* (1994); S. Mendelson and P. Crawford, *Women in Early Modern England* (Oxford, 1998), ch. 5. on work.

Printed primary sources: R. Houlbrooke, *English Family Life, 1576–1716, An Anthology from Diaries* (Oxford, 1988); M. St Clare Byrne (ed.), *The Lisle Letters* (Harmondsworth, 1983; Penguin, one-vol edn, abridged from 6 vols, Chicago, 1981); A. Wall (ed.), *Two Elizabethan Women: Correspondence of Joan and Maria Thynne 1575–1611*, Wiltshire Record Society, XXXVIII (Devizes, 1983).

6 The practice of authority

Tasks: A. Hassell Smith, 'Justices at Work in Elizabethan Norfolk', *Norfolk Archeology*, XXXIV (1967), 93–110; F. Heal and C. Holmes, *The Gentry in England and Wales 1500–1700* (1994), ch. 5. Administration: J. Samaha, 'The Recognizance in Elizabethan Law Enforcement', *American Journal of Legal History*, CCLI, 3 (1981), pp. 189–204 explains how recognizances were used, as does S. Hindle, 'The Keeping of the Public Peace', in P. Griffiths, A. Fox and S. Hindle (eds), *The Experience of Authority in Early Modern England* (1996), ch. 7.

Attitudes: R. Cust and P. Lake, 'Sir Richard Grosvenor and the Rhetoric of Magistracy', *BIHR*, LIV, 129 (1981), 40–52; V.M. Larminie, 'The Godly Magistrate: the Private Philosophy and Public Life of Sir John Newdigate', *Dugdale Society*, Occasional Papers, no. 28 (1982), esp. p. 15–17; H. Langeluddecke, '"Patchy and Spasmodic": the Response of Justices of the Peace to Charles I's Book of Orders', *EHR* CXIII, 454 (1998), 1231–48.

Printed primary source: *The Official Papers of Nathaniel Bacon of Stiffkey, Norfolk, as Justice of the Peace, 1580–1620*, Camden Society, 3rd series, XXVI (1915).

7 Obedience

K. Wrightson, 'Two Concepts of Order', in J. Brewer and J. Styles (eds), *An Ungovernable People: The English and Their Law in the Seventeenth and Eighteenth Centuries* for a now controversial view.

Local enforcement: J. Kent, *The English Village Constable 1580–1642* (Oxford, 1986); C. Herrup, *The Common Peace: Participation and the Criminal Law in Seventeenth Century England* (Cambridge, 1987); J. Morrill, *The Cheshire Grand Jury 1625–1659*, Leicester Department of English Local History Occasional Papers, 3rd series, 1 (1976); M. McIntosh, *Controlling Misbehaviour in England 1370–1600* (Cambridge, 1998), pp. 73–6; [and *JBS*, XXXVII, 3 (1998): special issue about the book and issues raised].

Failure or success: J. Cockburn, 'The Nature and Incidence of Crime in England, 1559–1800', in J. Cockburn (ed.), *Crime in England 1550–1800* (1977), ch. 2, and other essays in the collection; J. Sharpe, *Crime in Early Modern England 1550–1750* (1984).

8 Dissent

Prosecution: G.R. Elton, *Policy and Police: The Enforcement of the Reformation in the Age of Thomas Cromwell* (Cambridge, 1972) is a full study of opposition in the 1530s; J. Samaha, 'Gleanings from Local Criminal Court Records: Sedition Amongst the Inarticulate in Elizabethan England', *Journal of Social History*, VIII, 4 (1975), 61–79.

Circulation of opinion: Richard Cust, 'News and Politics in Early Seventeenth-Century England', *P&P*, CXII (1986), 60–90; A. Fox, 'Rumour, News and Popular Political Opinion in Elizabethan and Early Stuart England', *HJ*, LX, 3 (1997), pp. 597–620. Written criticism or libels: A. Bellany, '"Raylinge Rymes and Vaunting Verse": Libellous Politics in Early Stuart England, 1603–1628', in K. Sharpe and P. Lake (eds), *Culture and Politics in Early Stuart England* (1994), pp. 285–310; P. Croft, 'Libels, Popular Literacy and Public Opinion in Early Modern England', *HR*, LXVIII, 167 (1995), 266–85.

Printed primary source: *Poems and Songs Relating to George Villiers, Duke of Buckingham*, ed. F.W. Fairholt (1850).

9 Riot

R.B. Manning, *Village Revolts: Social Protest and Popular Disturbances in England 1509–1640* (Oxford, 1988) mainly uses Star Chamber complaints of alleged riots. B. Sharp, *In Contempt of All Authority: Rural Artisans and Riot in the West of England 1586–1660* (Berkeley, 1980), especially for the western forest disturbances 1628–1632; D. Underdown, *Revel, Riot, and Rebellion: Popular Politics and Culture in England 1603–1660* (Oxford, 1985).

Riotous shaming ritual: M.Ingram, 'Ridings, Rough Music and the "Reform of Popular Culture" in Early Modern England', *P&P*, CV (1984), 79–113, (a few examples also in Underdown, above).

J. Walter and K. Wrightson, 'Dearth and the Social Order in Early Modern England', *P&P*, LXXI (1974), 22–42 ([reprinted. in P. Slack, (ed.), *Rebellion, Popular Protest and the Social Order*] is an influential interpretation; also on subsistence problems, P. Clark, 'Popular Protest and Disturbance in Kent, 1558–1640', *EcHR*, 2nd series, XXIX, 3 (1976), 365–81. For London, K. Lindley, 'Riot Prevention and Control in Early Stuart London', *TRHS*, 5th series, XXXIII (1983), 109–126.

10 Rebellion

Introductory outline, and documents: A. Fletcher and D. MacCulloch, *Tudor Rebellions* (revised 4th edn 1997; but see ch. 10 above, n. 22).

Some of the many studies of rebellions: C.S.L. Davies, 'The Pilgrimage of Grace Reconsidered' in Slack, ed., *Rebellion, Popular Protest and the Social Order in Early Modern England* (Cambridge, 1984), ch.1; S. Gunn, 'Peers, Commons and Gentry in the Lincolnshire Revolt of 1536', *P&P*, CXXIII (1989), 52–79. S.T. Bindoff, *Kett's Rebellion 1549* (Historical Association, 1949) is an excellent short account of the East Anglian revolt, or D. MacCulloch, 'Kett's Rebellion in Context', in Slack (ed), *Rebellion, Popular Protest*, ch. 2.

Also on 1549: J. Youings, 'The South-Western Rebellion of 1549', *Southern History*, I (1979); 99–122; for a fuller coverage, with documents, F. Rose-Troup, *The Western Rebellion of 1549* (1913). On 1569, M. James, 'The Concept of Order and the Rising of the North', *P&P*, LX (1973) pp. 49–83, reprinted in his *Society, Politics and Culture: Studies in Early Modern England* (Cambridge, 1986).

For exhaustive (and somewhat repetitive) exploration of the organisation of the Pilgrims: M. Bush, *The Pilgrimage of Grace: A Study of the Rebel Armies of October 1536* (Manchester, 1996). For discussion of religion, including its role in Tudor rebellions: C. Haigh, *English Reformations* (Oxford, 1993), esp. pp. 143–50, 170–76, 251–9.

Early seventeenth century: M. James, 'At a Cross-roads of the Political Culture: the Essex Revolt, 1601', in his *Society, Politics and Culture*, pp. 416–65; for a brief view, A. Wall, 'An Account of the Essex Revolt', *BIHR*, LIV, 130 (1981), 131–3. J. Martin, *Feudalism to Capitalism: Peasant and Landlord in English Agricultural Development* (1983), Part III, Case study: the Midlands Revolt of 1607.

Index

Page references in *italic* refer to figures